AHEAD OF THE FLAMING FRONT:

A LIFE ON FIRE

AHEAD OF THE FLAMING FRONT:

A LIFE ON FIRE

Jerry D. Mathes II

CAXTON PRESS
Caldwell, Idaho
2013

Caxton Press
312 Main St.
Caldwell, Id. 83605
www.caxtonpress.com

ISBN# 978-087004-527-1

Library of Congress Cataloging-in-Publication Data

Mathes, Jerry D., II.
Ahead of the flaming front : a life on fire / by Jerry D. Mathes II.
pages cm
ISBN 978-0-87004-527-1
1. Mathes, Jerry D., II. 2. Wildfire fighters--United States--Biography.
I. Title.

SD421.25.M38A3 2013
363.37092--dc23
 [B]
                        2013003264

Printed in the
United States of America
by

Caxton Press

184122

DEDICATION

To the long-suffering girl posse: Sophia and Maddie Rose and their mother Kathy.

TABLE OF CONTENTS

ACKNOWLEDGEMENTS

This book took years to write. All of you firefighters who appear in its pages, thank you for whatever it was that you did—good, bad, or indifferent. I feel a deep kinship with many of you and the memories of the dead, from those at Rock Creek in 1939, to the crash of helicopter 5EV in 2006, and the others in between and after. To quote Charles Wright, "The dead are always with us," and I hope I have honored those I have written about.

I want to acknowledge my first nonfiction teacher, Mark Sanders, who read the original "Ahead of the Flaming Front," essay when I was his student and his suggestion to keep writing about fire and the people in it. Claire Davis read and helped me with "Falling into Fire" when I was trying to come to terms with the things that had happened and how to craft it into an artful narrative. It was no joke when she held up pages with red ink slashed through them, and I am grateful for it. Although I have had many writing teachers, it was Claire who inspired and forged the writer I would become. She showed no mercy, and I asked for none.

I need to thank Kim Barnes who steadfastly insisted that I find the story within the story, and Mary Clearman Blew who told me just shoehorning in action doesn't make a compelling story. I want to thank the poet Robert Wrigley for his poetry and his skill at looking at and reflecting the ordinary world with beauty, grace, and unexpected imagery and his suggestions to me about word choices and poetic language.

I appreciate my fellow students of writing and impromptu writing groups over the years: Ida, Dean, Ryan A., AnnE, Lucas, Kelly, Andrea, Matt, Lisa, Kim, Annie, Mike, Ryan F., Linda, and the others. A special thanks to The Southernmost Writers' Workshop in the World at South Pole Station and Andre Fleuette, Kate Macfarlane Javes, and Paddy Douglas who inspired me with their work.

A big thank you to Dean Ferguson who first suggested I contact *Caxton Press* and his reading of many pages of the manuscript. And another huge thanks and hugs to Debra Heironymus for reading and reading four versions of this book and her insightful comments. She too read early drafts of fire narratives as far back as 2002.

I must mention the Jack Kent Cooke Foundation and the scholarship they saw fit to award making it possible for me to study writing in graduate school at the University of Idaho. Grad school would never have been possible without their support.

The chapter "Ahead of the Flaming Front" appeared in an altered version in *High Desert Journal*. (2009).

The chapter "Falling into Fire" appeared in an altered version in *The Baltimore Review.* (2005).

Fire, water, and government know nothing of mercy.

Albanian Proverb

Author's photo

Krassel Crew 2007

Chapter 1

THE OLDEST ROOKIE

The rotor slap beats down through the trees and echoes off the century old houses in my neighborhood. I hear a helicopter, but from under the trees I can't see it yet. I look for it. The days break cooler now in Boise's fall. I scan the patches of blue between the greens, yellows, and reds of turning leaves. It sounds like a Bell 407, a light helicopter with four blades. My cell phone rings. My boss from Amundsen-Scott South Pole Station, Paddy tells me today or tomorrow I should expect a primary position contract as an Air Transportation Specialist to work in logistics.

I had skipped this fire season, 2011, to spend time with my daughters after having spent the academic year away from them teaching writing at a university in east Texas. The helicopter's rotors beat louder. It flies low, heading for the hospital on the other side of my neighborhood. I catch part of what Paddy says as the noise fluctuates with the wind. The flutter of leaves, the creaking of branches, sunlight bright in my eyes, and wood smoke from chimneys caught in my throat create a sensory puzzle, shifting and transforming over a decade of experience into series of film trailers out of order, jump cut, and loud.

"Paddy, can you standby, please?" She is my boss from when I first worked for her during the 2009-10 Austral summer at South Pole, but we are also friends. She is a poet, a chef, a judoka, and runs all things logistics at the South Pole. On my trips through Denver I have stayed at her house, and we share poetry.

She laughs. "Sure." She knows.

Like the flash of a signal mirror I see myself far off and bright during the thousands of times I tried to talk on a radio or cell phone as a heli came in or flared above a flaming front with a bucket of water slung below its belly, fanning ash into the air and shaking the trees. I feel the beat in my chest that is part thump of the rotors and part thump of something I've left behind. I flew, helitacked, to my first fire in 1997, and now in 2011, it feels as if helicopters had always been in my life, and indeed they worked their way into my consciousness in the stories of my father who was a door-gunner in the iconic Huey during the Vietnam War. It hits me hard and now. I feel a pang to be back with my crew. This summer I didn't leave to fight fire so I could spend time with my daughters before they grew up and had no time for dad. This morning I have escorted them to school, and now walk their miniature schnauzer, Soup. The helicopter thumps in my veins. I think of all the years and all the fires and even in this passion to put on my fire boots and feel the weight of my fire pack, I know it's over. Even in my first season as a rappeller some four years ago, the signals were marking the way out of the woods for me.

The helicopter passes and I hear it change pitch as it flares for landing on the hospital. I put my cell phone to my ear. "Sorry about that."

*

When I first stepped onto the skid of a hovering helicopter in 2007, the flight helmet muffled the whine of the turbine and the roar of air rushing around me, but not the blood beating in my head. We hovered at treetop level, nothing but air and grass between the hard earth and me. I leaned into the harness and it tightened around my back, shoulders, and crotch and pulled away from my chest, making me feel that maybe I didn't tighten the straps enough. My hamstring ached a reminder of how fast and unexpected trouble could come. I waited for my spotter to give the signal to rappel or re-board the ship. I was forty-two when I applied and was offered a position on the Krassel Heli-rappellers, a fire crew on the Payette National Forest in Idaho. Before rappel training started, I would turn 43 and Jen Feltner would bake a cake in McCall and brought it the two hour drive to our remote camp at Krassel. I was the oldest rookie in the thirty-year history of the program.

I had worked with the supervisor, Doug Marolf, and one of the crewmembers, Feltner, four years before. We had fought a few fires together, and I was excited to not only work with them again, but for the opportunity to rappel from a helicopter. Doug had offered me a position the season before when someone dropped out on him, but I had already committed to Nate, the supervisor of Musselshell Helitack on the Clearwater, and didn't feel good about leaving him short a person in May. Nate had been the supervisor of Doug and Feltner when I detailed to their crew, Grangeville Helitack, in 2003.

I gave my wife the news of being hired at Krassel as she read the newspaper and told her I'd have to train harder as I wanted to excel on the physical fitness test, which is more arduous than the standard physical test required of firefighters. My wife, Kathy, laid her paper down and said, "If fighting fire wasn't hazardous enough, now you're going to do this." I wondered if her infinite understanding was reaching its limits.

People have brought this up before, like when I first attended a class in North Carolina for graduate school in 2004, we were introducing ourselves to the other students, and I said that I had just arrived from a helitack crew based in Nevada. They didn't know what that meant. I explained that I was firefighter whose primary means of transportation was a helicopter and that we landed in remote areas got out and hooked a Bambi bucket to the helicopter that the pilot used to dip water from ponds, rivers, lakes, or free standing port-a-tanks set up in water scarce areas. The crewmembers then started suppressing the fire or set up helispots to support larger fires with cargo and personnel transport. Sometimes we were assigned to hand crews, worked as sawyers, on engine crews, worked with bulldozers, assumed fire staff responsibilities, and sent out on details to fill in other crews that could last anywhere from fourteen to twenty-one days. A blonde woman with glasses, a wife of a United States Marine, said, "It must be dangerous, fighting forest fires." I tried to wave it off, but noticed the other people in the class were nodding their heads.

I am always caught between saying no and sounding dismissive of a dangerous profession and being falsely modest or the alternative of saying yes and sounding like I am grandstanding or overplaying a mediocre hand for my own benefit. It is a strange place to be--not being a hero, but occupying a hero's space and knowing I'm only a guy doing a job that I loved to do and have mitigated the danger to an acceptable level. Am I lying to myself so I can perform, deluding myself to the real physical danger that surrounds me? After all, those who have been killed in fires must have believed they were going to be home at the end of the season. Is it neither and both, a complexity of urges and emotions--an attitude I step into like a costume on Halloween to fend off the dead?

When I meet the Krassel crew for the first time at the McCall office, I discovered there were five rookies all together, that I was the oldest, even older than the supervisor or lead supervisors. The only one older was the Fire Management Office (FMO), who was in charge of all things fire and forest on the district. Ours, Sam, once hiked a mile and a half to bring a crew in the field doughnuts. They were all in their thirties, and one of the rookies, a former Nebraska rancher, Craig, was thirty-eight. He later told me he was glad I was on the crew to take the pressure off him. I told him we were going to write the book, *Old Men and Fire*. Kat "Katzilla" Shell a former cross country runner from *The* Ohio State University who would run the mile and half four minutes faster than me and at five-five, the shortest on the crew, but the tallest on sheer energy. Dan "Dano" Crowell who had been a Garden Valley rappeller and worked on the Boise Hotshots, a type I crew--a twenty person shot crew stayed together all season, had more rigorous physical fitness standards and more work was expected of them on the fire line than twenty person type II hand crews. Jamie Dobbs had worked as the crew boss of the Bear Hand Crew on the Payette and had occupied a fire look out for several years and brought that patient temperament to the crew. Dobbs had a thick chest and would do a hundred push-ups in a minute. We rookies had fire experience that spanned forty years give or take.

According to the Interagency Helicopter Operations Manual (IHOG) before a person can work in aviation, he or she must have had at least a year of experience in fire. Most managers will hire people with more experience because of the added danger of helicopter operations, not only in the fire environment, but also in the dangerous world of aviation. It isn't all about physical fitness and the amount of push-ups a person knocked out or how fast someone ran. Everyone hired at Krassel had worked with someone from Krassel before and been vetted in the field and given a thumb's up as Krassel material. We rookies were all strangers at this point, but connected in some way by the people who had come back to Krassel after the wreck of Five Echo Victor.

That morning I hugged my twenty-four-year old friend, Jen Feltner after she set a dozen doughnuts on a desk, and I shook Doug's hand. They were the only two I had worked with on fire and that was in 2003, but we had remained in contact since then. Around them still hung the pall of grief, the turned down eyes, and lowered voices as we spoke of the Krassel helicopter that according to the NTSB had a rotor strike on a snag that stuck up above the canopy during smoky conditions as they crossed a ridge at "too low of an altitude" the season before. Two crewmembers, the pilot, and a fire lookout all died when the helicopter crashed and burst into flames on the road along the East Fork of the South Fork of the Salmon River.

*

When I first heard about the accident I stood at my last briefing for the summer before heading back to the University of Idaho for graduate school in August 2006. We had been operating out of Red River Helibase on the Nez Perce National Forest, just north of the Salmon River. Krassel was on the South Fork of the Salmon River. The helitack crews gathered by the blue shade tarp we used as a communications center. Over twenty people from the different helicopters milled about and my crew of four joked a little. We were going to forego military rations for dinner and drive the forty-some miles to Elk City and have pizza for my last night. Our supervisor, Nate, stood a little away. Tall and thin he always had the aspect of being deep in thought, which he usually was. When Heather, the helibase manager, finished her briefing she asked if anyone else had anything to add. I was anxious about going to town, and hoped nobody wanted to add much and drone on about something pointless. I wanted to roll.

Nate cleared his throat. "One more thing." He swallowed. I wondered if he was going to mention it was my last day, but his attitude didn't seem right.

"This afternoon the Krassel helicopter, Five Echo Victor, crashed killing all aboard."

My gut dropped. That was Feltner and Doug's helicopter.

"We don't have the names of the victims or any details, but you should call your families so they don't worry about you."

This was standard because even though we know what crews were with what helicopter, most of our families saw a crash on the news and didn't know if we were with it or not. We all reflect back on our close calls when we hear of tragedies or what might have been close calls that we never thought of except in retrospect. My own summer's flying had been with a pilot who flew nape of the earth, simulated gun runs to show us what his army days were like, and what we called fancy flying. Other less skillful pilots whose timid or haphazard flying skills made me feel uneasier than our hotrod pilot. Hindsight recalculated these risks.

*

Doug was glad I had turned down the Northern Cascades Smokejumpers to come to Krassel. When he hired the new rookies he wanted experienced hands to add a steadying influence to the crew for the rebuilding year ahead. It was my tenth season in fire, and at one time I had been the assistant fire warden of a district before giving it up to pursue my dream of being a writer and English teacher. At the end of the season I would be beginning my last year in the MFA program at the University of Idaho. Before wildfire, I had fished commercially in Alaska from Metlakatla in the Southeast to Unalakleet in Norton Sound for three seasons. I had seen a lot of bad weather.

Feltner's dozen doughnuts remained untouched. After we introduced ourselves and filled out the pages of paperwork, tried and failed to use the government internet sites, and went to the main forest office and back to our district office it was late in the afternoon. Flipping the box open she grabbed an apple fritter. "I'm surprised these are still here. You rookies must be afraid it'll give you a big, fat butt like mine." Many of us made jokes about not being up to the challenge of being fit enough to be on the crew.

"Whatever, Skinny Jenny," I said.

She laughed as she chewed. "You watch it rook, I'll have you doing push-ups."

At Krassel, the minimum requirements for the physical fitness test were—aside from the standard 45 pound pack test, 3 miles in under 45 minutes that every fighter must pass—were 45 sit-ups in 60 seconds, 25 push-ups in 60 seconds, 7 chin-ups, 1 1/2 mile run in 11:40 or less and the final test at the end of rappel training where the crew rappelled into the woods and carried 85 pound packs over 3 miles back to the helibase in 90 minutes or less. I was worried about the run. I had never been a strong runner and usually avoided it. I grew up in the house of a chain smoker before it became common knowledge that secondhand smoke burned out the lungs of innocent bystanders. And I'd chain smoked myself for seven years and had hundreds of fires worth of smoke lodged in the recesses of my lungs. I had done nothing but grow older and slower as time went on. I was lucky to find a training partner at the University of Idaho, Kelly "Blix" Blikre, long legged, fast woman of Mid-Western toughness from Gillette, Wyoming who'd run cross-country for Texas Tech. She kept my lazy butt running by exploiting my competitive nature. "Come on, JMath, you don't want people to think a little snow stopped you." Out into north Idaho blizzards we ran until snow covered us like the glaze and frosting on the doughnuts none of us rookies touched.

Through the winter I worked out hard. I knew the mountains were high and steep and coming down was harder on the legs than going up. Cutting brush and trees on those hills, constantly holding a sixteen pound power saw in front of me, cutting a fire-line strained the arms and the fire pack at around 30 pounds cut the shoulders. I was not worried about those things as there was something that kicked in after the first fire that set the mind and body into a gear driven state of old fashioned work day after day. An infusion. But I was injured during physical training (PT) doing an exercise I'd never done.

Truth be told, I never worked-out for a fire season until I was thirty-nine. I had always relied on being physically active through the winter, good genetics, and the first couple of weeks of working in the woods to bring me into fire shape. But the first year I applied to a federal fire helitack crew in 2003, I wanted to be in top shape when I arrived and hit the trails with 65-pound packs, ran, and did old-fashioned calisthenics.

*

On the skid for the first time I looked up. My safety glasses kept the rotor wash from blinding me, and then I looked back to Doug, the spotter, for the signal to either rappel or re-board the ship if things weren't right. He sat with his back to the pilot in the passenger compartment. Retread rappellers advised rookies that after the first step onto the skid of the hovering helicopter to look up through the rotor disk and the blur of sky, look down to make sure no knots fouled the rope, look back to the spotter for the signal, and when it came, "lean back and the feed the rope through your Genie, (a descending device

7

that uses friction to control the speed of descent also called the can because it is roughly the size of a pop can), and as you become inverted under the helicopter, look for the horizon." They reminded us that our exits must be swift and smooth. Our bodies should be perpendicular to the ground like a bat, and do not rock the ship by pushing off. Gravity would pull us away from the ship. The last thing they told us was, "Have fun. Not everyone gets to slide from a helicopter."

On the opposite skid stood Craig Utter who went by various nicknames like The Utter Buddy and Cowboy Craig. Before we loaded, Doug joked that we were the geriatric stick, a stick being two rappellers who go out of the ship at the same time, and he told the pilot we were headed to the Old Man Fire. Craig held his hand up to the earpiece of his flight helmet. "What's that whipper snapper? I thought we were headed to bingo!" Craig ran marathons and was capable of great distances, but no one would've suspected it because he had wide shoulders and thick chest. He also had the opposite hairline of mine. Whereas mine went all the way back, his went halfway down his forehead, but he kept his head shaved because it was so dense. He too had worked out all winter, running, lifting weights, and playing hockey.

I had always worried about the injuries suffered in training or on the job from falling snags, slipping on a steep hillside, or the shimmering curtain of fire rolling hard behind me. What mostly worried me was to have my body quit. Just one day have it say fuck it and stop, unable to hike or carry the weight of being a firefighter, whether the joints ground to a halt or muscles contracted against the anchorage of bone. Letting down the crew haunted me and I trained with that in mind.

For a month we trained to fight fire, went through refresher training, and worked on the station, which is two hours from McCall, Idaho, along the South Fork of the Salmon River. Until the snow melted over Lick Creek, we traveled to Cascade, Idaho, along Highway 55 and then 24 miles over the mountain range to the South Fork Road. The South Fork Road followed the river and wound 25 miles through the steep, forested mountains. More of a glorified golf cart track, the road brought precarious meetings with other vehicles on the many corners. Rumor had it that it was paved because it led to a politician's long time hunting spot. Given state politics, I never doubted it. Heavy rains sent trees, rocks, and boulders careening over it or washed it out completely.

We went through ground training and tower training for a week before we even mocked-up with the helicopter—configuring to rappel with the ship not started to run the rappeller through the procedures before going into live operations—for another day before we flew. The retreads taught to trust our equipment, to have confidence that it would not fail when we rappelled from 250 feet off the ground into the forest. We executed each step of the operation in our training, creating muscle memory for the procedures that made a safe and effective rappel, and taught the emergency tie-off (the ETO) in the event things went wrong and we became stranded between the helicopter and the ground.

We gathered in the concrete circle of our basketball court we used for stretching and calisthenics. It sat on the edge of a grass airstrip. Most weekends aircraft landed in the very early morning, much to the chagrin of the crew as they usually came in just after dawn and we didn't have to be to work for another two hours. Tall ponderosa pines line the airstrip and shade us as we started jumping and lunging to the commands of a crew leader—plyometrics. I hated and never do jumping exercises, as I don't like jumping. Besides I don't jump when I fight fire. When I trained over the winter I packed 50 to 80 pounds of weight over trails, lifted weights, did pull-ups and push-ups, ran, cycled, and carried my daughters around. When my hamstring spasmed, I swore, and kept trying to go on. Sweat burned my eyes. I had to stop and stretch it and try to join the group again. But the hamstring twinged and pulled against its bone moorings. The helicopter wasn't even at the base yet, but at least I had already finished first in the pack test with my pal Feltner.

After my injury, I swallowed anti-inflammatory pills and rubbed balm on the back of my leg. At PT, I lifted weights and did pull-ups, but stopped running for a week and then made the slow come back. Runs of a mile and a half in which the downhill portions hurt more than the uphill, and at Krassel along the South Fork of the Salmon River, most of the terrain ran up or down. At night I massaged it. In the field I refused to be the broken leg of a two to four person crew digging fire line and suppressing an acre fire through the night. By degrees I healed before my first fire assignment. No one wanted to seize up and be medivaced or packed out of the woods like a downed elk.

The risks we took, we took with others. We never risked alone.

I thought of life and its phases and where they began and where they ended. Many times a firefighter cannot mark a date as the end, the final week or day of a job, because even if he or she fought another fire or ten fires, they were all resolution to the climax. Only when we looked back at the seasons can we say that was the fire where it ended, the final fire beginning the long stretch to the finish, because we were never done with fire. Fire would be done with us, but it might take us a while to realize it.

*

In Boise the mini schnauzer tugs at his leash. I hear the helicopter above the East End neighborhood, and my mind races through the names, places, and fires from the sun-deadened deserts to conifer forests blowing flames at three miles a minute. In the Boise autumn, I again stand in the heat that stung my face like a polar wind. Doug wanted experienced people that year after the crash that killed his friends, but also wanted people who understood that bond and put the crew before self-glory or career climbing. That season I went to help my old friends, and meet new friends that would become like a surrogate family to my daughters. Doug wanted people who had each other's backs even when there was no fire except a campfire and the only thing needing suppressed were ghosts with a bottle of whiskey.

*

Doug sat with his back to the pilot in the helicopter's passenger compartment. He held his arms out to his side and brought his hands together in a sweeping motion in front of his shins: the signal to rappel. I undallied the rope from the Genie, brought the rope to my hip with my right hand, and leaned back looking for the upside down horizon, painfully bright and blue and jagged until gravity pulled my feet from the skid, sending me back to earth in the wash and thrum of rotors.

Chapter 2

AHEAD OF THE FLAMING FRONT

A ugust marks the peak-burning month in the Northwest. Even when things start going bad in July, fire folk know August is coming. Stories become cautionary tales to warn of summer's fury and lost lives and what went wrong. August is the month of the Big Blow-Up of 1910, which charred 3 million acres, killing 85 people. Ed Pulaski saved his crew by forcing them into a mineshaft and held them there at gunpoint. During the two days some firefighters got out of the path of the inferno and other groups of firefighters huddled under wool blankets in shallow creeks as the fire roared around them. It is also the month of Mann Gulch in 1949 where a fire crossed the creek and blew up, forcing Wag Dodge and his smokejumpers to retreat up canyon. Out of sixteen, thirteen died still running along the hillside. August is the month everyone buckles down. The heat and moisture combine in the alchemy of thunderstorms, which shed lightning over mountains and basins, and forests and ranges tremble in the acid dry air and smoke will hang thick in the trees long after fires have passed through.

On an August morning in 2003, Jenny and I stood on a rock outcropping a third of the way down slope to where the dozer had carved a firebreak into the ground. We were lookouts for our squad of firefighters--Chad, Hannah, Doug, and Scott--digging a hand-line--a trail cleared to mineral earth so fire can't burn across it--into the bottom of the ravine to tie into a line we had dug the afternoon before from the eastern side. Liza injured her knee and stayed behind to operate the base radio, while Nate stayed at the helibase to manage the helicopter. The crew called Jenny and I the fire twins, both of us blonde, tall and with a lot of energy, doing pushups when others sat around. The difference being that she was twenty-three and I was thirty-nine. I became a teacher to her and passed on my stories and knowledge of fire. The Milepost 59 Fire was burning east, up and along the south side of the steep and narrow canyon of the Clearwater River toward the small town of Kamiah. The fire had burned over 7000 acres, crews and aircraft from across the US were flown in and a special supervisory team from Florida had taken over from the local state district at Maggie Creek.

White smoke clouded the ponderosa pines in the bottom of the ravine like a heavy fog rising into the morning air. Two helicopters with buckets slung from their bellies flew round robins from ponds dug into the farm fields. Flames, slowed by the night and lower temperatures, crept up the ravine as helicopters dropped water on spot fires ignited from firebrands--embers and other burning debris like pine cones--blown ahead of the main fire. Up canyon from Jenny and I, forty acres of timber stretched to where the ravine rose up to meet the grass and farmland of the Hamilton Ranch. If the fire escaped us, the ranch house, barn, vehicle sheds, at the head of the ravine would be endangered.

The white smoke told us that it was burning through the damp vegetation and not moving fast. Now if the smoke were black and pushing a cloud column it'd be a different story. On our rock outcropping, I told Jenny that if the fire threatened the crew, I'd call Doug and have them retreat up the line and into the plowed fields. Because the ground was as steep as an a-frame, I'd have to give the crew a lot of warning. Both Doug and Scott had a lot of experience, and I knew they'd be checking the smoke as they descended into the ravine. Doug had been on a heli-rappel crew in Krassel, Idaho and fought fires in the South during the winter months, when it was the fire season there. Scott was an assistant fire management officer in southern Missouri where he had started, and kept going, a helitack module in a place where most fire fighters on his district thought they'd never need anything more than dozers. Doug called him Misery.

"We've got to watch the weather too," I said. "Right now the sky is clear and the breeze is one of the diurnals, meaning it's a local wind created by the heating and cooling of the terrain. If we saw castellanus clouds, which look like castle walls, we could expect erratic winds and storms this afternoon. Same thing if we saw any lenticular clouds, lens clouds. They look like domes or UFOs, all smoothed by fast, high-altitude winds."

She visored her eyes, scanning the sky. "I don't believe in UFOs."

I looked at her and laughed. "Good, they're indicators of instability."

She asked other questions. I explained about stratus clouds being a sign of stable weather, the puff ball clouds – the alto cumulus floccus-like a floccus of sheep, "bah, bah," showing us fair weather, the cirrus like the high flying mare's tails ahead of a warm front, telling us the weather will change in a few days, the Alto Cumulus Nimbus – the thunderhead.

The day was heating fast. If the fire flared up, threatening the crew, and they didn't have the time to make it back to the top of the ravine, one other option was to burn a safety zone, called the black, like Wag Dodge had done. Huge patches of grass yellowed between stands of ponderosa pines. Everyone carried fusees, and could torch a stretch of grass. As it burned the crew could step in and deploy their shelters. The difference between a burnout like we were about to do and burning an emergency safety zone is that firefighters don't care where the fire spreads. Only that it spreads fast.

I pulled some dry grass from some cracks in the rocks. I held the grass out and dropped it, and the blades trailed down canyon. The fire was burning into the wind, so it wouldn't advance as fast. As long as we paid attention to the smoke column and the wind, we'd have a good idea of how safe everyone was. I told her how we'd have to keep an eye on the wind, maintain our situational awareness, as it might switch as the day heated up.

*

On the first day of the fire, Jenny and I had climbed two miles out of a harvested wheat field, through a patch of dead coneflowers and star thistle, onto a ridge to scout the fire as it pushed out of the Clearwater River Valley. Two others and I flew in and established a helispot in a harvested wheat field on the prairie south of and above the river before the rest of the crew arrived by ground. We were in a depression, and from that position, we couldn't see the fire, only the convection column rising out of the canyon, darkening, and leaning east, up river. The fire illuminated the smoke as if the sun burned through volcanic ash. Jenny wore a thin tank top that rode up, revealing the Chinese character--Praise God--inked into the small of her back. She'd left her yellow fire shirt behind, and we had both left fire shelters in the heli-tender, as we didn't expect to walk far from the truck. The fire shelters, made of fire resistant laminates, were supposed to protect us in the event we got caught ahead of the flames. They looked like aluminum foil pup tents and everyone on a fire was required to carry one.

We called them shake-and-bake bags and anyone caught in one and to survive, a baked potato. The shelters worked, but a firefighter had to have an area cleared of fuel, out of reach of falling snags or trees, and a place where flames couldn't touch the shelter—it'd peel and burn, releasing toxic fumes. Heavy and bulky, they were a pain in the ass to carry, so the government redesigned them to be heavier and bulky enough not to fit into any of the existing line packs, but able to withstand harsher conditions. I had rarely carried one on the crew I had come from, a small cooperative association. Even though I was now on a federal fire crew, didn't think much of carrying one. Part of my fire education became reconciling the two ways of approaching fire safety and training. One an anal retentive obsession with guidelines, checklists, safety meetings and discussions, while the other held that common sense didn't need a checklist and contempt for anyone following too closely to the rules.

Because the incident commander (IC, the person in command of the fire) wanted to avoid using heavy equipment, like dozers, and use a minimum of personnel, the fire had gotten ahead of him, and they were calling for help from interagency resources like the United States Forest Service, other state districts, and the Idaho Department of Corrections hand crews. The fire had made the top of the canyon and stretched for one thousand acres along the river, burning through stands of ponderosa pines, alder brush and grass, to where the prairie rolled into wheat farms and cattle ranches, spotted with stands of pines. The fire burned from bottom of the river to the top of the canyon ranging from a quarter mile to three miles up and most if it folded with draws and ravines of feeder creeks as steep as 55 percent to straight up. It was a rugged place to fight a fire and the sky was high pressure clear without a sign of moisture.

Jenny and I went to scout so we would know what the fire was doing on the ground, and find out if there were any firebreaks, like roads, streams, plowed fields or any absence of anything that could burn between the helispot and the fire. In 1956, the government formed a committee who thought up ten standard fire orders and twelve--later expanded to eighteen--watch out situations as a reaction to a rash of fire fatalities. In 1991 Paul Gleason, the superintendant of the ZigZag Hotshots proposed to distill down the 10 and 18 to four basic things later summed up at LCES: lookouts, communications, escape routes, and safety zones. We didn't think we were in that much danger, but we climbed anyway. A contour road ran on the far edge of the ridge and we could see down a quarter of a mile to the fire running ponderosa pines.

Jenny snagged the Skittles from an MRE--meal ready to eat--we shared. A gaggle of volunteers at the end of a dirt road pulled back. Pick-up trucks with water tanks, combines, tractors with discs, and four-wheelers with farmers crossed the field or followed the road past us. Jenny unbuttoned and pulled her Nomex pants down around the curves of her hips, reached around into the crotch of her magenta panties and pulled out a stick.

She held the twig up and asked, "How the hell did this get there?"

I laughed as farmers swerved in passing. "I don't know. I didn't leave it there."

Fire crossed dozer lines and burned hard in yellow grass and alder brush. Engulfed, Ponderosas torched. The speed at which the trees blazed out amazed us. Bark, fire licked, exploded skyward like the torches of hundreds of enraged villagers looking for a monster. Smoke thickened over the trees, billowing and churning the blue sky dark. A single engine air tanker, a SEAT, flew a test run into the smoke and emerged like a bee from the center of a gray blossom. On final, the Air Tractor streamed red retardant. All the people had disappeared into the folds of the land, headed to eat dinner. Soon night crews would be in place. Jenny and I watched the fire, the wind still pushing it up river. The sun clipped the horizon, and we hiked back to the heli-tender. We broke down the helispot and headed back to our helibase.

Because we were close to our base, the IC released us from the fire to drive back to Grangeville. We would replenish our food, water, mixed gas, oil, sharpen tools, service the vehicles, fill out paperwork, and make sure everything was ready to launch in the morning. Some nights we went out to a local bar and had a drink and other nights if we got back too late, we'd head to sleep. One night Liza invited a couple of us detailers over for dinner with her boyfriend. After the fire Liza and I listened to Bob Marley and refurbed the equipment we had used and in the evening we went to the movies. Liza helped in many small ways to make us feel at home in a strange town.

*

Two days later six of us had been sent out from the airfield to dig a firebreak as a hand-crew squad. After tying into a dozer line, we set a backfire in Six Mile Creek that needed to burn through the dried timber, brush, weeds, and grass from our hand-line and join the wildfire, stopping it. It started in the grass, climbed into parched huckleberry and alder brush, and raced up the trunk of the white fir. In a matter of minutes, firebrands carried over the firebreak we had dug to hold the fire and into the timber. I was the last firefighter up the hill and below me my helitack squad, four volunteers, and one Idaho Department of Lands forester, who was the IC, of what was then a thousand acres were spread out. Several outlying homes, farmhouses and ranches had been evacuated. The crew worked down toward the river as the IC started lighting the grass and brush.

I stood on a small bench, before the hill dropped into timber at a 60 to 70 percent grade to the highway. The volunteers, backs to the fire, scanned the unburned side of the hand-line. They leaned on their tools trying to catch their breath after the hike up. Jenny was the last member of my helitack crew. She yelled, "You guys thought about a PT program? You know--physical fitness." She winked at me, "Scandalous." She brought her fists together in front of her, flexed and yelled, "I got your back."

I flashed a thumb up before keying my radio, calling the helicopter.

The helicopter pivoted above the river, the bucket suspended from its belly like a pendulum, and pointed its nose at me on the steep hillside. "I see you," the pilot said.

As he hovered close, I put down my power saw and stretched my arms toward the fir tree.

Jenny's long-limbed stride took her out of sight below the hill's horizon, ponytail trailing below her hardhat.

After Jenny disappeared below me, I watched as One-Echo Hotel nosed into the wind, stabilizing the bucket. Two other helicopters dumped buckets of water into the timber below where the lighting was still going on.

Several hundred gallons of water splashed into the hand-line, short of the tree. The pilot radioed that he caught a wind shift and would hit it the next time. I picked up my saw, slung it over my shoulder, turned and saw the volunteers pounding at flames with shovels and pulaskis. Firebrands sailed over their heads. They zoned into a shovel space of flames, beating and sweating, hard breaths coughing in smoke and dust, squinting into parched earth. They beat and scrambled at fire growing at their feet, missing the rest of the mountain. Fire surrounded us. The earthen thud of tools sounded larger than rotors overhead. Flames ripped all the way to the ridge's break, as far as I could see, and raced along the contour, a quarter acre wide.

"You can't catch it," I yelled. "Move down the hand-line."

I radioed Doug as I started through the flames. My voice screeched out, smoke and heat constricting my vocal cords, trees began to torch. The smoke and flames mixed with the greens and browns of earth and foliage creating a burst kaleidoscope. Blue slices of backdrop between the trees were stark, and the dull thump of helicopters beat bass to the flame's tenor and the whoosh of trees consumed in seconds. Sap sizzled and popped. I could feel my skin turning red, the fusion of flame and flesh. Walking turned to running. The volunteers had already started their flight and disappeared over the break.

I had read the books by both Norman Maclean and his son John, read the reports by government investigative teams, complete with interviews and speculation, and I had been around fire and knew no one quits with the fire at their back. People always struggled to outpace flames. Even crews in the midst of conflagrations, about to be burned over, kept running, hoping for the fuel break, the ridge top, rockslide, or a pond, as flames sucked the oxygen out of lungs, replacing it with toxic gasses--scalding alveoli. The dead must have believed they could've beaten the blow-up--even those huddled into fire shelters alone with voices around them calling out the names of those they'd never see again.

My boots slid out from under me as I crested where the hillside dropped off. My forward momentum carried me until, for a second, I hung weightless. The power saw, my line pack and gravity pushed me, and I tried to avoid piling into a tree. Dirt kicked up around me. Wild rose thorns punctured my pants, tore my legs, as loose rocks and gravel clattered ahead of me like a bow wake. The air cooled, flowing from the river, drafted by the fire's heat above us. An ash branch slapped my face, and my eyes watered. My line pack helped drag me to a stop as I dug in my heels and grabbed at branches with my free hand. I stopped in the midst of my crew, dust and smoke swirling. The volunteers kept going until they hit the highway, where, in a pullout along the closed Highway 12, three, twenty person hand-crews staged too late in the eastern shadows.

Jenny leaned into the hill closest to me. Above us, trees with leaves of flames looked like Brancusi's *Bird in Flight*. Polished blades the color of tigers lunged skyward, driving black smoke where the flames couldn't follow. The saw rolled off my shoulder, and she stuck out her hand to help me to my feet. By the end of the day, the fire would grow to 6300 acres.

*

The blades of grass I had dropped to show Jenny the wind direction still floated on the air current when the others began their climb back to the top. We left our lookout to join them with the division supervisor (Div Sup, pronounced soup). After Doug briefed him on his plan, we were given the go ahead. From the corner Jenny and I burned along the top of the field. The fire would back down the slope and create heat, which would draw in the fire we would set along the hand-line across the slope toward the wildfire. This also created an anchor point to start our operations and as we burned from there, increasing the blackened area as we went, if anything went wrong we could retreat into an area already scorched clear. We called it one foot in the black or dragging the black with you. When Jenny and I rejoined the crew we all lit the burnout down into the ravine, the five of us took turns lighting and the fire burned away from us. The timber was tall and the brush thick in the dried creek. The wind kept blowing down canyon. We slid one at a time into the rocky creek bottom, scattering rocks and dust, to where we had dug the night before.

The burnout's smoke column still bent away from us, obscuring the sun, carrying bits of grass, leaves and twigs in the updraft. Spot-fires burned down canyon. Grass was up the east side was sparse. We hung out in the bottom and got the brush burning under the trees. Thunderheads built to the west. Over the fire, cumulous developed, but hadn't grown into thunderstorms. Chad climbed the east side of the ravine to a point fifty yards up, where a rockslide blocked the fuel to the top of the ridge, to wait for Doug's radio call to start burning back down. The rest of us watched for spots flying out of the timber.

Before Chad was halfway up, a firebrand flew across the ravine and started burning just below us. Doug and I yelled for Chad to climb faster and start lighting, as we popped fusees—like highway flares. I labored up slope to make the mid-point and burn down to Doug, who burned up toward me. The small ember grew fast like watching a rose bloom in high speed.

Jenny and Hannah scouted the timber upstream.

We didn't bother with long strips in the thin, dry grass. We wanted to create a buffer of black between the hand-line and the increasing spot fire. The wind pushed it and the heat from the fire drew it down canyon. The three of us met at the mid-slope. The fire we had hastily set consumed the spot and kept it from crossing the upstream line. We climbed back down to the creek bottom.

The heat from the west side of the ravine sucked wind down canyon. Jenny pointed at the storm clouds building over the fire, and yelled, "Those aren't sheep clouds." We all laughed, but knew if the storm matured before we were done high winds could blow the fire over us. Fire climbed and cracked and popped in the dried alder brush, syringa, wild roses, and burned up the bark of ponderosa pines as if following a trail of gasoline. Sweat ran down our faces and the trees began waving and creaking in the convection column. I smiled at Jenny, but she looked unsure.

"Do you think we ought to climb up?" She had never held ground against such a big fire. Her eyes watered from the smoke and tears dried before reaching her chin. Thunderstorms loomed.

I saw myself in her seven years before, when I stood in the bottom of a clear-cut, as fire galloped over a hundred acres and two guys flanked me, smiling into a night fire, empty drip torches hanging in our hands. I had a twinge in my bowels, yet I trusted those guys wanted to make it home too. "No, things are still carrying down canyon."

Her nervousness made me chuckle a little. We had first met at a helibase on the Red River two weeks before, operating for a complex of fires in the Clearwater National Forest and in the Selway-Bitterroot Wilderness. I had been detailed from Winnemucca Helitack to manage a helispot, which was a laugh to me because I had fought fire in that part of Idaho for six years before returning to college and giving up my year-round, assistant fire warden position in Elk River. I had spent 2002 going to summer school at Lewis-Clark State College, in Lewiston and studying Spanish in Cuernavaca, Mexico. I applied to the BLM in Winnemucca for the 2003 season because my parents and my sister and her family lived there and my wife and I thought it would be nice for our two young girls to be close to cousins, as well as the aunt, uncle and grandparents. When we flew to the Milepost 59 Fire, it was like I'd never left, hearing the voices of some of the state firefighters I had worked with since 1997.

When I was en route to Grangeville, my resource order had been canceled, and I got reassigned to the Clear-Nez Helitack. The first day I flew to the Red River Helibase with Doug, the assistant helitack manager. The base was in a large meadow. A barbed wire fence bound the helibase on the north, and a stream flowed west, lengthways down the center of the pasture. Logging trucks rolled down the two-lane road and local kids cruised by. A late '80s, white Mustang slowed, and a girl yelled, hanging out of the passenger window flashing her tits at the firefighters.

On the other side of the stream, a farmer mowed hay with an old Case tractor. By the access gate, a crew had pitched a tarpaulin and set-up some tables for the aircraft radio operator, the helibase manager, and anyone in transit with logistics or in need of a flight. To the east of the command post the heavy helicopters--a Sky Crane, a couple of Sikorsky S-61s, a K-Max, and some 212s--flew into the pasture for fuel and out with up to 2000 gallon tanks or up 1000 gallon buckets to siphon or dip water out of rivers and lakes. Ground crews moved around service trucks and fuel trucks. One crew was working on switching the rotor blades between two Sikorskys on contract from a logging company.

To the west of the command post, the smaller ships, Jet Rangers and Long Rangers, ferried people and equipment to new lightning starts, or in support of the 26,000 acre Slims Fire. The rugged, timbered mountains, deep, narrow draws and river canyons combined with the remote roadless area, made helicopters a perfect tool. A Hotshot crew from New Mexico staged in the vehicle area, close to the command post, waiting for a resource order. Some kicked a hacky-sack or wandered around, and others lounged around their two crew-buggies, which looked like armored cars with passengers windows.

I was manifesting cargo and crews to smaller fires when Doug pointed to an F-250 six-pack pulling through barbed wire gate: "Here comes Chad and Jenny. She's a hair trigger."

Jenny jumped out of the truck shouting, "We kicked that fire's ass." She and Chad had helitacked to a tenth of an acre fire, worked it overnight, and hiked to a road after mopping it up all morning. She was about 5'10" and her blonde hair was sooty and French braided, her sharp facial features looked both hard and refined.

I had to take care of an inbound ship, so Doug introduced me to both of my new crewmembers. Chad looked like a guy who you'd find on any beach next to a surfboard--tall and wide, with curly blond hair and even when he wasn't smiling, seemed like he was. He spent six months on the crew then traveled. He had planned for Central America after lay-off and loved to hike in the wilderness on any days off from the helibase. Jenny's second year in fire, and first year on helitack, she fought fire during the summer and went to college the other nine months of the year like many seasonal firefighters.

After marshalling the ship in and unloading the passengers and equipment, I returned to the shade tarpaulin. Several of the shots stood talking with Jenny about snowboarding.

Chad smiled at me and said, "She always attracts a group."

A longhaired guy asked where she was from.

"McCall," she adjusted her macramé choker.

Dirt and soot covered everyone, except Doug and me.

"No shit, I'm from Cascade. Brundage is my home mountain."

She pointed at him. "Your home mountain? I own that mountain. Nobody shreds it like me and no one will. Got it."

Before the shot could answer, she turned and strode behind the command post, where her line pack lay, and stretched out with a disc player and fell asleep.

Doug and Chad chuckled. "Told you, man," Doug said, "a hair trigger." But she'd always have your back on the mountain and in life. She was full of an almost wild energy and not afraid of anything.

But now in the canyon she looked up, the fire tempered her zeal, hoping the fire we set wouldn't kick our asses. Ten feet separated the crowns of torching trees and unburned trees, spotted red by retardant. The heat rose in the creek bottom. This was the hard part, waiting for the fire to back away, standing in the base of all the heat with sweat soaking us, and our fatigued muscles stiffening. The air sucked down canyon cooled our backs as the fire heated our faces.

The fire burned hard in yellow grass and alder brush. Engulfed, ponderosas torched. Trees exploded skyward like rockets consumed by their own boosters. I thought of the fall campfires I had labored over, spark after spark--flame after flame on insensible wood producing coal smudges and frustration. Below us flames were conjured out of dry air. Smoke crowded the trees and obscured everything down wind.

The wind gusted, the fire burned away from us as the smoke billowed and blended into the cumulus clouds pushing up over the fire. We stood in the canyon's shadow, and below the clouds, sunlight still shone on the eastern ridge. I shivered.

We scaled the steep hillside onto the ridge road and gathered in a staging area by a tanker truck, various other vehicles, and where two inmate crews, and groups of volunteers had watched us descend the far side and rise out of the smoke and fire on their side with scuffed hardhats, smoke stained faces. The thunderstorms came and everyone crawled into trucks as the wind blasted and the sporadic rain hit the ground. Jenny challenged me to the most push-ups in a minute before we ducked under cover.

The next day, August 23, a light rain covered the fire. At its peak, the fire had 431 people configured in sixteen crews, fourteen engines, several dozers and five helicopters and burned 8139 acres, including someone's house. Two fire fighters had deployed fire shelters. They lived. Accountants figured the cost at 3.2 million dollars for the one fire and if asked, I believe the ranchers, farmers, and the citizens of Kamiah would say it was money worth spending. All of that damage and expense from the whim of teenagers and for what reason, I never found out.

On August 13, 2006 Jenny and Doug were working on the Krassel heli-rappel crew on the Payette National Forest, while I was on Clearwater National Forest, when I heard their helicopter went down, killing all aboard. The next day when I found out they were not among the dead. Nate called me, saying, "Michael Lewis, Monica Zajanc, Lilly Patten the fire lookout, and the pilot Quin Stone" had been aboard. I'd be lying if I said that I didn't imagine what it was like in the helicopter as it careened out of control into a road along the East Fork of the South Fork of the Salmon River. When I started work with them at Krassel, the stories Jenny now told me about her lost crewmembers made me realize how stories create a remembrance to the dead and all the things they did right, and not the things that went wrong, on the fire line and in friendship. How one crew member was fanatical about using only wood utensils or the other's stash of hard candy in a flight helmet bag, or maybe another had a never ending stream of movie quotes, and all of the small actions and quirks of speech that develop into the micro-culture of a close fire crew. The stories we repeat are not just so we can learn to read the weather or recognize when a fire is going to blow-up, but so that we are able to weather the storms and keep ahead of the flames that threaten us even in the winter when mist drifts through the trees like last summer's smoke.

Chapter 3

Buddy check

Jess Martin smiled and shook her head. "Rookies." As tall as Feltner, her brunette hair stopped at her shoulders and her sharper features accented her darker complexion. She had grownup in the remote Idaho town of Elk City, which began as gold rush town in the late Nineteenth Century that converted to lumber when the gold ran out, but shrank as timber disappeared and tens-of-thousands of acres surrounding it became wilderness. She had grown up working in the woods with her logger father and tending livestock.

Money, gave a snicker, an honest to God, heh heh heh heh, as I crunched the Doritos chip. A grin opened his Nordic face. "That will be fifty push-ups my rookie friend." Money held the assistant supervisor position on the crew and had worked at Krassel for over a decade. He had a fondness for Scandinavian speed metal when working out and looked like a Viking.

As soon as he said it, I realized I had been lured into breaking a rule: a break in concentration that could result in an accident or a situation with potential. In this case I had taken a bite of something while wearing my harness. No food, no drink, except water, no tobacco, no push ups or sitting with the leg loops clipped around your legs, and no putting the harness anywhere except in the rope bag or hanging it off the ground. All these rules mitigated dirt and foreign material from getting on the harness and abrading the threads. This was the first day of rappel training at Krassel.

Jess reminded me of a woman I worked with in Alaska. I'd arrived on the ferry and after a night camped out on the muskeg, I walked the docks. The first boat I saw with people on it, I approached and the skipper, Dave, hired me. Julia had come to Alaska from Germany and was Dave's girlfriend. Because I hadn't fished before, much less went to sea, she taught me how to run gear, mend nets, splice lines, and cook salmon in every possible way. One of the first nights out on the deck, the boat swung on its anchor chain rippling the moonlit water. The net strung up between the mast and the gunwale. I held the fid in my hand running it between the monofilament, trying to tie the same sized diamond shapes into the hole that had been torn by rocks. "No, up and then down and use your fingers to keep the size consistent and all the edges the same length." The other deckhands lounged in the wheelhouse reading magazines. Her German accent attracted a lot of other fishermen to mill around the dock when we were tied up and on deck cleaning and mending, as did her German features.

We gathered in front of the shack at Krassel, a long building with the office/training room, a bathroom, and a locker lined ready room where we all kept our equipment. We all wore the green Nomex fire pants and various colored t-shirts with the small Krassel logo on the chest and a full back logo of two rappellers descending through the trees, modeled on two trees in front of cabin one. Krassel was the only crew I knew of that allowed its members to choose the color of the shirt they wore. Except for red, because Price Valley Heli-rappellers, our cross-forest rivals, wore the color exclusively, and as we joked, red was typically the color of communists, streetwalkers, and inmate crews.

Jenny was up on a ladder painting the office the same chocolate brown with white trim as all the buildings at Krassel. Sprucing up fire camps and remote bases was a rite of spring across the West. Parallel to the shack a 1500-foot grass airstrip had been built on a spur ridge. Between the shack and the strip two concrete helipads had been poured a hundred feet apart. Because the helibase had been built up on a flat spot on the ridge, many people who traveled along the South Fork of the Salmon River missed the helibase.

"Nice paint job," I said.

Feltner joked, "There's only two things you need to know, cabana boy. The back of my hand and where the kitchen is."

When I first went to Krassel, before I worked there, Kathy and I were driving to Moscow from Boise and I wanted to go by and see it because Doug had returned to be the supervisor of the crew. Coincidentally years before, Kathy had stayed in the ranger house for a couple of weeks when one of her sisters was a lookout on Miner's Peak, a mountain up the river from Krassel. Downstairs, as we called it, across the road from the river was the original ranger house and a couple of other houses with rail fences. A narrow dirt road that looked like a driveway cut between a storage building and a house, switch-backed up the hill through the trees. Halfway up a shed and a barn made of hand hewn logs made up Middle Earth (a barn the district ranger got into trouble for constructing). At the end of the road our camp spread out in an area the size of several football fields scattered with centuries-old ponderosa pines. The mountain continued up another couple of thousand feet and loomed up behind the camp, as did the mountains across the river. We couldn't see the river from the helibase, but in the evening when things quieted we could hear the water rushing for the ocean. The road forked at the top and the fork paralleling the airstrip went by the communal campfire a circular sunken rock lined pit called Lake Saleen, the physical training area, two propane tanks, the generator building housing two propane generators, hose supply house, fuel tanks, and then the office. The other fork snaked past five cabins and looped around, but a hundred or so yards away to trailer row: two unused single-wides and several FEMA trailers. A narrow trail extended off the loop to a six by six building where our water was filtered after being pumped from Indian Creek by two Amish gravity pumps. Our communication was only a satellite phone and radio. Krassel was self-contained. We all lived, worked, played, and depended on each other to keep the camp running and each other's morale up.

That morning we rookies were given a rappel guide and a schedule for the next two weeks. We were also told to bring in our rope bags. Small orange or yellow canvas with black reinforced bottoms and loops for handles like round reusable shopping bags. Inside: rappel gloves with reinforced palms and extended six-inch gauntlets, the full body harness with leg loops with heavy-duty tri-link that joined the two soft loops in front the solar plexus securing the harness around the body, the descending device called a Sky Genie, developed for skyscraper window washers, and 250 feet of woven rope.

One side of the tri-link triangle opened and closed by means of a barrel nut. Unscrewing it created a gap and screwing it closed the gap. Some rappellers kept it closed and pulled their harness over their head like a tank top, while others removed one soft loop from the link and slung the harness on like a coat, returned the soft loop to the safety inside the link.

Jess stood facing me and asked, "Have you had your buddy check?"

"No."

"Want one?"

I nodded and she put her hands on my flight helmet's locking nut for the visor. "Flight helmet in place. Visor up and locked." She ran her hands down and pointed at my safety sunglasses, "Eye protection in place." Then pointed at my neck. "Chin strap secure, collar up, top button of the shirt buttoned. She placed her hands on my shoulders and before running them down to check my gloves and shirt cuffs made sure my harness wasn't twisted or the stitching wasn't coming undone. She brought her hands back to my shoulders and traced the harness to the j-hook. "Two soft loops captured by the tri-link with the nut tight and to the rappeller's right." She unlocked and locked the j-hook. "Functional. Leg straps buckled and untwisted." She put her hand between my thighs and forced my legs apart to insure they were good to go. She patted the Raptor knife, which is flat piece of aluminum with razors clamped in a hook for cutting away rope. Just put the rope in the crook and pull. After she pointed at my boots and said, "Pants cover boots," she motioned for me to turn around and went head to foot again looking for twisted straps, worn stitching, un-tucked shirt anything in the right side pockets like knives or pens that might get caught in the rope, and that the tops of the boots were covered. She patted me on the shoulder and I turned and pointed to my rope bag where she inspected the rope and Genie for cracks, frays, and that it was assembled correctly.

The Genie was aluminum and lightweight. It had a cover that slipped off, exposing a metal rod that rappeller wrapped the rope around twice and then slid the cover back over. The rope entered the bottom and exited the top ending in a metal lined eye, which was attached to a carabineer fixed to the helicopter. The rope from the bottom of the Genie dangled into the rope bag. Any break in this chain and a firefighter could fall from the helicopter, which was why we learned the buddy check.

I then did the same for her, but she told me to not be shy and put my hands on her and make sure all the straps were in working order.

When I didn't check her leg straps close enough she stopped me and made me do the whole buddy check over from the top and said, "get your hands on the harness and make sure." Any time the buddy check was broken policy required that we started over from the top.

That was not the only check. When Jess and I were given the nod by the pilot, one of us went to the right and the other to the left side of the ship. The helicopter at Krassel was a Bell 407, a light helicopter that carried two rappellers, and the spotter/manager. We attached our ropes to the carabineers fastened at the top of the rear passenger doorway, locked the rope off to the Genie and leaned back, waiting for the spotter to give us the next check. We were fully tied to the machine. Money's blond braid hung below his flight helmet and his grin widened as he walked up to me. "Have you had your buddy check?"

I held my arms at my sides, the rope taut as it held my weight at a forty-five degree angle to the ground like a marionette controlled by one string. I nodded and said yes. If I had said no, I would have been required to unhook from the ship and get a buddy check. He started at my helmet and did everything Jess had done when we had checked each other before going to the helicopter, with the exception that he checked that my rope was properly locked off to my Genie and that all the carabineers were locked and facing the correct way where they attached to the helicopter. To catch rookies off guard occasionally they would put one of the carabineers on backwards, and not correcting it was worth fifty push-ups to reflect on safety.

Money gave me the thumb up and I set the rope bag in the floor of the ship and climbed in. He walked around the nose to check Jess. When he came back to the left side, I gave him a buddy check to make sure his harness and personal protective equipment was on correctly. He sat across from me and hooked the safety strap in to a ring fastened to the seat frame. After he waved his finger for our attention he went through the final safety checks, insured our seat belts were fastened and that our ropes were secure and untangled. We were ready to fly. But in this case the helicopter remained stationary, rotors drooping in the sun. This was a mock-up. Money went through the signals. First we dropped our rope bags out the door. Then he hooked his fingers together as if pulling and Jess and I went to the skid and leaned into our harnesses. He swept his arms in front of him touching his palms together after checking that all systems were safe and Jess and I undallied the rope from the Genie and simulated rappelling. After a week of tower training we had to perform three mockups before being give the opportunity to rappel.

The buddy check was a regimented procedure that reminded me of the katas of Hwa Rang Do. The kata was a choreographed series of kicks, punches, blocks, and sweeps and throws meant to instill muscle memory to defend oneself in case of a physical attack. At Krassel we were defending against the overlooked small thing that would send a rappeller plummeting to the earth in a rush of wind and arms flailing as hands tried to grab a rope hanging inches away. If he managed to catch the rope as he hurtled to the ground, the friction would burn through the double-palmed gloves, skin, and tendons to the bone like a wire through cheese, which had happened. In 2009 a rappeller on the Chester Flight Crew, Thomas David Marovich, Jr, fell to his death from a medium helicopter, a Bell 212, at Willow Springs helibase in Northern California because he had connected his j-hook to his tri-link with a rubber o-ring and it broke when he put his weight on it in the air. If he had been on a light helicopter couldn't have happened as we rigged up while the helicopter is still on the ground and put our full weight against the rope and harness. In an earlier instance on another medium helicopter, a rappeller managed to arrest his fall enough to live, but in this case he wasn't even hooked into the Genie. As with other near misses of this type, rappellers moved to the skid without being hooked into the genie, but they were all in medium helicopters where the genie was not hooked to the rappeller during the flight. It dangled from the rope attached to the upper doorframe and the rappeller must unbuckle his seat beat, hook in, and then remove a gunner's strap (a small web strap that fits around the waist and fastened with a quick release buckle) as he moved to the skid with the ship hovering 250-feet above the ground. We cross-trained with the Price Valley crew on their mediums and learned how the system worked. After having trained on our Bell 407 it was disconcerting not to have been fully rigged before the flight and have to make that transition while in the air.

*

Jess and I removed our ropes from the carabineers and secured our equipment. Training like that brought all of us closer together, rookies and retreads alike. We looked to each other for help and guidance and Jess remarked, "Our least experienced rookie has five years in fire.

Another is a crew boss and yet another is a crew boss with ten years fighting fire." It struck me later how what led to Marovich's death at Willow Creek Helibase was not only overlooking an incorrectly rigged J-hook, but a system that put twenty rookies together who only have two years in fire, and have not worked around helicopters--most of the time at helibases they sat around in their crew-buggies because they were unqualified to pitch in and help or they were sent out on the line and never gained any extensive helicopter experience. The crew had managers and lead persons, but lacked mentors who were crewmembers to help when managers and leads were busy managing. Jess and I knew we had earned our positions at Krassel and not assigned them because we expressed interest in being a career firefighter and desired the fast track. In a team, that meant we knew we had each other's best interest and safety in mind, down to the smallest o-ring or stitch that when torn could start a chain reaction like a levy breaking. The accident investigation into Marovich's death drew the line from the lack of experience and the development of situational awareness to the accident.

After Jess and I stored our gear, Doug waved me down. "I got your red card."

"Cool." We'd need those cards, which list our qualifications and training positions.

He handed Jess hers and before handing mine over, said, "Looks like you're the least qualified guy on the crew."

I laughed.

"No, seriously. The office has a problem with your paper work. You're missing certificates."

I rolled my eyes. I had gone through this in Montana with a training officer. I had moved so much and had stuff in storage that I wasn't sure where some of the certificates were and when I worked for the Clearwater-Potlatch Timber Protective Association (C-PTPA), a state, private and federal fire organization in north-central Idaho, I had been to some classes, and hadn't received certificates for them. They did mostly on the job training and by working. For instance, I was forced to take the basic power saw class in Nevada even though I had more experience than all of the instructors in timber, brush, and felling snags and had fallen up to a hundred snags a day on projects including one that measured 7'8" at the stump. The upside, though, was that I discovered some bad habits I had learned from the old school sawyers. To Winnemucca's credit they saw my experience record in fire and forestry and signed off on my qualifications, but the Montana officer had a fit, and I took it the FMO whom I had fought fire with in Idaho. He approved me. On the Clearwater National Forest, they approved me and sent me out with the Assistant Fire Management Officer as an Engine Boss Trainee and he signed me off and gave me high marks as a boss in figuring out solutions to problems.

But on the Payette, like the Montana officer, they couldn't see past the paper trail even if the Incident Qualification and Command System (IQCS, a computer database listing a firefighter's qualifications and fire experience) had me listed as qualified in the position. I also needed to have a special saw card for the Payette above the supposed national standard and couldn't be certified in the next level (saw ratings are A, B, C and based on tree diameter, although some take complexity into account as some large trees were easier to fall than jack-strawed smaller trees), without a special class only given in the spring. There seemed to be a unique trait amongst some fire folk when they get into administrative positions and that was to add more layers of bureaucracy. There was supposed to be a national standard and what was good in one forest or district was good for another, but many forests decided to add extra paperwork or made the firefighter start over.

In 2007 I was an Incident Commander Type 4, a Crew Boss an Engine Boss, a Faller B, Helicopter Crew member, a Burn Boss because of my extensive experience in not only burning, but because I had planned them when I was the Assistant Fire Warden in Elk River, Idaho. My first red card on the Payette only listed Fire Fighter Type II (a first year firefighter), and they didn't want to give me that, but had to so they could keep me at Krassel. Some of those qualifications I had lost for good and it set me back for making money and going out on assignments and often I was on a fire with a crew boss or incident commander with a quarter of my experience.

Doug handed me the card. "Dino said you can teach the squad boss class and get credit, and we'll put you through pump class."

"Oh the irony. I'm not qualified to even be a squad boss, but I can teach it."

I went in to the office to talk with Alexis. "All your old district has to do is send us a letter saying they'll vouch for you."

"Have you called him?"

"Yes, and left messages, but he doesn't seem to even want to talk to me."

"What about my red cards from the Clearwater, Miles City, and Winnemucca since 2003? That's documentation that others have signed off on me, plus my fire record shows I was and IC type four."

"You haven't gone through the proper channels. Get your fire warden to write you a letter."

Dino stood shuffling some papers.

I said, "I thought the IQCS was supposed to take the place of all this chasing down of papers."

Dino said, "You could hack in and change the system."

"You've got to be kidding me." I guess I should have just taken a bunch of the blank certificates they had in the file cabinets when they weren't around and printed up a bunch of records.

The following Monday morning when I was driving back from my home in Moscow, Idaho, I drove to the C-PTPA office. The building sat along Highway 12 on the bank of the Clearwater River. Just over two hundred years previous Lewis and Clark built canoes out of ponderosa pines with the help of the Nez Perce tribe. In tribal history when the Corps of Discovery emerged onto the Wieppe prairie out of the Bitterroot Mountains, starving and lost, that some members of the tribe wanted to kill the explorers, but a woman who had been held captive and lived in Canada among whites, stopped them. The tribe hoped in helping the explorers that they could acquire guns to defend themselves from the Blackfeet and the Atsina tribes. In the end lost more than they gained. I had flown to a butte on rainy cloud strewn day above the North Fork of the Clearwater. We had landed to let some smokejumpers ready their gear so we could fly it off for them. On the edge of the butte I saw the rock with its dished out pockets for mixing war paints and, according to local legend, this was the last place the Nez Perce ceremonially prepared for their fight with US Army in Idaho before retreating toward Canada.

I pulled my Isuzu Trooper II into the parking lot at the Association office. The day had already begun to heat up. The river flowed heavy with run-off. Some of my old friends were there, but Walter, the Chief

Fire Warden and my former boss at the Elk River camp before his promotion, was out of the office. It was odd to be in the office again. I smiled and waved at Tim, who was the assistant. His family had been in the Association for three generations. He looked away as if I had walked into formal restaurant wearing a torn t-shirt and flip-flops. Another friend, Stan who had been out in the Floodwood when I had been forgotten on a fire, asked, "What can we do for you?"

"I wanted to talk with Walter."

"He's not in today."

"Great. I have to go back to Krassel. Can you have him write me a letter assuring the Payette that I have fought fire for more than a month?"

"I'll ask him. But, you know, that woman's been calling down here an awful lot." His contempt for her reflected the "Old Boy" nature of the Association that believed women had no business in the woods.

"That woman is the Assistant Fire Management Officer and she just wants to be able to red card me so I can fight fire."

"Their problem is that they don't believe a person can work when they can. They keep their noses inside regulation manuals and do more harm than good."

"Look, I just need you to send them my certificate or have Walter write them a letter."

Stan walked back to his office. After picking up a file folder, he thumbed through it. "You went to that class the same time as Tim, but I don't know. We have his."

"I worked for you guys for five years. All of you know the work I did. Jesus, I was the assistant warden at Elk River."

"You know, a bunch of our people have the same problem. The Payette told John he wasn't even allowed to use a drip torch. They need to modify their system." John had been a Fire Warden and had more than twenty years experience.

"The Payette doesn't care. Just ask Walter to do this for me."

The Federal Fire Service wasn't going to change to suit how small co-operative fire unit in Idaho believed things should be done, I thought as I said bye. As I left he told me good luck. I believed that it'd work out because there wasn't a reason to think everyone didn't have my interests in mind. I even thought, given the opportunity, the Association would write the Payette just to back up the credibility of their training and out of organizational pride. But I was wrong there too.

I drove the highway back down Idaho. US 95 split Idaho, running north and south, and was the main transportation artery for highway traffic in those directions. Two lanes over prairies and down into river gorges, like the mighty Salmon River, cut through forested mountains, the Snake River plain, the rugged Owyhee mountains, and the high desert into Oregon. The landscape never failed to stun me and made me reflect.

In the early days of the Forest Service they'd go into bars and ask for volunteers and now the training to become a supervisor in fire would require enough classroom time to earn a college degree, if not more, then there was the field experience and having task books signed for assignments. Across the Fire Service a few years ago great fire management officers without some kind of biology or forestry college credits were being told they had to take those college classes or be demoted, no matter the quality or how much field experience they had. The 401 series, as the program was known, was rescinded, but not before wasting the time and money of people and taxpayers. In a small irony I wanted to try to get into dispatch and with a Bachelor's in English and a minor in Spanish, a Master of Fine Arts degree in writing, several years teaching writing and communications, and over a decade in fire talking on radios to aircraft, crews, and dispatchers, I was less qualified than somebody with biology credits and a season in fire.

The task book system was devised with the best intentions, and good in theory, but like most things became modified by piling on or a splitting off of jobs that should be included in one book. If one assignment was good then three was better. Sometimes due to another assignments or a slow season, a person might not get signed off for years. Then it went to a committee and they deemed if the assignment was worthy of being counted in a closed meeting where the candidate was excluded. On one forest, if a trainer signed off on an assignment, then the trainer also needed to write an evaluation in addition to the comments in the task book because more paper equals better instead of redundant. In some cases individual jobs were split out, requiring an additional task book or task books. For instance, a person becomes a helicopter crewmember and then has to complete task books for helispot manager and long line specialist. A helicopter crewmember should already be able to do these things or he wasn't much of a crewmember.

Even then, with these requirements in place we still had "red card whores" who tried to put as many qualifications on their card as quickly as possible and by doing so acquired the minimum experience operating in those positions, but had all the paperwork in order. Supervisors signed off their task books rather than dealing with them or maybe they just signed out of rote obligation. It was ironic to me that some get signed off because they had connections or that they were a problematic to have around, and to get rid of them the supervisor just signed them off. Lack of experience was no problem if you had the office work looking snappy.

The highway rose up out of the Salmon River canyon and into the high valleys around New Meadows. The forested mountains bracketed ranches and pastures on each side of the highway and I turned left at the junction where the small town split US 55 and US 95 at a gas station with an A&W restaurant. Highway 95 went southwest and Highway 55 went east past the house with the "Don't Tread on Me" flag and another with a Confederate flag painted on his mail box and stars and bars flag over the junk pile surrounding a rundown house. The other houses were newer, well kept and in a perfect Idaho juxtaposition of backwards thinking in the midst progressive values being built up around them. The highway rose into the high country and McCall. At McCall I'd still have two hours to reach Krassel and a long time to wonder if my desire to rappel and work with Jen and Doug again would cost me in unexpected ways. I'd given up my chance to try and be a smokejumper, but that was something I had been willing to do. It was easy to think a person kept moving forward instead of being knocked back. Even as I drove and having had people try to destroy what I'd worked for in the past, I felt that they were the anomaly. I kept thinking that at heart all people were inherently good and would help me in my journey.

During my first season in Alaska, Julia taught me the ways of the seiner and how to long-line. Dave showed me how to navigate and pilot a boat. Julia showed me the ways to live upon the sea and ride out storms filling the sea with ship crushing waves and we taught each other. It wasn't just that the stakes were so high that they worked with

36

me. No they hired me knowing I knew next to nothing, but saw past that and lifted me up and made me part of a crew. The first day we left the dock, we sailed under a sky clamped down with clouds. The wind carried the rain and it pelted the sea. The boat waddled through the swells as I stood on the back deck, electrified with possibility.

At Warm Lake Road in Cascade, I turned east again. Fifty miles from Krassel. Almost like a time machine the further I traveled, the houses giving way to forests and mountains with the final destination still standing as it had been for many decades. I rolled down the Trooper's window. The air carried the crisp reminder that spring hung on between the greening up of the forests and shaking off the snow gathered in the peaks and summits of the mountains. Patches of snow receded into the forest shade or the north side of ridges. The ebbing and flowing of flux and change that brings renewal and growth, but also a leaving behind, because not everything survived the winter to see the blossoms of spring.

I hated the cynical turn of thoughts in my head. I knew of plenty of people who did have other's best interest in mind and fire administrators who worked their level best in trying to make the system work better to help firefighters as it was intended to do and not as a weapon to beat them down. In my career I'd been lucky to work with some of the finest firefighters. At Krassel I pulled in front of Cabin Three. The crew worked at one of the many jobs at a remote post. The fire crew took care of all the maintenance of the camp, even where the trails, recreation, and other forest crews stayed. We mowed the grass, ran the weed eater, painted the buildings, sharpened fire tools, maintained the power saws and pumps, worked on the water system, organized the fire cache, made sure the plumbing worked in Cabin Five where the trails crew stayed, mended gear, charged propane tanks, tuned up the generators, installed solar panels, cleaned the communal areas, checked the Jet-A fuel quality, repainted the helipads, organized records, planned training, and the odds and ends of running a crew and camp.

In the evening we lit a campfire in the fire ring—Lake Saleen. When the supervisor of the crew at the time, Merrill Saleen, had the crew excavate the about 12 foot diameter hole to line with flat rocks and make a sunken area for the fire and a place for people to sit in the round, his crew filled it with water at night so that in the morning it would appear flooded, putting off construction another day. They revealed the practical joke after a couple of weeks and finished building the gathering place. We all brought food to put into a three foot wok that was a gift from the mother of a previous supervisor, Willy Acton. Alone, but for ourselves, we cooked a communal meal and shared stories and drinks and dinner. We might've played volleyball that night or maybe someone broke out a guitar or three and played music and sang songs or maybe both. The night deepened and the sky spread taut between the ridges like a glittered tarp. The sound of the South Fork of the Salmon River rushing by in its spring frenzy rose up canyon sides making a soundtrack to the noise of voices, guitars, and clatter of plates, utensils, cans and bottles.

Krassel was one of the few remote bases left and one of the few places where a crew lived together all week. At the time most crews had been moved into town or moved into town to create super bases of over 40 people who drove home every night, or as many have said, upper level supervisors putting all their eggs in a basket to keep their thumbs on them. For now Krasselians gathered as in the early days of the Forest Service and worked and lived together, and created a team of people who knew each other's strengths and weakness and filled in the gaps. After the crash and the investigations, Krassel became a place to get away from the scrutiny and questions of others. A place of solace as well as remembrance. Around the fire ring as flames lit our faces and kept the chill of May air back not much could be said, and as Adam Stark put it later: "One way or the other one of my friends made a mistake and killed other friends, and I don't need to know who it was, just how to stop it from happening again."

In the end all of the rules and dictates, that in some cases were absurd, others well intentioned, but pointless, and some bona fide, but later to be perverted and twisted by micromanagers, made little difference because no matter how fire managers tried to provide a net to keep them from liability, those of us still in the field were already implementing changes in how we viewed the world and how we would train the firefighters following after us. We sat around the fire sharing tales of our past and of a future we all planned to live to see. We in the field thought two steps ahead of the administrators, and they never bothered to ask us what we thought. Unlike them, we had to live with the consequences, so we staked out the pragmatic from the bureaucratic. At Krassel they shared stories of the dead. We all became part of an extended family story and what binds families and cultures are webs of stories, even the myths, that let us know who we are and where we came from, divine or not. The fire popped and cracked. Money said, "This is the earliest form of human entertainment. To watch fire burn and tell stories about the best way to bring down a mammoth or where to find the most delicious roots."

Yes, I thought, to share stories of survival, mental and physical and bond the clan of the fire crew. The buddy check at its finest. To make one conscious.

In one week Jess, Money, Kat, Dano and Keg, a thickset Mormon guy who had worked on the Sawtooth Hotshots a couple seasons before coming to Krassel, and I rolled for the Horse Creek Fire in western Wyoming as a squad assigned to a twenty-person hand-crew called the Payette Regulars--a crew made up of firefighters from different districts on the Forest including engine operators, heli-rappellers, smokejumpers, hand-crew members, and sometimes trail-crew folks. We were lucky on the Payette because we had such a deep roster of experience to pull from that even if we ended up with several first year firefighters that it was likely that even the squad bosses had crew boss level experience. The curse was to be assigned experienced firefighters who were difficult to lead because if an operation wasn't planned to what they thought was right or if it wasn't their idea then they might fight it a little. Overall they joined together once the plan was ordered and got the job safely and effectively.

Jess had a squad boss task book, and because I was an experienced crew-boss, Money assigned me to shadow her and train her. There were a few jokes about making sure her reports were grammatically correct, as I'd been teaching English composition as a teaching assistant at the University of Idaho. We arrived in the ICP (incident command post). It had been set up in a meadow by a gravel road that led up a drainage. All the camps had the quality of a carnival in that yurts were erected for offices and in some cases trailers, like construction office trailers were hauled in, lines of port-a-potties (the blue rooms), semi-trucks with mobile kitchens, showers, fuel, water, and supplies collected in a tight group. Generators ran all night and the ground churned to dust filled the air. In some places they try dust abatement by having water tenders spray the main routes around the camp, but often times it just made mud or slippery clay. Parking was usually tight and with the people wandering around we took extra precautions by having someone from each truck get out to ground guide us. We parked and hoped to be out in the field soon. No one wanted to stay in camp with the dust and the noise.

On this assignment I met some of the other firefighters on the Payette. The Warren Hand Crew's supervisor became a close friend, Ryan Flegal. Tattoos covered his body and arms. Insignias of crews he had belonged to, nicknames, the zip code where he grew up, and has favorite tree he studied in forestry school. His skin a full color resume written with a needle. Thin and wiry, he never stopped moving and ran a power saw the way I imagined a samurai wielded a katana: grace, strength, and efficient. If we weren't on a fire, he PTed his crew with runs and calisthenics. After the fire in Wyoming the Geographic Area Command Center (GACC) transferred us to Camp Williams in Utah. In the morning on a fire on the Fourth of July we'd climbed high up some ridge over looking Spanish Forks. The IC said the climb would be short and we'd be able to see the fireworks in Salt Lake City. At midnight we reached the top and then spiked out with space blankets in a rock patch. The morning dawned freezing. All of us shivered under space blankets in the rocks. I stood stamped my feet. Keg stood close by, hands in his pockets. Down the hill from us Flegal and one of his crewmembers, Morgan, had sandwiched themselves between two space blankets and huddled up for warmth. Keg looked at me and shook his head as if telling me, "Don't you even think about coming over here."

*

At the command post in Wyoming, Jess and I took a hand-held radio to the communications tent. The technician hooked a cable from his radio to ours and cloned it to the frequencies being used on the incident. We took it back and cloned all the radios in our crew. We went to the operation's tent to get a briefing on the fire, the weather, and where they wanted us to go and who to make contact with.

I showed her how to use her notebook to organize what information she needed and how to brief the crew. She laughed as she wrote the weather forecast for the afternoon. "Last week you were the rookie."

"I'll always be a rookie," I said.

"Me too, buddy. Me too."

Jess and I trained each other over the summer in different ways. Because our district covered part of the Frank Church: River of No Return Wilderness I learned how to fall and buck trees using crosscuts, known as misery whips, like the old time loggers. Jess competed in logging sports at the University of Idaho, as did Jen Benedict who would join our crew the next season. When Benedict graduated from the University of Montana, collegiate competitors sighed in relief because of her fierceness in the arena. They both smoked me in chopping and bucking. It made me think about how far the fire service had strayed from its early days and even how people have been hired to do work in other professions. Missing a certificate didn't take my experience away or my ability to do a job or teach the best way to do that job to another. It also spoke to the mistrust administrators had of the crewmembers. Julia could teach me to be a fisherman and a sailor in the fishing fleet, but a crew of seasoned and experienced firefighters was forbidden to vouch for another without calling a committee and submitting reams of paper.

Jess reread her notes. "We need to make sure we have plenty of water. It's going to get hotter." We began walking to the trucks to brief the waiting crew on our mission. She had all her paperwork in order and ready to learn and develop her skills through experience, as was I. "All right, let's do this," she said and gathered the squad around her.

Chapter 4

FALLING INTO FIRE

In 1997 I fought my first wildfires. My rookie year I worked alone
and as a part of smoke chaser teams in helicopters and on ground
attack, fell my first snags and trees, begun to learn forestry, and
had been assigned to my first prescribed burn. Fire flooded up from
the bottom of the main draw, and when it hit the two tributaries, split;
at the head of each, fire whirls, cyclones of flaming debris, arose. It
was dark. The upper fire line held and the heat in the bottom of the
draw continued to surge air upward, feeding the embers sucked from
the logging unit's timber litter. A cold October breeze, drawn by the
heat, drafted out of the darkness from the unburned timber on the
ridge's opposite side. Firebrands glowed out of sight, carried by the
wind whirls, into the damp and cool night where they would not start
another fire outside the line.

At the bottom of the burning clear-cut, my drip torch was empty
and all I had to do was make sure that the fire didn't find a dry patch
and burn some bonus acres on my section of the line. It was unlikely,
considering the conditions and the wet year, one with low wildfire
activity. But, it was a hazard nonetheless.

I had climbed the steep ridges of north-central Idaho with the fire
crews of the Clearwater-Potlatch Timber Protective Association, called
CT or the Association. The organization was an amalgam of two co-
operative organizations, the Clearwater Timber Protective Association
and the Potlatch Timber Association, formed before the Idaho
Department of Lands had gone into the forests and fire suppression
and before the USFS had found its way into serious fire fighting in the
wake of the 1910 conflagration. The summer before, I had finished
my third season as a commercial fisherman in Alaska, but that April I

had moved to north-central Idaho, and instead of fighting the weather and the sea; I fought the weather and land. A relative by marriage to my fiancé had gotten me on as an emergency fire crewmember when a slash abatement fire had gotten out of control in Bat Creek, outside of Weippe, Idaho. After the fire was contained, I stayed on with the Headquarters crew and began to learn the intricacies of forestry work, logging, fire suppression, and the politics of governmental agencies.

My first prescribed burn, I had been allowed to run a drip torch. Two others and I strip fired the unit, walking length wise, top to bottom, wading slash while dribbling fire behind us until the diesel and gasoline-initiated fire raged through cured limbs, tree tops, brush, and logs that hadn't made the grade. Alder, huckleberry, service berry and syringa still growing within the unit slapped me and tore at my sleeves as the slash shredded the cuffs of my pants, demonstrating why loggers cut the cuffs of their pants even with their boot tops and their sleeves at about mid-forearm. I started using my hardhat to bore my way through the brush. I'd dip my head and hope for as few thorns as possible. Wild rose and blackberry vines and weeds like Canadian and Scotch thistle left thorns and stickers in my clothes to worry rashes and scratches on my skin. The effort of wallowing through brush and the slash had me wishing for a pair of caulk boots, like the assistant fire warden's moving uphill from me, never slipping. The small spikes on the boots dug into the wood and prevented him from sliding on the bush and limbs. A pair of the boots would not only keep me off my ass, but save energy and wear and tear on my knees and ankles. It was like trying to get my sea legs all over again.

We had started out spaced several yards apart downhill. The assistant fire warden Paul, at the top, would start lighting the slash and brush, and, after he had walked ahead about ten feet, the second guy, Bill, would start lighting, and finally me. It was impressed upon me, whatever you do, do not pass the man above you; it would cut off his escape route, downhill. The fire burned in strips as I negotiated the draws and ridges of the unit. I remember seeing the man above me, stopping to wait for him to move on. The assistant fire warden was on the top and he set a brisk pace. At that time, I thought it had something to do with the fire, but it didn't.

I huffed and sweated, and when we reached the far side, we spaced ourselves below my strip and crossed the unit again. As we watched the fire, I shivered; the cold night hovered at my back and I thought it odd to be standing below forty acres of fire and be cold. The air started to move up slope and the smoke pushed into the air. Later, I would find out that often convection cannot be sustained and the smoke will lie over, choking any one on that side of the line.

The point of the burn was to reduce the fire hazard, promote nitrogen release, and clear the slash so that the tree planters would have an easier time getting trees into the ground the following spring. A perfect burn would leave the ground the texture of black velvet, and all the organic material would remain unburned just beneath the surface. For me, this had become the culmination of the unofficial motto, *we fight □em and we light □em*. It was beautiful. In the case of Bat Creek, it had been we light □em and *then* fight □em.

We were on the final pass. I would weave between the road and several yards into the unit until the unit boundary climbed the ridges above the road; then, I would light the edge of the road's cut bank or natural drop offs to several yards uphill. We passed above a cut bank that had a thirty-foot drop, and as I reached the mid point of the cut, weaving downhill, the fire sprang up before me. Bill had dipped down and lit the slash in front of me and to the lip of the cut bank. Because I had fired the area behind, I was trapped in a pocket of slash with fire on three sides and on the fourth, air that was being consumed.

An overwhelming heat displaced the alternating shivers and warmth. The smoke and scorched air caused my eyes to slam shut. Tears sluiced down my cheeks, unable to wash away the abrasion. The overwhelming blast that comes from a fire shocked rookie firefighters. I had heard several say, "I didn't realize how hot it would be." It felt as if I worked at sea on a seiner again. It wasn't only the salt spray that stung your eyes. Jellyfish caught in the seine dropped out as the net passed through the power block, suspended above the deck on a boom. Sometimes they slid off my hood or the bill of my cap and splashed into my face. The poison caused temporary blindness and it burned, and no matter how hard I tried to open my eyes, arching my brows until the muscles cramped, I couldn't. The skipper yelled to keep my head down and keep pulling and piling the net. If we stopped the boat would drift into the gear and not only foul the prop, but collapse the seine. Afterward, Julia held my blind eyes open and poured milk into them to relieve the pain. Thirty minutes later, I could see again.

Smoke and fire provoked the same, eye-gripping response. I brushed my eyes with my gloved hand. The cotton logging gloves were sooty and reeked of diesel and white fir. I could feel the fuel mix with the sweat as it wore into the corners of my eyes. Ahead, Bill picked his way through the slash, and I cursed him, but he kept going, and I fought to keep my eyes open. The flames gathered height at the ridge top, my space was shrinking, and I became the center of a convection column, the wind no longer at my back or in my face, but all around me and moving upward and not across. Sweat puddled under my hard hat and rivulets ran down my head. Flames wrapped themselves around individual needles and branches, then around the tree trunks in columns of fire streaking into the dark, whirling like a dervish trying to spin his way to communion with God, a twisting, sensuous dance that mesmerized the eyes, a cobra that swayed back and forth before striking. Fire chanted in cracks and pops as it burned, and as certain fuels sang their hymn, a savvy fire fighter could tell what was burning by the sound and how fast the fire ran. I looked down my escape route and saw some of the pick-ups pulled into an old log deck, but the guys who were supposed to be watching that part of the line were gone.

I took six long steps through the fire as it started to close my corridor. The cold air wrapped my body, raising goose bumps, as I slid-fell to the road. Gravel and powdered clay filled the air with dust and left red streaks along my calves, elbows, and ass. I walked up the road, climbed back into the unit and finished my strip. My lookouts had wandered down to a stream where they had sunk some beer and had moved down slope for a little fresh air and a cigarette.

I confronted Bill and the assistant fire warden about being entrapped, they both shrugged. Bill said, "Fire's a dangerous business."

When the fire died down, the embers and small patches of brush and slash continued glowing. Concentrations flared up and died down as they reached the point of ignition. The unit looked like a city seen from an airplane at night or Los Angeles seen from high up in the San Gabriel Mountains, sprawled out lights glimmering orange against the black in a natural geometry of lines and blocks--its own universe with a thousand withering stars.

The crew was an odd mixture of kids right out of high school who didn't know where else to go, guys who had grown up in this region—the north-central woods of Idaho—and looking to retire in a few years, men who had tried to leave, but remained, working the summers on the CT crews and logging through the winter until the CT called them back. If they held out long enough they could get one of the few permanent positions when one came open. Others couldn't leave; they had trapped themselves and couldn't get a job anywhere else. In cities like Los Angeles, they would have been seen sleeping in cardboard boxes, vying for space under a bridge, or a shut-in waiting for the social security check to come. A few of the firefighters had come in from the out of the area, and, after many years, came to be accepted; still as likely as not, they were treated as inferior. Of the outsiders there were two groups, those who had come from logging backgrounds and those who hadn't. The organization was founded in 1905 by timber men who conceived of fire suppression as a means to save lumber--the fuel of their manifest destiny.

I was an outsider brought in by the forbearance of a relative and had become one of those people who, when they reached out and touch fire, had to reach out again. When it burned, it cauterized the urge to see it, to confront it, to control it. Maybe it was in the way it moved or raced, but harnessing, taming, something wild and dangerous was something necessary and elemental. Perhaps it was because of its elemental nature—one of the big four of antiquity—and by grasping it, we somehow came to terms with our own inner fires. Or maybe it was just a kick in the ass. Whatever it was, it made me wonder what it took to walk away.

When the fire died down, we gathered at the trucks. Most of our fire vehicles were converted military rigs: M-880 pick-ups, 2½ ton trucks (the deuce and a half), and Gamma Goats fitted with water tanks, tool boxes, and painted red. The CT was an organization protecting federal, state and private timber lands and had the same authority as a state district and answered to the state for some funding, although an autonomous entity ruled by a board of landowners and a chief fire warden. They charged a fee for each acre under their protection and contracted forestry work: thinning, pruning, hand-line construction, applying herbicide, maintaining forest roads, gate work, and prescribed burning. In fact, the oldest wildfire lookout stood on Bertha Hill in one of their districts, and was maintained and operated by them. I leaned over the hood of one of the trucks and listened to what the veteran firefighters were saying. I had become used to operating on the sea, but I was still getting used to the environment beneath the trees. I came to learn experience didn't equal competence.

*

Bill wore a goofy looking welder's cap, and would bum smokes and bite them off at the filter when he was out of snoose. He had once been on a Hotshot crew--the highly trained ground crews--and used to be an assistant fire warden on the Boehls' district until he'd been fired for drug problems. It was said that he had been the best saw in the woods at one time, but something had happened. Some claimed he'd always been screwed up, some said he started using drugs after his father was killed on a logging job. The tree his father was working barber chaired--that's when a tree cracks vertically as a sawyer is finishing the back-cut, and its weight forces the butt of the tree straight into the sawyer like a battering ram, squashing him onto the hillside or into another tree behind him.

Bill was short and wiry, wore his hair shaved close and always had five o'clock shadow, even in the morning. When he walked, it was fast; he leaned forward into his suspenders as if he was bucking a stiff wind. Although the regulations called for all leather boots, he wore the rubber bottomed, Maine boots, even on fires. He had the habit of cutting up his clothing: he stagged off his jeans, like most loggers, cut the sleeves up, and sliced out the front of his Mackinaw so it looked as if he was wearing plaid tails. He always wore thermal underwear, whether on the hottest fires or the hottest days.

Bill carried the power saw on his shoulder and led the crew over the road bank. We were out at Gold Dollar Flats, preparing a clear-cut for a prescribed burn. A storm was threatening. A triple topped cedar was leaning hard up hill. It would be nearly impossible to fall it downhill. The unit was "steep as a cow's face," as they'd said, and there was no way anyone could fall the tree into the lean and get to safety before it would slide down on him. But the tree needed to be felled; it was close to the fire line, and should fire run up it, it would broadcast firebrands out of the unit. There was the additional possibility that if the tree fell during the burn, it would roll out the bottom, spreading fire into the timber. Bill intended to climb the tree, and cut two of its tops out so that it would fall the way he wanted, without trying to wedge it over. The crew boss thought it was a bad idea, but Bill, in his forties, dismissed the twenty year old; "Don't you worry, I was topping trees when your dad was a pup."

The wind filled the treetops like sails. The howls across the top of the canopy, made me feel like I was in a jar. The thunderstorm was drawing in air, but the downburst was probably twenty minutes away yet. We expected harder winds, rain, and as it turned out, hail, and lightning loomed over the next ridge. The crew boss led us up the hill to a safe location to watch.

Bill tied a length of rope to the orange and white Stihl, snapped on his saw chaps, cinched down his hard hat, and began to climb the cedar. I watched closely. I had never seen a tree topped and had just started to learn how to use a power saw. Most of my experience had been on prescribed burn firebreaks, cutting brush and deadfall around a fire perimeter. I had tripped a couple of snags, including a rotted white fir that was three feet on the butt. An accomplishment, but I was no sawyer. Bill worked his way into the tree through the branches, and situated himself with his back against the main trunk. He wasn't far off of the ground on the uphill side, twenty feet or so, but on the high side it was forty feet off the ground. After hauling up the saw, he started it. He gunned the motor a few times, cut away some limbs, and began cutting one of the tops close to the bole of the tree.

We had hiked up the hill about 60 feet. From our position, it was like sitting in a balcony watching a one-act play. Bill kicked some of the limbs out of the way and gunned the motor again. The top started to crack and seconds later, he and the saw plummeted to the ground in a storm of limbs and fronds. The saw landed on its power head with the bar pointed into the air, and he scrambled midair, grabbing at limbs on his way down, flailing, and trying through body English and will power to miss the idling saw. He crashed to the ground even as thunder rumbled from somewhere over French Mountain.

The crew boss yelled for him to stop, but Bill dusted himself off, shut off the saw, adjusted his hardhat, and climbed up again. He pulled the rope and, within a minute, he and the saw fell to the ground again in a surreal moment of déjà vu. I had seen some crazy shit in my life, like the 2nd lieutenant who gave a machine gun safety lecture, then fired it without the barrel being secure, launching it downrange, or a deckhand who had tied off a line, leaned over the side rail as the line unwrapped, dumping him into the sea. They all got the same look on their faces, and Bill had it then, the shocked look as though he had given what he knew was the correct answer and had been proven wrong. What I remember clearest is that fear did not cross over his face, even as he rolled through the air missing the saw a second time. I later learned that when he was the assistant fire warden in the Floodwood, he led a crew over a hill and trapped the firefighters in a bad spot, as he would later do to me. He had had his boots burned off his feet and, luckily, the crew escaped with nothing more than emotional scars. I imagine he had had that same look then as he had now plunging for the ground above the power saw in a reverse of Damocles.

He always had that same look, an accidental nonchalance, and I understood he would never be hurt badly, though he would scatter crews with trees felled at them and then climb up to the next one as if he were alone on the hillside. Undeterred, he climbed back into the tree a third time and pruned off some limbs to show the cedar that it hadn't got the best of him, climbed down and fell the tree as hail drove the rest of us back to the crew-cab.

A convection column will punch straight up through cold air and create its own weather. It changes what was there before into something entirely different and reshapes the environment at the local level. Something similar happened to the Clearwater-Potlatch Timber Protective Association. The Association thought of themselves as rogue firefighters, the guerillas of the fire world, who wore tin hats after they had been banned by other agencies, who would let men operate power saws without saw chaps, ear plugs, or safety glasses, and who opted to wear the clothes of the logging industry in lieu of Nomex (fire resistant clothing required by all other agencies), that was rarely worn, if at all. They eventually conceded to wear the shirts most of the time.

*

The helicopter, a Bell Jet Ranger 206, had a thirty-foot cable hung under it, and suspended from it was a fifty-five gallon drum with an igniter, filled with alumagel. The napalm-like substance would ignite the slash in the steep clear-cut for the broadcast burn. This was in the Floodwood above the Little North Fork of the Clearwater River. It was anything but gentle, country of forty to sixty percent slopes that jutted up from the river and climbed a thousand feet over a couple of miles. Our pilot would discharge the flames just as we had done with drip torches. With the helicopter we walked less, and watching it stream fire was as close as I ever wanted to get to seeing a dragon. It hovered close and then flew across the top of the unit. The ship had backed off to watch and wait for the firing boss to tell him to make another pass. Five fire fighters, including myself, were in the top north corner of the east facing clear-cut. The top and bottom firebreaks, and the north line were roads. The west line was a hand-line. The upper line was a dead-end logging road that was narrow and chewed up from trucks and heavy equipment.

We watched as fire ran up unfelled stobs. They turned into Roman candles and broadcast fire over the line in flaming parachutes. Snags in the green timber are known as fire catchers and the reason sawyers fell all snags within thirty feet of the line in the timber. The fire created its own wind and started pushing more smoke and firebrands over the line. Luckily, it was late in the year and the rate of spread would be slow, but it was going to be a long affair; if we waited the spot fires could join other spots and gather its own intensity and change the conditions. While the crew boss called in the spot fires, I noticed that all across the mile and half front, fire was spotting over the line. There were five of us on the crew, though three said almost simultaneously, "I got a *bad* knee, back, knee and back, so we'll stay here and watch the trucks." That left me, a rookie in my first year, and Mike, another rookie.

Mike climbed onto the back of a deuce and half and opened the toolbox, as I grabbed a power saw. I wanted to begin tripping the burning snags so that they would quit flinging embers. Then we could wet them down and move to the next one, but before I could start the power saw, Mike called that there was no rigging in the truck. The other three began to look in the pick-ups, as Mike climbed onto the other deuce and a half, and came up with a first aid kit, but no hoses or fittings. Close to 2500 gallons of water ready to be carried by one guy in his hard hat. The burn boss called off the helicopter, believing that more fire wasn't the answer. It was backing down the hill at a steady rate and it was fortunate that the ground cover under the timber was damp, but we couldn't let the fire change that.

One of the men with a bad knee volunteered to drive the forty minutes to camp to retrieve hoses and fittings, a second offered to give him a hand and the third offered to act as our lookout.

I looked at the sky overhead—a habit I picked up on the sea. On summer mornings, sometimes banks of clouds form battlements and towers, called alto cumulous castellanus, castle clouds. Free floating fortresses in the sky. When the firefighter saw them, he knew there'd be trouble in the afternoon. It was also true in the fishing fleet—red sky at night a sailor's delight; red sky in the morning sailor take warning—except now the red sky was filtered sun through the clouds of black smoke of green timber and brush burning. The equipment arrived three hours later, and I was still tripping snags and grubbing them out with my pulaski, as they lit grass, weeds, and shrubs.

I backed a deuce and a half down the logging road that was supposed to be the upper firebreak. The smoke was thick, and the heat was intensified in the all steel cab. Sweat and smoke burned my eyes as I tried to keep the truck rolling steadily down the torn up road. Below me was a forty-degree slope; if I went off the road, I wouldn't stop rolling until I hit the Little North Fork of the Clearwater River some several miles down. Visibility was reduced to a little beyond the mud-flaps, and part of this was due to my watering, burning eyes. The bandana that I sucked air through became wet, and contrary to popular belief, it's more dangerous to breathe smoke through damp cloth. Moisture mixed with smoke increased the airway and lung damage.

The air was dense with smoke—at times, it felt like the Bering Sea when I had been pitched overboard during a particularly grueling herring fishery two years before. The whole world became focused into the amount of space I existed in, introspective in the first seconds, and then the consciousness ranging out and in supra-awareness. I remembered whales seining herring. They dove under a school of fish, swam in great circles blowing air, driving fish into the center of the cyclone, swimming toward the surface to stay ahead of the bubble net. Whales swam upwards, mouth gaping to gorge on fish. The whole time I was only forty feet from shore, caught in a tiderip, trying angle away from the certain death of gill nets. I saw the gulls like they were painted on a porcelain sky, circling and waiting to dive into the center of the sea where the whales sounded, breaking the surface with concussive blows.

Currents of smoke breathed in like water—it felt as if I were drowning. I swam in the truck cab and could hear a bull elk bugling over the ridge as he challenged another bull to duel or to get lost.

Bull elk can be twelve hundred pounds with bone sabers on their heads, crashing brush and destroying small to midsize trees. The herd galloped through a stand of trees, sounding like a cavalry charge busting through pickets, impervious to steep ground and thickets. As I heard them moving away, in my mind I could see the herd bull bugling at the smoke streaming up the ridge as he herded his harem toward Gobbler's Knob.

I and the other fit firefighter worked on opposite ends of the burn and pursued spots, trying to work our way to the center. It became dark as I kept relaying the hose, packing my saw and pulaski forward, and dealing with each small fire. I would take small breaks to scout the terrain, to make sure other spot fires weren't about to flare up, or that I wasn't about to be entrapped. The later it became, the more the temperature dropped, and the fire danger decreased. I thought about calling on the radio, but in the outfit it was common to work for hours without using the radio. An unwritten rule: do not break radio silence at all costs. This was a reaction to guys like Bill who would stand 20 feet away and call a crewmember to see if he had any smokes he could chew.

The night was quiet except for the muffled sound of the pump filtered through the forest. Occasionally, I heard the creak of a tree and it toppling over, crashing into the ground. It was eerie, the cracks and pops echoing in the dark, waiting for any rush of wind, any warning that a snag was falling for me.

It was around eleven p.m. when I got a radio call from the warden. He didn't know where we were. He had seen the three other crewmembers back at camp and assumed that Mike and I were at the camp or in the bunkhouse. It seemed that as the two of us had worked securing the fire, the others had decided to head back to dinner at the fire camp, have a couple of beers, and go to bed. The fire warden drove out to get us and back at camp, he took us to the cookhouse, said, "It's all you can eat boys, so make yourself at home." It wasn't his fault that the state forestry crews and injured CT guys had left nothing but squash, mashed potatoes, and the stripped, greasy carcasses some type of fowl--small turkeys or large chickens, but I'll never forget the night--forgotten on the fire-line and then the all you can eat squash and spuds at the Floodwood fire camp.

We sat on the benches at the long tables. We were black and sooty, and smoke hung heavy on us stifling our sweat. I ached and my nose was clogged. We were wet and might as easily have died from hypothermia as an escaped fire. We looked at each other across the table, loading our mouths with tablespoons of squash. Mike smiled and I nodded; we couldn't wait for morning.

The food didn't need to be chewed, I could swallow it as fast I could put it in my mouth, but I chewed and took my time. My hands ached from being molded onto a pulaski handle and the vibration of running a power saw; I almost couldn't hold onto the spoon. How could I know then, tired as I was, that the next afternoon my hand would be wrapped around the cork of a fly rod as a 19-inch cutthroat trout rose to a royal coachman—the reward for our perseverance, a two-hour trip to the river. For now, I looked up, and the cookhouse windows reflected my image. My blond mustache was black and the smoke and charcoal streaked my skin, gathering in the creases and pores. My eyes stared out of blacked out sockets. I twisted my head and popped my neck as wind shivered across the glass. It was a portent for sunrise five hours off, because wind at night will keep a fire active and threatening. I knew it would be like the endless hours in the Alaska fisheries, where at any minute the weather could change, or personnel and equipment failure could twist an easy day into a hard scramble. But there was something in the challenge of a precarious existence that would make sure I would be up at 4:30 and work long into the next night. Fire runs through the blood like it rips through dry grass in August.

Chapter 5

TEN AND EIGHTEEN

A hard wind drove a storm up Dworshak Reservoir scattering lightning and fire in north-central Idaho, blowing white caps on the water and knocking down trees in the creaking forest. The Association dispatch called us out of Elk River at around 2300, along with a crew from Orofino. It was going to be my first complex fire as an incident commander. Mike and I drove in an M-880 pick-up followed by two deuce-and-a-half fire-trucks. We could see the fire's glow as we came to the breaks of the reservoir. Homes situated on five-acre plots, called ranchettes were scattered on a bench above where the fire burned in grass, brush, and ponderosa pines. Mike and I pulled into a driveway and backlit by the glow the fire a woman in her thirties held onto a trembling and wide-eyed bay horse by its halter. I couldn't tell who was more frightened. The woman was afraid the horse would bolt through the fence and down the hill into the fire. I told her the horse would run the other way and she risked being stomped if she kept holding onto it. "You guys," she said, "have to stop the fire."

"We will," I said, while I thought, holy crap, the fire's ripping. Some rain had fallen so the fire didn't carry as fast through the grass. As we started to make our way into the pasture three trucks from Orofino fell into line behind us. Against the black of night the flames curled up and flames further down the mountain made shadows of smoke and flakes of ash swirling up on the heat columns like the bodies of sinners in a Bosch painting of hell. The fence had already been cut at the back of the lady's pasture. We drove onto a bull-rocked road developers had built. Neighbors slapped at the flames in the grass with burlap sacks.

I hoped the public listened to me and stayed out of the way because I had no authority to tell them to evacuate. Only the law could do that.

I worried about the locals, where I needed to put the trucks, and how to deploy my people. The previous wildfires I had been the incident commander of had been small low intensity lightning strikes in the middle of the woods. Single trees I walked around and dropped, fires two people could dig a hand-line around in a couple of hours, fires with ten people and a couple of engines. We often joked that we worked on the asbestos forest. The weather through our area had been wetter. I had been a crewmember or a squad boss on larger fires with dozens of people, engines, helicopters, dozers, and worked the big slash abatement fires that consumed hundreds of acres in an afternoon, but nothing near a home.

*

During the Fire School in June, I had taught "Standards of Survival," to incoming firefighters, not because of my vast fire experience, but because they needed someone and my fire warden had noticed that I had a knack for training people. It helped that the more experienced firefighters in the Association didn't want to teach it and some went so far to say that it was only the government trying to teach common sense and a waste of time when we should be working in woods. "Bunch of damned college boys. They'd have us spend more time checking off lists and consulting paperwork than fighting fire." The SOS as we called the section was made up of teaching rookies and refreshing returning firefighters on the Ten Standard Fire Orders and the Eighteen Watch Out Situations (or Situations that Shout Watch Out!). The fire orders had been organized under the handy mnemonic device, F-I-R-E O-R-D-E-R-S:

F Fight fire aggressively but provide for SAFETY FIRST.

I nitiate all action based on current and expected FIRE BEHAVIOR.

R Recognize current WEATHER CONDITIONS and obtain forecasts.

E Ensure INSTRUCTIONS are given and understood.

O Obtain current information on FIRE STATUS.

R Remain in COMMUNICATION with crew members, your supervisor, and adjoining forces.

D Determine SAFETY ZONES and ESCAPE ROUTES.

E Establish LOOKOUTS in potentially hazardous situations.
R Retain CONTROL at all times.
S Stay ALERT, keep CALM, THINK clearly, ACT decisively.

The government has since done away with the mnemonic device as a committee felt that orders were emphasized incorrectly, so they organized them to reflect the priorities in the fire environment.

The Current 10 Standard Fire Orders:

Fire Behavior
1. Keep informed on fire weather conditions and forecasts.
2. Know what your fire is doing at all times.
3. Base all actions on current and expected behavior of the fire.

Fire line Safety
4. Identify escape routes and safety zones and make them known.
5. Post lookouts when there is possible danger.
6. Be alert. Keep calm. Think clearly. Act decisively.

Organizational Control
7. Maintain prompt communications with your forces, your supervisor and adjoining forces.
8. Give clear instructions and insure they are understood.
9. Maintain control of your forces at all times.

If 1-9 are considered, then...
10. Fight fire aggressively, having provided for safety first.

It was taught that the 10 Standard Fire Orders were firm. We don't break them; we don't bend them. All firefighters have the right to a safe assignment.

According to the legendary ranger, Bud Moore in his book *The Lochsa Story*, they developed 13 situations that shout watch out, but the government had since added five more and now firefighters have 18.

The 18 Watch Out Situations:

1. Fire not scouted and sized up.
2. In country not seen in daylight.
3. Safety zones and escape routes not identified.
4. Unfamiliar with weather and local factors influencing fire behavior
5. Uninformed on strategy, tactics, and hazards.
6. Instructions and assignments not clear.
7. No communication link between crew-members and supervisors.
8. Constructing line without safe anchor point.
9. Building line downhill with fire below.
10. Attempting frontal assault on fire.
11. Unburned fuel between you and the fire.
12. Cannot see main fire, not in contact with anyone who can.
13. On a hillside where rolling material can ignite fuel below.
14. Weather gets hotter and drier.
15. Wind increases and/or changes direction.
16. Getting frequent spot fires across line.
17. Terrain or fuels make escape to safety zones difficult.
18. Feel like taking a nap near fireline.

It is interesting that from the Situations That Shout Watch Out, the fire service had developed watch out cards for aviation, prescribed fire, and working in the Mexican border region.

The classroom at the fire camp in Headquarters, Idaho was a common area in an old bunkhouse. The air stifled from the closed windows and so many people breathing in the close and dusty space. Everyone wanted to be outside, and I thought about combining the classroom with field exercises to get the firefighters in the habit of looking at the environment, and developing their situational awareness before we went to a practice fire (and a practice fire wasn't always to be had making the drills more important for training). In front of the class I couldn't help but think of a watch out for learning outcome, napping in the classroom and nothing learned. Even though the some members of the Association thought the week of training a silly formality, some of us took it seriously and tried to engage the students.

*

Above the fire I stopped in the middle of the rocked cul-de-sac after turning the truck around so we faced our escape route. At least we had a safety zone. The engines began to position themselves on each flank. Where the roadbed met the cul-de-sac, another CT pickup was parked. By the water jugs mounted on the back, I could tell it belonged to the assistant fire warden from Orofino. The eight firefighters with me gathered and ten others from Orofino mixed in. I knew I needed to act decisively and not look like I didn't know what I was doing. I felt unsure in that moment, mostly because I didn't want to make a mistake, but also didn't want to be seen looking through any pocket guide looking for answers.

I saw Tim, the assistant from Orofino come up the east flank of the fire and onto the road bank. It ran flat that direction beyond the fire. The mountainside faced south, so it baked under the sun all day. To the west it dropped off into a steep gully clogged with alder brush, syringa, Oregon grape vines, thickets of small trees and power lines ran up the east side of it. The fire wasn't there yet, but if it reached it the gully would become a chimney, funneling smoke, heat, and roaring flames into the houses built at the top of it.

"You engines, start hitting the head of this with water and start working down either side. Mike standby, I want to talk with Tim." I felt that all the locals were staring at me and wondering why I wasn't throwing my guys into work.

Tim and two guys that rode with him were starting to dig a hand-line on the east flank.

"How did it look down there?" I asked.

He didn't look up. The fire flared his blond hair and wispy mustache. In his baggy fire clothes and fire-pack on his skinny body, he looked like a kid wearing oversized football pads. "Like it was on fire. Why don't you go look?"

"I will, just thought you could let me know. I'm worried it'll get into that ravine."

"Then I suppose you better do something about it."

I felt pressure to lunge and take any action, to, as the woman begged, stop the fire. But my inexperience also gave me hesitation. It always seemed odd that we trained very little. We attended the five day basic fire school in June, but then spent the rest of the summer digging hand-line around clear-cuts for burning in the fall, slashing brush, working with dozers to build fire breaks and road improvement, pruning white pines against blister rust, installing gates on forest roads, spraying weeds, and whatever odd forestry job arose in the course of the year. We rarely sent people out to work on the big fires managed by the United States Forest Service or Bureau of Land Management.

The engine operators had their pumps whining and water started knocking down flames at the edge of the rock. I wanted to scout it as soon as possible. I didn't know how long it'd take me to get around the fire and I didn't want my crew to be standing by with the locals watching. I certainly didn't want them to fall in with Tim and leave that ravine unsupported. I went to Mike and told him that I was going to scout down the eastern flank. I wanted him to lead the remaining firefighters and start digging their firebreak on the western side and have a couple of guys follow with hoses from the engine to begin a hose-lay. "I don't want it to get into that ravine." I pointed at the brush. "It'll take out everything above it."

The fire flared as dried brush caught fire in a sudden burst. "Remember, it hasn't been scouted. You'll scout ahead of your crew until I meet you coming around from the other side. We just can't let it get into that draw."

"Sounds like a plan," he said and took off to join his squad.

The Ten and Eighteen were developed in 1956 and first implemented in 1957. USDA-Forest Service Chief Richard E. McArdle put together a group of seasoned firefighters in response to the rise of fire fatalities in the preceding years, most notably Mann Gulch in Montana where 12 smokejumpers and a ranger were burned over and killed in 1949, leaving three others to sort out the aftermath of their lives. The task force reviewed the records of 16 tragedy fires that occurred from 1937 to 1956 and searched for the common denominators in all of the disasters. They compiled their findings into the lists and incorporated them into training. One of the things the majority of the Association firefighters remarked about how the Forest Service spent more time checking lists, filling out paperwork, checking lists again, and letting fires escape and grow, while they shuffled papers. They didn't consider drought, climate change, fuel loading, urban sprawl, that lead to large fires, to them it was only bureaucracy. They had a point, because all the lists in the world couldn't replace common sense, practical field experience, and internalizing reactions to a dynamic environment that demanded a leader keep his or her head. Lists couldn't constantly reassess the fluid conditions instead of focusing on individual elements. Training somebody to see a break in a pattern seemed difficult at that level or in any of the things we did at the Association. Even the chaos of a wildfire has a particular pattern, just as a person could look into a thunderstorm and see when the winds changed.

That June, the section I taught at the fire school was filled with a bunch of guys, with glazed over eyes or nodding off, who only wanted to get out into the woods and fight fire. Almost everyone came from logging industry families from the local area and wore woods clothes. Having grown up in the surrounding mountains, many saw the class as a waste of time, and especially a mandated class from the U. S. "Nanny" Service. "Too many sue-happy city boys and not enough real woodsmen anymore." I'd heard from the mouth a kid just out of high school.

People still died on fires. For years reports always read that the incident commanders were deficient in protocol of the 10 and 18 and that the "take home lesson" was to continually refer to the Incident Response Pocket Guide, IRPG, and pocket cards. It was interesting to consider how people in office situations always fell back to reference material as the ready solution to tragedy. "If they had only followed these guidelines disaster could have been averted." It seemed to me overly simplistic to arm people with reams of paper as if a talisman against panic and freak weather switches. Some firefighters began to argue that it was impossible to fight a fire and not have several watch outs present, and the sometimes the situation so fluid as to make a fire order null and void, but they still had to keep at it. At the Thirty-Mile Fire, investigators found that most didn't even follow the fire orders because they were unwieldy. Some felt the rules were iron, but that didn't allow for fluid conditions, while others considered them guidelines. The fire I was thrust onto was at night, on a steep hillside, and we were above it. We had no lookouts, and as soon as I started to scout, I'd have unburned fuel between the fire and me. The worst part was that I had no clue how many other people were running around in the dark.

I worked my way down the eastern flank of the fire. It cracked and popped as it curled leaves and charred grass. The brush grew in thick stands in places. Even as the flames burned several feet high, the night air and high humidity kept the rate of spread low. I looked up to see if I could tell against the back drop of the stars if any of the trees were leaning together or if any of the tops or limbs had been knocked loose, but still hanging above the ground. Another problem I wanted to find was snags. During the last couple of years I had felled hundreds around clear-cuts and on fires. Each species had different characteristics in how it rotted, so a sawyer had to be aware of that and be careful of dead limbs and tops that could tumble out from the vibration of the saw or pounding in wedges to push it the direction it needed to fall.

With the wind, they could topple over and kill or cripple a firefighter, fire weakened trees can also fall, snags cast firebrands like sparklers in a kid's hand, as I had discovered on a prescribed fire during my rookie year. Sometimes a snag just fell. No wind needed. The first time it had happened, we had been helicoptered into a remote helispot and hiked a couple of miles through a thick forest of fir. The lightning had hit a tree about a third of the way down the slope, and the fire crept in the thick moist duff layer. We even dug through of layer of ash from the Mt. St. Helen's eruption some 18 years before. The night was calm and cool, so cool that when we bedded down after midnight we still had to get up and move around to generate warmth. One crewmember, Mark, waded around in the ash to find any hotspots to warm his feet. One of the times I woke up I heard a long creak like a rusty hinge and a tree slamming into the ground. The noise came from up the ridge and the air was still.

Another thing the Association mocked about the federal firefighters was their rule to fall the direction of the tree's predominate lean and not directional falling, because "they had too low quality sawyers and just as inexperienced teachers. How can they expect to be any good when all they do is fall their trees in one way?" The truth, though, was that both organizations had great and poor sawyers. We also worked all day falling snags and cutting brush and had the conception that all the government firefighters did was sit around their station and workout. "No better workout than work," any one of the old-timers would say after a fire leaning against the pick-up with a beer brought in by supply. Another thing the "Nanny" Service would frown on.

Before signing on to the C-PTPA, I didn't know anything about forestry work or fighting fire as I had spent my formative years in the treeless desert, seeing fires from a great distance. My landscape included far mountains like gray and rusty ships on a sandy sea. For me, I had listened to the locals the way I had listened to my father. As we grew up he had a habit of telling moral/lesson stories about survivors and non-survivors. His stories were also cautionary and, because he had grown up a poor country boy in the hills of Kentucky, carried the feeling of country-vanity. But it just wasn't him, it was everyone he associated with.

When I was in the eighth grade, we lived in Skull Valley, Arizona on a small farm with a dairy cow, a beef cow, chickens, rabbits, and the assorted trappings of tenant farmer life in a tarpaper shack down by a dry wash. I cleared the overgrown grass from the yard with a scythe because it was supposed to be good for me.

One night he brought in a large cardboard box. He called my two younger brothers and me. When we gathered around, he opened the box and pulled out various military hats and pieces of uniforms he had had from the Air Force. He put a green field cap on my head, a dress uniform cap on my youngest brother's head, and a flat cap, a "piss cutter," on the middle son's head. He leaned back in his chair as if Caesar surveying the Praetorian Guard. "I don't know why I gave you that one," he said to me. "You're a too much by-the-book guy. I seen Lieutenants in Nam busy fucking around with their field manuals--worried about breaking a rule instead of leading--and get their platoons killed. That's what happens when you let a bunch of college kids lead men." Two things always cropped up in our family. One was a mistrust for anyone who went to college, which given he told us to go to college set up some psychological confusion, and second that following the letter of any rule was bad, which given that he had been a cop and small town judge seemed odd. These two things always led to incompetence and me getting people killed. I wanted no one to die. As a junior high kid, standing there with the military detritus of a helicopter door-gunner who had been shot down five times, I had no idea of a how to respond. He looked over to my next youngest brother, "I should have given it to him. The second son of a second son." For some reason he thought the second son accursed, but superior to first son. It was no small to wonder how a single sentence from a father could influence a boy's concept of leading a crew decades later.

On the mountain, I kicked up dust. The decomposed granite and rocky soil was loose under my feet. I tried to keep my balance and look for hazards. During Standards of Survival training, I warned students about walking off bluffs or walking into porcupines on night fires. I had heard of people walking off of bluffs at night, but I didn't know about porcupines. It always got their attention and broke the stream of their hypnosis and hopefully created a chain of associations. I could've tried to force them to memorize the 10 and 18, like I had done, but some wouldn't have bothered, some couldn't, and others would begin to forget them in a week. I also knew the overhead would mock me for making the boys waste time (and yes guys as the Association still hadn't hired a woman firefighter in its history until after I left).

Somehow they needed to internalize them and needed to start a series of mental associations so that when something presented itself in the field, they could recognize it and take action. With the lack of training and utter disdain for sending people to larger fires, we created few opportunities for that internalization to take place. Above me I could hear the clink of Pulaski's and shovels and on the far side of the fire a power saw fired up.

At the heel of the fire, I began to hike east and the land rose and then dipped again on the contour and the ground became less steep. The mountain still dropped away another 800 feet to the waterline of the reservoir. The fire wasn't backing down very fast, but I knew that a flaming pinecone could be kicked loose and tumble below, spreading fire with each bounce through dried grass. My crew was a quick radio-call away if something happened, but it was good to catch it early so I wouldn't have to call dispatch for more people and equipment. Where the finger ridge dropped into the ravine I met Mike.

"How's it going over there?"

"Fine," he said. He had never been very talkative.

"What's it look like?

"It's brushy and the trees get thicker in the bottom."

"Do you have it handled or do you need anything else?"

"We got it."

I always felt odd talking with him and this summer I had felt more resentment and I wasn't sure if it was because the fire warden had given me more leadership roles in both the project work and fire or something else. Sometimes I thought I was misreading him, but he'd be laughing and joking with the crew, and when I came up it'd be a change of attitude. He was a local and I was an outsider and I was older and had traveled and worked in a lot of places from Europe to commercial fishing in Alaska. He hadn't been anywhere.

"Okay," I said. "I'm going to climb back up this side and check on Tim and the engines and go reassure the locals that we'll get this."

"Sounds good." He hiked back from where he came, a shadow among the branches of brush and trees.

By four in the morning we had a firebreak scratched in around the fire. It would be good enough until light when so we could strengthen the line and begin mopping up the interior, making sure not one coal was left smoldering to put up smoke later. Our standing order for mop up was put the fire "dead out" and we got on our hands and knees and felt every square inch of ash. We were lucky, because a pond had been dug up the mountain on an old logging road as part of the fire warden's resource plan. We could just keep adding water until any heat had been "washed off the hillside."

I had radioed for everyone to eat and get some sleep. In the dark, before dawn, I sat in the front seat of my pick-up, thinking I was doing all right. We had kept the fire out of the chimney, didn't lose any houses, and nobody was hurt. In all, it was a good night's work.

When the sunlight lit my face, I woke. My eyes itched from the smoke. I stepped out of the truck and stretched, trying to release the tension wound into my muscles. All the locals had gone home and I had firefighters scattered down the eastern flank of the fire. No open flames wavered anywhere, but smoke still smoldered up from clumps of grass, downed trees, and thickets of brush.

I have found that many people have a misconception that when a fire burned through an area that everything was left like the wood consumed in a fireplace. While that can happen, it is the norm that the fire doesn't burn everything off and smolders in logs, in the roots of trees, stumps, snags, grass, brush, and even high up in standing trees either from a lightning strike or fire climbing up the trunk into the tops. It burned incompletely because of weather, fuel moisture, and topography, all the elements of heat and speed. Wind blew it past too fast, humidity levels didn't allow for complete combustion, dead fuel moisture content was at a level that resisted the flame, or not enough wind to fan the flames or drive the fire in a direction leaving the edge barely burning, or the air temperature wasn't conducive with all the other factors, the ground wasn't as steep to let the fire burn completely in relation to all those other factors. I have seen fire leave nothing behind except ash, but that was during a hot dry day in fuels baked in weeks of drought.

This morning we'd move slow and conserve our energy for later in the day when the sun's heat on the hillside would cause hidden smokes to start popping. During the cool of the day, we'd clear brush and limbs of trees away from the fire's edge, and we'd strengthen the line by making it wider and reinforce a cup trench with a foot-high berm on the downhill side to catch any rolling debris. All the while, we'd keep an eye for any smokes.

Tim's crew had returned to the top to sleep, and was eating canned food and drinking coffee heated on the fire. I hiked down the line found Mike with our crew huddled together on a flat spot near the heel of the fire. Mike was talking with a new guy when I stopped and knelt down. "How's it going?"

All the chatting stopped and everyone stared at me. I had that odd feeling again about Mike. It was that feeling a person gets when they interrupt a conversation that is about him. "Fine."

"Anything else?"

"Nope."

The glares and silence made me wonder what was up and I figured I'd talk with Mike later away from the crew while they were working so it wouldn't look like I was calling him out and undermining his authority. I also wanted to be careful that it wasn't just me misreading the crew and undermine my authority with the crew. I wanted to avoid saying something when nothing was wrong and look foolish. I didn't work with the crew that much during that summer. I spent most of my time "pimping for the cat" as a sawyer for the dozer. My primary job was to follow the dozer as it plowed firebreaks around clear-cuts, fell snags on each side of the fire-line that could potentially cast or catch sparks, cut downed trees so the dozer could push them out of the way, and help the operator with whatever he needed.

In his book, *Young Men and Fire*, Norman Maclean observed that one factor in the Mann Gulch tragedy had to do with how well the foreman, Wag Dodge, had known the men on his crew.

The fire in Mann Gulch had crossed their side of the creek below them. When they realized it was blowing up they ran back up the gulch. Dodge knew they weren't going to make it and yelled for his crew to stop. He took matches from his pocket as he knelt down in waist high grass and lit it. As the flames leapt up, forty-mile an hour winds drove the fire ahead of him. He called his men to follow him into the burnt off area, but his crew didn't listen. They ignored him because they didn't know him very well and didn't trust his judgment. One of survivors, Bob Sallee, said, "We thought he must be nuts." No one had ever seen a burn out before and it wasn't part of the training. Burning away grass to use as a safety zone had been used by Native Americans to create a buffer against flame set by their enemies to burn them out, and mentioned in fiction like the James Fennimore Cooper's *The Plains*, but none of the firefighters scrambling for their lives knew that and they didn't think Dodge was on to something. The third survivor, Walter Rumsey told investigators, "I remember thinking it was a good idea, but I don't remember what I thought it was good for. I kept thinking the ridge--if I can make it. On the ridge I will be safe."

The guys on my crew almost all knew each other from high school or their families were connected to the area and people knew them through local lore. I came from Boise, by way of Nevada, California, and Arizona and California. These provincial kids looked at me as a carpetbagger coming up here and taking jobs one of the locals deserved. And like kids with provincial attitudes who had seen nothing of the wider world, they believed their way was the only and best way to look at the world. They also wrapped that attitude with talk of tradition of the woods, of loggers and mill workers' sons and a way of life, even if the way of life wasn't sustainable and even Potlatch, the monolithic employer, was selling off land for tourist homes and closing mills on private land not connected to the government. As all fears borne of conservative values it was a fear of change and unknown future, what will we do? The answer was hostility against anything and anyone representing change. I heard it in the way they talked, and it ran right up the chain of command to the chief fire warden who resented federal fire fighters so much as to ignore any policy he saw fit to ignore, and could get away with ignoring. The man openly disdained my boss who called for federal help on his district when lightning sparked seventy-some fires in one night. To him, it was like a small town police force admitting that they needed the FBI after all.

*

Along the fire line we were all exhausted. There were no work to rest ratio yet in any of the fire services, and no clear guidelines of when to start and when to stop. We worked to contain the fire, took a nap in the dirt along the fire line, and then hit it again. After the Thirty-Mile tragedy in Washington State, during the 2001 where four firefighters were killed, investigators determined that one contributing factor was firefighter fatigue. The crew-boss and crew were determined to be too fatigued to make sound decisions, and in their fatigue, failed to identify the hazardous situation as it developed before them. Sleep deprivation hindered processing information and making judgments as much as would a blood alcohol content of .20. In fact, as the fire roared up the valley at them, firefighters were snapping pictures instead of clearing a safety zone. It was reported by some of the crew that other firefighters ignored the crew boss and deployed shelters on a scree slope that drew smoke up into their fire shelters and burned plants and brush growing under the rocks. The fire that blew by them was so intense it melted a truck into a lump of metal and plastic. The heat on the rocks baked and seared the flesh from the bones of those on them. A loss of command equal to trying to control a scared, drunken mob.

The NWCG responded with guidelines that called for every two hours worked one hour off. A firefighter can work 16 hours in a day and then take 8 off, which at first seemed okay, until you have a fire start in the evening below a bunch of houses and catching it will mean you break your work to rest ratio. Now it's developed to where you need special permission to work past sixteen hours or take a shorter break than eight hours. Even out on a fire in the middle of the woods, we would wake up after sleeping a few hours and if we wanted to work, we were technically prohibited from doing so until eight hours had elapsed. We'd work anyway and get the job done because no firefighter wanted to stand around just to please paper pushers.

I stood. "I'd like to have the line reinforced and we'll start mopping up."

Mike just nodded.

I walked down the east line to circle back up the other side. On the western flank I followed power lines up the mountain until I came to where a tree had fallen into the lines and hung up. Mike hadn't said anything about this. I side-hilled away from the fire line to stay out from under the tree. It'd have to come down. Blackened to the ground, it smoldered near the top where it had arced out against the wire. I was bothered by it. Why hadn't Mike reported it so I could tell everyone else on the fire? A tree leaning in a power line could come down without warning and kill or hurt someone. It could scatter more fire down the hillside or knock other trees down in a chain reaction. The power company needed to be notified. After the storm I imagined they were all over the county trying find where the power outages were.

Except for the tree in the power lines, everything looked good. Before I could get all the way around the fire wardens in Elk River and Orofino called wanting to know when I was going to release people and equipment back to camp. No other smokes had been reported yet, but it was still early and they wanted to get people refreshed and equipment refurbished for the late afternoon. The morning patrol flight was about to launch and the planners were already worried about being overextended.

I got off the radio and tried to figure how many people I needed. Too few and they'd bitch and moan that it'd take longer than needed. Too many and I would be taking resources out of the rotation that might be needed. I felt in an awkward position.

At the top I met Tim. "Figure I'll keep everyone until after lunch and start letting folks go."

By his sigh and the look on his face I knew he didn't want to stay longer. No one wanted to stay and crawl around on their hands and knees, searching for coals with their bare hands in the dirt, ash, and surviving grass and brush. They all wanted to go home, get rested, and hope to initial attack another fire. That was where the excitement and glory was for all firefighters.

"Let's start gridding. Also there's a tree hung up in the wires on the west side. I'm going to have Mike cut it down."

"I know, Mike told me about it."

"Good. As long as you know." I wondered why he told Tim, but not me. Tim was another guy I liked, even though many gave him a bad time for getting a college education in communications, his vegetarian tendencies, and the fact that he may have been fast-tracked into his job because his family had worked for the Association since the Nineteen-teens. While many of the others dressed in logging clothes all the time, he wore the clothes of any normal suburban guy. He didn't exactly fit in, but he did have the three generation family legacy.

The day wore on. The sun baked the fire-scorched hillside as we patrolled back and forth in a grid for hot spots. All the shade had been burned to the black ash on the ground we sifted through. Everyone began to drag under the weight of the heat. I pulled Mike aside and asked him why he didn't tell me about the tree. "I thought you knew," he said.

"I told you I hadn't scouted that side and that you were my eyes."

He shrugged and clammed up. It was hard to have a second-in-command who refused to speak. It was even harder to have a second-in-command who suffered no consequences for insubordination, much less encouraged to be insubordinate. Given the Association's habit of protecting their local boys and those who might not be able to find work outside the county, what good was it to have a second in command you couldn't replace?

In 1949, Wag Dodge's second-in-command was William Hellman. Dodge left him to lead the crew down to the river while he climbed back to the cargo spot with the ranger Jim Harrison who had been on the fire all morning to grab some lunch. During the twenty minutes they were separated, the crew became spread out and lost sight of each other. After he reached the cargo spot, Dodge looked over the gulch realized he needed to hustle back as fast as he could run. Norman Maclean writes, "and sure enough, it happens as it nearly always does when the second-in-command takes charge. The crew got separated and confused." Even in as short a time as twenty minutes things went from being manageable to being outside the bounds of control. Not so much that they could control the fire, but control the decisions to keep them safe before all the options evaporated. All but three would die in less than an hour. The fire cut their options down to two: run and hope to make the ridge top or stop and light the grass and lay down in the hot ash as the main fire blew over like a million horses out of hell.

These things haunted me for years. There but for the grace of God go I. The ranger Harrison had given up being a smokejumper because his mom worried that it was too dangerous and there he was. I had already been left hanging on too many fires and here I thought of flames in the chimney or a hung snag in shorted out power lines falling hard into a squad digging in the dirt all jacked up on fire and smoke. No one looking up or around or spotting the break in the pattern, just hell bent for work. For the grace of God.

Most of the crew, as with many crews, had limited experience. We sent them to a one-week class and then dropped it until a fire because we had a push to do project work and anything that halted production was a waste of time. I asked about revisiting it and drills, but we had other work to do. When I became the assistant fire warden I ran a readiness drill where I had the whole crew turn out for a fire call and then inspected the equipment and fire packs, which was found wanting. I had always been aggravated with the lax nature of the crew towards readiness and showing up on fires without gear or enough food and water to remain unsupported in the field for three days. The result was my being called into the fire warden's, office and told we didn't run exercises or drills. "That's for structure firefighters," Jody said.

On my fire, I still hadn't learned. I was caught between forces that didn't allow me to command and trying to help nurture others into leadership. I was still in the contradictory position of holding the federal fire service in contempt, but like Walter, seeing how they were right and how the old rogue woodsman image was not only never true, but harmful nostalgia that retarded forward progress of the Association. I saw what a joke I had become trying to walk in both worlds with my second undermining me, and my immediate supervisor not supporting me.

Tim caught me by my truck when I went to refill my canteens. "We got to get back in case of a fire on the breaks." I ran my tongue over my teeth. A couple of other guys had made comments about how good it would be to get back to a bed or a hot meal. Both Elk River and Orofino offices had called again looking for the return of resources.

"Look man," Tim said. Ash and carbon clung to his fine blond mustache hair. "You don't want to be that guy who hangs on to resources too long or that guy who can't handle the fire with as little as possible or be that guy who couldn't put the fire to bed in a reasonable time or look like that guy sandbagging a fire for overtime."

"That guy."

He nodded. I didn't want a lot of things, but I didn't want to be that guy who balled it up. I knew if I asked Tim his opinion, it'd be to send everyone home, which I didn't want to do.

"All right then." When I gave the word, they left as fast as they could. I called out over the radio for one of the engines to slow down. I kept one engine from my camp with two guys. Jason, an overweight man with bad knees and bits of chewing tobacco at the corners of his mouth, had been a logger until a back injury had washed him up and ended up with the Association much like Bill. He had rolled his ankle in the bull rock, making him limp. The other was a rookie, and a high school kid who was tall and doughy whose family attended the fire warden's church. On an earlier fire, I had to yell at him when he took off running through the woods toward the fire. An excited rookie, he didn't realize that the fire might be scattered over a wider area or that snags or fire-weakened trees might be ready to topple over on to him.

I was going to have one crew standby until Jason had refilled the engine at the pond, but I was tired of feeling that I was putting everyone out. I followed the deuce-and-a-half in my pick-up to help.

On top of the truck, I fed the fill hose into the top of the tank. A high-pressure system stretched blue over mountains and reservoir. No wind to cut the heat. Jason fired the fill-pump and adjusted the idle. I sat back on my heels as water splashed, and exchanged a few jokes with Jason when he hobbled up to the truck. The rookie squatted by the water's edge and splashed his face.

Down the hill, below the houses, smoke rose up. "What the hell," I said as the column smudged the sky. I stood and shaded my eyes and blinked. Jason turned. It billowed up from my fire area, but I knew it couldn't be mine. Mine didn't have enough life in it to generate a column like that. The smoke was still thin, but building.

"We got to get down there." Jason killed the fill-pump. I reasoned it must be a holdover--a different lightning fire just down the hill from mine. A hold over could pop up two and three weeks after a storm had passed over. I tried to call back the trucks and people I had released, but only Tim and his people responded. I called dispatch and requested the helicopter. They asked if this was a new start or my fire flaring up after I'd turned loose resources. I told them that I was still above it, but couldn't imagine how it could be mine. I imagined the homeowners above the fire looking out a kitchen window or feeding a horse, and seeing a new smoke column. I knew the elemental fear that burned the bottom of their guts. It seized mine.

Jason backed the engine up to where we had disconnected the hose. Luckily, I had left the inch and half trunk line, and inch laterals and three quarter inch laterals in place around the fire. The trunk line fed water to the laterals that could be extended or split with wyes to create more laterals to spray water on the fire or mop up. The rookie and I scrambled down the east hand-line in a cloud of dirt. At the bottom corner just on the outside of the firebreak flames had started in pile of branches, pine needles and grass. One of the crew when digging the line pulled embers from my fire into the pile where they lay in shade of trees until it had smoldered and crept, worming its way out from under the suffocating timber litter to the life giving air. With the influx of oxygen and the afternoon heat it grew and found a second wind. Flames whipped and snapped from the grass and into the brush, then leap-frogged up into the branches of small trees crowded around larger trees.

"Get that nozzle." I pointed to the end of a canvas one-inch hose that had been laterry from the trunk line. I knew if we could get water on it we could stop it. Suck the heat out of it while smothering it. The rookie picked it up. "When Jason charges the line I want you to hit the base and work up into the trees to wet to tops of the trees. "

He nodded.

I keyed my hand-held radio. "Jason, we need the water. Charge the line."

"I can't get the pump started."

Shit. The rookie looked at me. The fire climbed higher.

"Jason, we can catch this, *pump* the water." My radio hissed and I adjusted the squelch.

"I'm trying."

I said to the rookie, "You stay in the black until you get water."

"Alright." His voice sounded small.

"As soon as you get water, hit it."

I ran up the hand-line. Bull-rock on the exposed roadbed made walking tough. My feet ached. At the truck Jason pulled at the starter rope.

"It has an electric start," I said. I laid the throttle back, opened the choke, and hit the starter button. A sick clicking noise. Wires smoked.

The taste of electricity bleeding from grounded out connections filled my mouth. Sweat burned my eyes.

"It shorted," Jason said. Below me flames soared in the treetops. I stared at the pump, and banged the panel. Switches and lights jabbed my fist. I tried the button again, as if a second time would miraculously make it work, but nothing. I shifted my hardhat back and ran a sooty hand over my forehead.

Jason pulled the rope the motor chugged to life. I checked to make sure he was hooked into the hose lay, but water isn't drafting from the tank. I pulled at levers. The hose remained limp. What the fuck now, I thought. Over my shoulder, the smoke column changed from white to black, punching the atmosphere. I turned my disbelieving eyes back to the pump.

The rookie waited in the steep canyon bottom. Flames arced through the ponderosa pines. Jason pulled the rope and the pumped coughed and fired. I jerked the choke mistaking it for the throttle, and killed the motor. *Shit.* I hit the motor with my palm. It hurt.

"We *need* water." My voice cracked, and sounded like a worn father calling after kids.

He pulled and pulled on the rope. I messed with the choke and throttle. The pump spit and coughed. We switched off and I pulled. Down the hill, the fire had climbed into the treetops. I was relieved there wasn't any wind yet, but it was high and I needed to get the rookie back up because it was too late to catch it from the bottom.

I toggled the throttle. Over and over, I punched the dead button in a reflex. Jason grabbed the pull-rope and pulled. The motor coughed. I adjusted the choke, opened the throttle, as Jason pulled the rope again and again. The motor sputtered. It belched a white cloud from the exhaust. It flooded. I smelled gasoline.

Jason bent over and rested his hands on his knees. His breath wheezed. I pulled the rope again and again and again. My arms ached and something was working loose in my shoulder and muscle in my neck cramped. Finally the motor kicked over. Jason took the line for discharge and hooked it into the hose-reel, and I pulled the lever. The pitch of the motor changed as water drafted from the tank filing the hoses.

"Dump foam into the tank, and get ready to switch to the tank on my truck when you start sucking air."

Jason nodded. "Can do." His unshaven face still harbored all the dirt and ash from the night before and the long day, and it didn't hide the pain he was in. His ankle and back had both let him down, but his will kept him driving forward. I thought of all the young firefighters who had mocked him as an old washed up logger living in a pull trailer the size of a cat carrier, scraping by all winter.

About fifty feet below the roadbed, an old skid trail cut along the side hill. I knew we needed to try to catch the fire there. After calling for the rookie to hustle up the hand line, I grabbed four sections of inch-hose, a gated-wye, and two nozzles and bailed off the roadbed for the skid trail. I hooked the hose into the trunk line and then made two laterals. I was in front of the fire and planned to spray water into the trees and brush, hoping to drop the fire out of the treetops from the moisture, raising the humidity and dropping the temperature in front of the fire. I don't remember why I thought about it like that or even why I thought about it at all. It just came to me out of nothing, much like I figured Wag Dodge stopped running and knelt in waist deep grass to strike a match in a hope to save his and his crew's life.

The rookie yelled from the hand-line and I waved him over. I told him the objective and to spray water and not stop. "If it gets too sketchy, we'll run for the old fire."

I hustled back to the trunk line and pushed the lever to the wye and the water rushed toward the rookie. The echo of the pump changed pitch on the forest hillside. I thought of Jason, limping behind the engine and spitting tobacco into the rocks. The cul-de-sac of under-construction road for a woodland development would keep him safe and the trucks backed to the edge of the steep drop off unburned brush and trees. If the fire jumped us, it wouldn't stop until it hit the top and it would scour everything in its path. Earlier I had wanted to sleep, and now, with the fear and adrenaline, I felt like I might never sleep again. Now I think about the Thirty-Mile fire tragedy and fatigued cited as a contributing factor. The crew-boss, Elleresse Daniels had been awake and working hard for over thirty hours. Then mind numbed and the senses constricted down to what might be a blackout. I had caught two hours of sleep in the front of a pick-up in the last 34 hours of working the fire. I stood spraying water with a rookie in hopes to stop a fire, and I wonder now if I looked like a drunken fool before the flames.

I strained my ears for the helicopter and the other crews. They couldn't be that far away. I tried to massage the twinge in my neck. My greasy skin kept the grit and dirt trapped. The dry air tasted like parched grass and leaves, and the wind kicked up, rasping the dry stalks against each other as the fire came up the slope like the voices of T. S. Eliot's Hollow Men. The fire front stretched a hundred feet across. I looked upwards--the sky had never been so cloudless, clear. *Why can't it rain?*

The crack of fire overflowing wood rushed through canyon air, blistering bark with the roar of a blown dike. Heat slapped me like an angry lover and sucked sweat out of my body. The wind changed, sucking toward the fire. The fire arrived. Noise from the radio became a buzz and jumble of ape noises. A tornado of smoke threw a shadow over us--flames hung motionless, suspended from trees, as if shimmering in reflection of the sun. It reminded me of the long bright scarves a girlfriend used to wear. My sweat evaporated.

Some firebrands lit behind us in the grass. The rookie hit them with water and kicked at the spots to root up tufts of grass to mix them up and work the water into the clumps. The raw hum of a forest burning rattled branches and drove birds scattershot through the flashing timber. I wanted to yell for the rookie to run for the hand-line and run into the old burn. To take cover before it was too late. But before I opened my mouth, the fire hesitated and slowed in the wet timber and brush. The fire dropped from the treetops. Flames suffocated in the saturated grass and hissed against leaves and needles, steaming as if an ancient purification ceremony. We rushed back and forth along the skid trail hitting it wherever it was close. Vapor and smoke mingled. The smell changed from the dried thirst of a smoking forest to moist pine incense.

Someone hollered. Tim stood on the skid-trail, his crew strung out behind him. He met with me while I was still dousing spots. I told him where it started and why.

"On your crew's section of line," he said. In fact it wasn't.

They hiked into the bottom and each passing firefighter had the look of a kid unfairly punished by having his dinner taken away. They began to dig line around the fire. The helicopter flew over and started dropping buckets of water on the new east flank where the fire was still growing. We caught it. I kept thinking of the woman with the horse, and those she spoke for all along the bench with some homes in the top of steep brush choked draws. If the fire had gotten away the buildings wouldn't have stood a chance. They had no defensible space. Brush, grass, and trees crowded close to the wooden structures and they all had piles of cured firewood stacked around them. They had propane tanks and fuel tanks and the barns were filled with hay. In the fire business, we joked that structures are just another fuel type, but they aren't.

Before the sun had gone down, the fire had been lined, and I released everyone back to station. I too drove back, called in by the assistant warden. I struggled to stay awake. My head nodded and then snapped up, sending an electric shock to the base of my crotch when I realized I'd been asleep for longer than a millisecond and had travelled a hundred yards of gravel road. I drove off the road a couple of times and was lucky that it was on the flats crossing meadows and not where the road overlooked the 1000-foot drop-offs. I considered pulling over, but that was one of those unsaid things that led to disasters. We all knew the language of men: "Not tough enough to go on."

I shifted into low gear so the truck crept along at its slowest possible speed. I had left the engine at the cul-de-sac with some fresh firefighters who had not been on the initial call. When we made it the 19 miles back to fire camp, I stopped by the office. Jason and the rookie staggered to the bunkhouses. In the office, I filled out some paperwork and went home to shower and sleep.

The next morning Jody informed me that I had willfully endangered my crew by letting them work under power lines with a widow maker in them and then turning loose resources, only to have the fire escape. Mike had complained that I had sent them into a deathtrap. I told Jody that I had assigned Mike that flank and told him that he needed to scout it because I hadn't been down there. I thought about the icy stare I had received from the crew and wondered what had been said.

Jody shrugged his shoulders. "The whole crew backs him up."

"Can we get everyone together and review this?" I asked.

"No time for that. We have work to do." He had made up his mind.

Later I would find out that a crewmember saw the tree as dawn lighted the mountains. Mike had missed it and when confronted told them I had sent them down without telling him. No one had heard me tell Mike I hadn't scouted that flank. I wasn't going to try and convince anybody, as it sounded pathetic. I have always wondered why the truth sounded false like a kid making excuses after a lie has taken root. No one cared because they have already passed judgment.

Paul Gleason's LCES: Lookouts, Communications, Escape Routes, and Safety Zones became a quick way to lookout for safety since 1991, but it hadn't been reinforced into my world yet in the Association. I thought about the Association and how it mocked the federal fire service because they required briefings before fighting fires instead of getting on them quickly and putting them out. That night I was acutely aware of their ridicule, and in my rush and, not wanting to look like I was dawdling, I only communicated to one person instead of making him gather the crew and tell them all. Just identify and go on.

The NWCG also required that after every fire the people involved have an After Action Review. For the Association, this was more nonsense by the nannies. It was designed to be educational and not be used as a disciplinary hearing so that firefighters could talk freely. We began by asking what was planned and after we set up the situation and the plan, we asked what really happened. We discussed the tactics and effect they had on the fire and what went right and what went wrong. In the end we asked, what could we do differently next time to better accomplish our mission. This was a good thing in its conception and I believe strongly in using the AAR, even when some IC or fire supervisor tried to use it to fix blame on somebody, but even that is telling because not everyone has another's best interests in mind for reasons of career or jealousy or both or the fact that a person came from nowhere and had no roots in the place. Fighting somebody's sense of entitlement is worse than a crown fire.

I left the office and climbed into my pickup truck. Mike and I would never regain the camaraderie we had during our first two years. The days of all you can eat squash and spuds after working long nights on a fire had been burned up. Even as the day stretched hot and dusty before me, I knew I needed to do my job as best I could, and if I needed something from him, I needed to say it in front of other people. I had a scorched hillside to scout for smokes and make sure not one coal lived where it could fan into a flame and take flight on a hot wind across the fire-line. It would be a full day of searching for burning things in a dry land.

Chapter 6

THE DEAD

By the time we rookies had driven the two hours from the district office in McCall, to Krassel Work Center it was already evening time. Fletner brought her doughnuts. My roommate Patrick Bageant had arrived ahead of me to Cabin Three. He was a good looking guy with a smile like the western sky who had just graduated from the University of Idaho with a degree in philosophy and headed to Berkeley Law School in the coming fall. He and another had devised the Misery Index for working and the threshold at which firefighters were allowed to start bitching about the job:

[(% Slope) + (% RH) + (Temperature) + (RMP) + (C)] / 3.25
Where variables are defined as:
% Slope = 1-100
% RH = 1-100
Temperature = Degrees Fahrenheit
RMP = Relative Misery of Project, subjectively assessed, 1-5 (5 = most miserable)
C = Correction from special charts (0.0 in most cases)

For all temperatures above 0.0 degrees Fahrenheit, the MI produces a numerical rating on a scale of 1-100. MIs above 50 are considered significant, 72-78 are considered severe, 78-90 are considered extreme, and 90+ are considered intolerable. Can be used as an indicator of firefighter morale (and thus firefighter safety) or simply as a justification for extended bitching. The latter is more common. It should be noted for non-firefighters that some firefighters consider mowing a lawn more miserable than climbing steep mountains and burning out.

Bage wrote songs and played the guitar with wild Bruce Springsteen abandon. He examined and questioned the status quo if it needed questioning. He could help a person physically and emotionally with his emergency medical technician skills and philosophic attitude or he might just mix you a cocktail and call it good. He had been the one to arrive at the wreck of 5EV and take control of the scene after Adam Stark had driven upon it by coincidence right after it hit the road and called him on the radio. I felt about Pat the way Apsley Cherry-Garrard felt about Shackleton, "if I am in the devil of a hole and want to get out of it, give me Shackleton every time."

The dark brown cabin had a kitchen with two propane refrigerators, a small living/dining area, one large room with two bunks, and a bathroom with shower. On Pat's refrigerator were taped two photographs. One was of him and Feltner and the other of a man giving the rock and roll horns hand salute in a fast food restaurant. His unshaven face contorted in a grimace of victory.

"Who's that?" I asked.

Bage grinned. "That, my friend, is ChaHow."

Chad Howard was dying. Shortly after the crash of 5EV he lost consciousness behind the wheel and wrecked his car. A tumor caught like a small ember in the undergrowth of neurons and dendrites of his brain and thrived. I met him a couple of times during my rookie year when he and his fiancé, Julia, had driven several hours from Missoula, Montana to our remote helibase. He joked, "We'd have been here sooner, Bu Julia had to ooo and ahhhh at some sandhill cranes." His frail skeleton and weak handshake did not indicate he had one time been a heli-rappeller or on a Hotshot crew or could have managed to put out a small leaf. He was called ChaHow by us and no matter how shitty the situation, whether being smoked in at a helibase or getting stuck on mind-numbing mop-up for the tenth day or being able to fly to a fire in the high country and spend the night working with some good people in the cool hours of a dark mountain night he would always say, "It's all good."

In his face during those visits he wandered about the compound like patient on the yard. In his puffy face and hollowed eyes we could see the desire to tool up and go on the first fast helicopter. We kept his locker with all his gear ready for his comeback. He smiled when he opened the metal door and saw his gear still hanging on the hooks and organized on the shelves. "My locker is still ready to go."

"Ready for your come back," Doug said.

The locker door's click snapped in the ready room as he pushed it closed. "Next year." His mouth tightened, but he did not cry.

He did come back the next season in 2008—my second season at Krassel. The cancer had gone into remission through a combination of macrobiotic diet, exercise, and modern medicine. We arrived at the McCall office ready to work on the same day in May. It had been cool and rainy, but snow still clogged the high passes. The most direct route, Lick Creek still harbored deep drifts over it, so we drove through Cascade. We all made the paperwork tour around to all the offices to fill out the stacks of government forms, and then drove out to Krassel after lunch and shopping for food that we would need to stay out there for the week.

We all arrived at Krassel at different times, but by five we were all there and getting situated in our cabins or one of the little FEMA trailers further back in the woods. ChaHow made his way back to Cabin One, closest to Lake Saleen and the PT area. After organizing our gear and dinner, we started a fire in the pit and gathered around for the evening to catch up and drink beer. A breeze stumbled over the branches of the ponderosa pines and the sound of the South Fork of the Salmon rushed by in snow-melted torrents below in the shaded canyon. The high ridge tops blocked the sun by early afternoon, and the chill put us into light jackets. ChaHow stood with a PBR clasped to his sternum, a stocking cap pulled down over his fly away hair, while his clothes hung on his body like a parachute caught on the willows. All but Kat returned from my rookie class, although as before the term rookie only to position of rappelling. Five new rookies oriented themselves to the crew. As we sat and chatted, tending the fire, ChaHow's grin creased his unshaven face, a face flush with the fire and hope. Although he had been a rappeller before he had to start over as a rookie again.

Someone asked how he was doing and his grin turned into a broad smile, "It's all good."

He couldn't do as many pull-ups, push-ups, sit-ups, or run as fast as anyone else on the crew, but even as he struggled to do the minimums he never stopped until he couldn't go on. The morning of the pack test we gathered 45-pound vests or loaded our line packs with enough metal plates to make the 45 pounds. I always used my line pack if I could. We loaded everything into the back of a pickup truck and jogged the quarter mile down the switch-backed road to the river. We would walk a mile and a half out and back. The road rose and dipped, but we figured it evened out by the end. The air held its night edged cold and the river tumbled hard by in its banks, pushed by the warming season.

Test administrators leapfrogged ahead in two pickups and called out times at half-mile positions and cheered encouragement and picked up anyone that might go down. The year before I had finished first. "Packing," I said, "is my event." The first time I took the pack test was along a gravel road and we sucked Elk River dust as logging trucks rumbled by scattering gravel and bark. The fire warden, Walter at that time, didn't believe we should take it in running shoes and shorts because that's not how we worked in the woods. We legged it the three miles in work boots and Carhart dungarees. Typically everyone wore running clothes because that was how they designed the test, but not in the Association.

As we gathered at the back of the truck on the road and slung the weight onto our bodies ChaHow announced that he was going to be the pacesetter. Which meant he would walk the pace needed to pass. The last time someone told me that, he was a distance runner who could have easily smoked his way through the three miles, but as the assistant felt he needed to make sure his crew finished ahead of him and passed. In the helitack crews that I had been lucky enough to be a member, they all shared the code of run back or hike back. When someone finished, no matter how fast or how hard a person ran, she caught her breath and ran back to the last person to run or hike to the finish. We finished as a crew. Some people didn't like it as it made them feel inferior or weak. It made others feel they wouldn't left behind. But love or hate it, everyone understood they were part of a thing that was larger than the job and individual pride.

*

When I finished first, I dropped my pack, turned and ran back. Everyone I jogged back by cheered way to go and stuck out a hand for a high five. When I reached ChaHow, strain and sweat covered his face. His eyes did not look bewildered so much as caught between the remembrance of how he had always stormed the pack test and his current labor to keep the ahead of the minimum pace. His face was written with will.

As a young man I studied martial arts and growing up fell prey to all the myths and legends surrounding the mystical aspects. Monks who resisted cold and heat or pain and bleeding so that they could continue on and fight, and martial artists who developed paranormal powers like a sixth sense to detect ill intent or the ability to move invisible amongst enemies. Some claimed even to skip through time and space in quantum leaps to reach destinations in seconds rather than days. I chose to study Hwa Rang Do in Los Angeles because I had seen a television special where the grandmaster Jo Bang Lee, stuck sharpened bicycle spokes through the skin of his neck and forearms and suspended five gallon buckets full of water from them. The grand master's face was calm and without contorted grimaces I was used to seeing in Kung-fu movies or from American martial artists. During that same show he did other feats to show his control of his mind and body, that he could stop his bleeding and ignore the pain on beds of nails, spokes, axe bits, and 2x4s. Seeing the grandmaster and then his brother in action and then their demonstration of their martial prowess as they kicked, punched, and used joint locks and hip throws against their student attackers convinced me I needed to study with them. It was an odd quirk of life that I was able to study at the International Headquarters, but life can be that full of quirks.

When I finally stuck the bicycle spoke in my arm and suspended the water filled bucket, it became more than a step in the training or a validation of the training I had accomplished. It became the first crack in breaking the fortress of myth. Because later I would lose the metaphysical trappings and do it on will power, or at least what I called will power. After the first time it didn't take any will power at all to force a bicycle spoke through your arm again. Will power was getting up one morning and saying this cancer don't have me yet and train a year to come back to a crew a shadow of the firefighter he was. Will power was overcoming the image of who he was to be the person life allowed him to be. The whole crew had turned back at the finish line to walk the last leg with ChaHow. Elk had been spotted on the ridge above us, and we watched them ghost through the timber heading downstream to a meadow that snow had melted off recently. In the next week snow would fall again and it'd be the

83

first time rappel training began with snowfall, and ChaHow would be there having finished the first pack test in under 45 minutes. We still had the minimums and the 85-pound pack test, but having finished the first, he was set.

*

For our last rappel we readied everything we had and made sure our packs weighed 85 pounds. We rappelled into Krassel Saddle across the river and readied to hike back to camp. We went out in sticks of two and had the whole crew on the ground in thirty minutes and all the gear ready to pack out. Money came in on the last stick as the ship came over somebody yelled. "They have the pipe wrench."

The four-foot long, forty-five pound pipe wrench had been strapped to a pack in the cargo net that hung from the helicopter's belly. Ursula, as it had come to be called, had multiple uses in training. We clipped it into rappel ropes during tower training to create enough weight for a rappeller to have the feel of pulling up 250 feet of line when only twenty feet off the deck. My rookie buddy Rich had to sling it over his shoulder and do two hundred lunges to help him reflect on his continued errors of checking his buddy for life threatening twists or items that could foul a rope. Now the big red wrench was being slung in for several people to take turns packing out in addition to their eighty-five pounds.

"Rich," I said. "What did you not do this time?

"Not me, I got everything dialed."

"Right," As he was my rookie buddy, I had to do the requisite push-ups for his errors. I had already done over five hundred and knew he was prone to mistakes. He was a good kid, almost twenty-one amongst a crew where the average age hovered around thirty. Rich had both strength and brains. Like all of us, he too had the desire to succeed and be the finest rappeller possible, but he still had the youthful inclination to overlook small things or not take everything into account that experience would eventually give him. In the saddle watching the ship come in with the sling load dangling beneath its belly, I was waiting for the announcement of general reflection.

He was right. The wrench was to be split for disregarding an order given to everyone at the outset of training, which will remain a secret, as if I tell I'll owe Money a thousand push-ups. ChaHow was one of the offenders. When it was his turn, he slung the wrench over his shoulders and humped it down the trail. Another to carry the wrench was my other rookie-buddy, Aaron, who had been on the Chena Hotshots and during the off-season performed stand-up comedy. As a fellow English major we embarked upon Steinbeck Summer and read all of his works we could during the season.

We marched down the mountain, across the pack bridge, spanning the South Fork, across the road, past the houses of downstairs, and up the switchbacks until we reached the office where we halted. All of us finished together. Another rookie, Rachelle who had worked on a fire use module out of Utah previously, had Ursula by this point, but her smile still filled her face as her long legs powered her up the road. The retreads went into the office and told the rookies to go out in front of the heli-pad. With a little ceremony we pinned on an oval pin with the Krassel logo.

ChaHow's grin spread across is drawn and sweaty face. "So good I had to do it twice." During rappel training he asked anyone who had a taken a picture of him sliding down the rope to send it to him so he could show everyone back home that "I *am* back, baby."

Someone else pinned Aaron's pin on him, while I pinned Rich's on him. "Good job," I said. I knew we still had work to do and the training was only beginning.

The next morning we received two resource orders and the crew was broken into two, one as a rappel crew and the other as members of a hand crew. We were all dispatched to northern California and the Lime Fire Complex and would be at the same helibase. I was assigned to the crew going as rappellers, and I was hopeful I'd finally get an operational rappel.

ChaHow, Rich, and I drove the heli-tender. ChaHow played a song from the *Into the Wild* Soundtrack. Even though I thought the mythologizing of Christopher McCandless lame, I liked the music. Every truck we had left the helibase, and the lucky up-team got to fly and be there the day before us. Also with us was the fuel truck driver's Air Stream RV. His wife drove it and because she possessed a commercial driver's license, she acted as the relief driver. Ahead of us stretched a two-day drive with a layover in Bend, Oregon. Aaron grew up in the area we were going. His first crew had been Mad River, not too far from our destination of Hayfork, California. We cut across the Oregon desert and stopped at a rest area.

ChaHow slipped behind the wheel to drive. Rich had just made the comment, "We do all the driving and he just sits in the passenger seat running the iPod."

"He can sit over there the whole trip as far as I care," I said.

At the exit a man stood with a cardboard sign, Needs Gas Money.

"Needs to get a job," Rich said.

"My aren't we judgmental, Richard. For all you know he had a job and got laid off or maybe he got sick and laid low and his boss replaced him because he was more worried about profit than people. Maybe you should give thanks that you're blessed and haven't been put in a position to stand along a desolate stretch of highway with a cardboard sign as the sun sears your brain."

We wound our way through the mountains to Hayfork, California. The valley suffered under an inversion of smoke billowing from thousands of acres of fires. An Area Command had been set up due to the size, complexity, and numbers of fires in the region and to help with the different ownership boundaries the fires crossed so as to reduce duplicating resources and mitigate confusion in the region. The heat hit us as we stepped out of our trucks. A bunch of empty water bottles clattered to the ground behind ChaHow. He picked them up tossed them back into the floorboard with a grin.

We gathered in front of the trucks. Some crews had arrived at the helibase. Salmon-Challis, Sawtooth, the Chester Flight Crew, Price Valley, and some heavy helicopters. Other crews and people would mix in and the team had helibase personnel in place. We waited for a briefing before parking our trucks. The helicopter had flown in the day before and was parked on a gravel strip between the airstrip and the parking area.

We broke the crew into three modules. One was to remain with the helicopter for initial attack, one was go out with other helitack squads from the base to make a hand-crew to go out and work on the fires, and the other was going to do helibase work. My assignment was to be ready for initial attack. Ryan Flegal and I were first up and put our gear in the helicopter, wrote the manifest for the weight of the load, made sure our radios had the correct frequencies, and started reviewing maps. ChaHow and Rachelle made up the second up-team and staged their gear with the truck.

The weather forecast predicted temperatures in the nineties and possible afternoon thunderstorms with high, erratic winds. For the majority of the day an inversion kept aircraft grounded, but most afternoons a break occurred for a window of a couple of hours. Sometimes the mornings were clear and we always hoped to fly. Flegal and I had worked together the year before on a hand crew assignment when I had been Jess's trainer. He had been the crew boss of the Warren crew, but this year he went to be a smokejumper, but had washed out because he couldn't operate a chute to the satisfaction of the trainers. He told me at the Krassel pig roast and when he said he didn't know where he was going to work I asked Doug to offer him a position with us. Craig and I took him on Monday and worked him through ground training and tower work as the other rookies began to do mock-ups on the helicopter. Once I stepped in front of a thug in a bar who was picking fight with him because he wouldn't fight. Flegal organized everything and once he had the truck inventoried and checked for serviceability he knew where everything was and in what condition it was in.

Then the days at Hayfork became unbearable. The heat and the smoke pressed down on us wrapping us in a gritty cocoon of dried sweat and drift smoke. Every hour we Krasselians languishing on the helibase did push-ups and ChaHow cut a cardboard strip from an MRE box and drew handprints on it to protect his palms from the hot asphalt while the rest gloved up. We rigged a pull-up bar in a connex box. The Price Valley Rappellers came over to do pull-ups with us—two people on the bar to do two pull-ups until we reached 100 and after reaching 100 doing a set of maximum repetitions. Once we were shocked when two from the Chester Flight Crew came over, while the rest sat in their crew buggies.

Every two weeks, if a rappeller didn't rappel she had to perform a proficiency rappel. At the helibase the Chester Flight Crew spooled up and their medium helicopter hovered 250 feet above the deck. They tossed the ropes and we noticed one of the ropes had a knot. The rappellers went to the skids and the woman didn't look down her rope and began to descend. Neither she nor the spotter saw the knot. "Holy crap," someone said. "She's not stopping." We cringed as she hit the knot, trapping her on the rope. She hit it hard and lucky the force of the impact didn't bust her Genie. We all sucked in breath as she hit. "Holy fuck, what was she doing?" The helicopter lowered her to the ground so she could unhook. On the next stick a guy went to the skid without being hooked in. At first we saw him move out of the hovering helicopter and then jump back in. The rappeller on the opposite skid reentered the ship. The spotter unhooked the ropes, letting them fall to the ground. The helicopter flew back to its pad and shut down. Somebody said, "Chester Heli-Slack strikes again." The manager's disciplinary action was to force the crew to sit in their crew buggies and read the rappel guide for the rest of the day like a bunch of school kids in timeout. A dubious punishment at best.

It was the next season Marovich fell to his death or as the government said: "sustained fatal injuries from an uncontrolled descent." The main finding for the accident was lack of situational awareness and the lack of experience within the Chester Flight Crew because they were a Jack Crew. The Joint Apprenticeship Committee Program (JAC). They hired twenty young men and women who wanted to be career firefighters and put them on a crew. Unfortunately when they first started they had zero aviation experience. When rookies showed up on a crew, like Krassel or Price Valley on the Payette, they had almost an entire group of people, aside from the squad bosses and the crew boss to show them how to be an effective firefighter. The Jack crew couldn't function in the same environment or at the same level because of their inexperience. Their second year they are all sent to a helicopter rappel crew, one of which is the Chester Flight Crew. They arrived with almost no experience fighting fire in some cases, and no experience with helicopters and started rappelling.

With a supervisor and two spotters to keep track of them, they made a lot of mistakes. The Purpose of the program was "to fast track" people into leadership roles. Rookies were lumped into a crew and sent to work in different fields so they could have a taste of each of the fire specialties. Twenty rookies and even with a span of control of three to five was still twenty rookies. They ended up with people who had a superficial knowledge of a specialty and the false sense of how that specialty works. The Willow Springs accident report cited the need for experience and training in the fields of situational awareness. Marovich only had one season in fire before being allowed to rappel from a helicopter. In all honesty, he should have had more and I have interviewed Fire Management Officers and Assistant Fire Management

Officers, Helicopter Managers, and Helicopter Crew Supervisors and they agreed with the report that not only the experience of the individual, but the crew as a whole played a crucial role in the tragedy, and that perhaps the best thing would be to disband the crew or make them a non-rappel crew.

The Forest Service response was to ban rappelling from light helicopters, which had never had a near miss with a rappeller or an injury from uncontrolled descent, because it was impossible to enter the helicopter on the ground not attached to the ship. The bureaucrats in Fire and Aviation took not one real step in the aftermath of the death of a young rappeller and instead used it to go after light helicopters and kill a vital asset in fire suppression, fire monitoring in the wilderness, and for back country rescue as every year Krassel was called upon to fly to the aid of some one in a bad way in a remote area. In 2009 an airplane crashed in the wilderness and two Krasselians, including EMT Jess Martin, rappelled into to forest, stabilized the victims, cut out a helspot in the trees for a rescue helicopter and extracted the people. By the time this was done, the smokejumpers finally arrived on scene. The next day the newspaper read: smokejumpers rescue plane crash survivors or some other such report.

The government panel decided that because you could "standardize" all medium helicopters, then they would discontinue the light helicopter rappel program. That logic assumed that standardization equaled safety and a catchall to solve their problem. It was not and a faulty premise in the logic. The next season still saw rappellers attempting to go to the skid of medium helicopters without being properly hooked in and training cadre devolving into screaming drill instructors as if yelling a screaming were the best way to teach, which it wasn't and pointed to a failure in thinking about how to train firefighters.

When I first heard of the loss of the light rappel program and the reasons I thought of high school kids wrecking a full sized pick up and the response was to ban middle aged drivers from driving light trucks. It made that much sense. With all the vehicle deaths I am surprised the Fire Service let anyone drive given how they approach implementing safety standards. The upshot of all of it was that as the Fire Service eradicated rappelling from the safest helicopters with experienced and dedicated crews, while the Chester Flight Crew was allowed to continue its rappel program with same culture of fast tracking without building experience and continuing to be the least desired crew to arrive on an incident.

Many explorers from Cherry-Garrard to de Saint Exupèry have lamented their nations becoming nations of shopkeepers, but what to do when the job called for a person of imagination and flexibility to be met instead by a rigid bureaucratic shopkeeper who can't see past the cans on the shelf and most administrators didn't have to live with the consequences of their decisions as others suffer or die.

*

Flegal and I boarded the helicopter. We had a mission to meet some operations people so they could recon parts of the fire without having to drive four hours to the helibase. From the air all the marijuana plantations around Hayfork were exposed. Plywood fences and well-spaced plants spaced out like the grid of a pegboard. Our pilot hovered over one. "How bizarre is that?"

Below us a guy in cut-offs, a tank top, and a shotgun slung over his back watered his plants with a garden hose.

"Pretty bizarre, Man," Flegal said. "But we should fly along before he takes a shot at us."

"They can have up to 999 plants growing."

"For medicinal?" I asked.

"Yeah."

The helicopter nosed forward and flew over more plantations as we wheeled north. After the recon we were called for bucket work and flew to Hyampom northwest of Hayfork. The ship landed on a sand bar by the river. Flegal and I unloaded our gear and hooked the Bambi bucket to a 100-foot long line and the helicopter. We cleared away toward the riverbank. As the ship lifted I got a picture of Flegal holding his hand so it looked like he held the bucket in his palm. After the ship left Flegal dug into his pack and came up with a water bottle wrapped with fishing line and a hook. He searched around for a piece of driftwood for a bobber and began casting it. "I just made this and wanted to try it out."

"You'll need some bait." We scrambled around for some grasshoppers and caught a couple. He cast and drifted it back for fifteen minutes without luck.

"I don't get it. My buddy on Salt Lake caught fish like this."

"I don't know. Maybe they're just not hungry."

90

"All the weed that's bound to wash down into the water should give them the munchies."

Crews had found illegal plantations as they hiked to fires or dug firebreaks. Rachelle found a Drum tobacco pouch packed with marijuana in a dozer track. The woods were full of unexpected turns. The local fire folk gave us a briefing on what to look out for and if we saw black tubing in the middle of the woods that it was for watering plants and booby traps could be anything from light fish hooks hung at eye level to trip-wired shotguns and homemade bombs. Once outside of Bovill, Idaho, I had responded to a smoke report and discovered a small drug lab. We pulled back and called in the sheriff. A few years before three BLM resource workers in Northern Nevada wandered into a plantation in a remote ravine. The three Hispanics held them hostage, discussing whether to kill them or not, and in the end let them go.

As Flegal kept trying to catch a fish, I found a couple of nice river stones for my daughters. "One of these days, I'm going to catch a fish on this rig. Just not today." The pilot called that he was five minutes out and get ready "to turn and burn." Flegal wrapped fishing line up and put it in his helmet bag.

"It's still good times, bro."

I gave him a thumb-up. "As long as we're breathing."

We rotated off the initial attack squad and went out on a squad with ChaHow to help support a burnout operation. We dumped our gear into a pick-up truck and drove to a crossroads and after reaching it were re routed to get a lat and long of a helispot and upon finding it found the numbers painted on the pad. After we called it in to dispatch, they sent us to a pullout along a road to wait. We climbed out of trucks along with some other firefighters we hadn't met. A white pick-up sped by and braked. It turned around and came to a dusty stop, sliding in the gravel. A guy in a clean yellow fire shirt kicked the door open.

"What's going on around here? Where are you supposed to be?"

He slammed the door on his truck. "I need people to work and not sit around."

ChaHow leaned against front fender. "Your self-important attitude isn't working for me."

The man stopped and looked at ChaHow, his mouth open as if he lost all muscle control in his jaw.

ChaHow's deadpanned face measured the man. "I'm failing to see how your complaint is helping the overall operation. We were told to stage here after a driving to find a lat and long that was clearly marked on the pad. Unless you have something constructive to add we don't need the surplus drama."

The man paused. "I need you all to tie in with Union Shots up the road." He pointed from where he had come from. "There is a parking area and a huge set of power lines."

"This we can do," I said. We loaded into our trucks and drove away.

Later ChaHow told us, "Those petty men who need to bluster about to show they're in charge need to be brought down a peg. I survived brain cancer. I don't need to put up with their minor shit with the time I got left."

We finally got directions and met up with a Hotshot crew to do a burn out. Crews had been losing burns and having to fall back. We worked late into the night and got back to the base late, but we felt good to have been out and working the fire. ChaHow scooted off to his tent. In the night we could hear him pop the top of a beer can. We weren't supposed to have beer where we camped, but ChaHow figured he was off duty and as long as he kept to himself, "fuck ☐em."

*

In the austral summer of 2009/2010 I worked at Amundsen-Scott South Pole Station. I found out ChaHow had succumbed to the cancer that had dogged him since 2006. He simply lay down and said, "I'm tired of this bullshit," and died. He was the fourth friend I'd lost that year.

I kept working in the cargo yard and reflected on the dead and how they lived. ChaHow didn't have to come back. He didn't have to climb the mountains or suck the smoke and dig around fires anymore. He didn't have to run, pack, pull-up, work in the heat of smoke choked draws, or endure the days living in tents or spiked out on the ground. Maybe he did it to prove something to himself and the crew, and I think to the memory of those killed when 5EV crashed. On his calf he had tattooed the Krassel logo with four shooting stars. He knew he wasn't alone either; quite a few of us have some form of the Krassel tattoo. He came to a crew who would sling him on our backs and pack him up and down mountains if we had to, because the real essence of a crew isn't how much line it can dig or how tough they think they are, it's the quality of being able to fill in the gaps of your weaknesses as you fill in theirs because they know you and if you were down, carry you and the freight of all your hope. Oh sure a person might take some ribbing about it, but in the end no matter if we had to pick up some slack along the way, he'd repay it to us.

The striking thing for me that summer was the lack of complaint about the hardship. His Misery Index was calibrated by death and survival. He reserved his complaints to administrative snafus, and bad command decisions, and small-minded people. He never complained during any of the PT or the pack outs, or during the fires about his pain or mentioned his cancer as holding him back even though the pain and struggle crossed his face like spider-webbed glass. He pushed forward and showed a peculiar grace. We were able to plug in one guy on a sixteen-person crew and give him his shot at a comeback. I found myself kneeling on the Polar Plateau, weeping. Tears froze to my face as I tried to wipe them from under my goggles. Shelby on the Waste Crew called my name and asked if I was all right. I thought of his motto, "It's all good," and nodded, getting back to work under the frostbitten sun.

Chapter 7

THE DEAD II

But sometimes it's not all good. Sometimes you sit in a lounge in McMurdo Station, having just worked four months at Amundsen-Scott South Pole Station. You're drinking with Polies and in the morning your flight leaves for New Zealand. It is February 15 at the bottom of the world and February 14 and Valentine's Day in North America. You smile and drink, think about playing cribbage. You are going home and excited to see your girls. Your friend, who you were with on fires and more fires and more assignments than you can count, is dialing a phone number that doesn't pick up. He is distraught, this man you feel you can lean on. This man dials and dials and his girlfriend doesn't answer.

You are in McMurdo and no one can call you. You drink and think about playing cribbage with other firefighters. They fight structure and aircraft fire and great folk. Your friend, who you love and have fought fire and fire and fire with slams the door on himself. The neighbors must've heard the gunshot. You are in McMurdo drinking in a lounge in a cushy chair. You tell jokes and laugh, when a woman taps you on the shoulder. You jump up and smile. She works fire on your district too, a runner, a woman who can write sports columns. A woman happy in tough situations and tight spots. Mel's eyes well with tears. She mumbles. She never mumbles. She always speaks loud and clear, this friend of yours in McMurdo. Mel tells you Flegal is dead. She tells you he is gone from the earth because he found no way to go on.

You will meet another friend, a firefighter a woman already in New Zealand from South Pole. Trudy and Mel will drink with you. These women of the Ice and of fire will cry with you as you cried the night before because you are a maudlin and sentimental drunk. You reminisce about an easy grin, a bow legged walk, and wonder at a burned up inside we never knew. You wish to be tougher. You will get drunk, but will not miss your flight. The next morning you fly almost 3/4s the way up the globe. You travel and you go on. All the signs were there, looking back. The manic ways, the overheard phone calls from creditors, the rocky romances, and the all night brooding by the campfire. The slivers of black between the quick smile and the hand always ready to lift a friend up. Meriwether Lewis killed himself along a trail, alone in the woods. A man who didn't just make the arduous journey across North America and back, but led a Nation's quest. The toughest are sometimes the most sensitive and die and you got nothing in your will power to breathe the hope into the collapsed lungs of a life no matter how hard you train to save lives in the haze and heat of winter. But that won't keep you from trying. How did William Clark react upon hearing the news of the death of his co-commander? He wrote, "I fear the weight of his mind overcame him." Clark went on.

Then the news comes that Liza is dead.

Chapter 8

WE RIDE FOR THE BRAND

I leaned against the bar at the Black Rock Landing Saloon, in Gerlach, Nevada, facing a crowded dance floor. On my right side stood a man--more a Sasquatch--with a huge Montana crown cowboy hat and USMC tee shirt, and to my left was my co-worker, Wendy, a wiry brunette with wide cheek bones and a narrow jaw. It was around midnight and I was ready to head off to sleep. The town's population was usually just a handful of people and the surrounding 94 square miles topped out at 499 people. That night, the number in town had swelled to over a thousand in the town with the 1945 to 2003 high school reunion that was in full swing. 2003 marked my first year working with a federal fire crew after leaving the Association in 2001. I took the 2002 off to go to summer school, but right back into the swing of putting out fires and learning the language and attitudes of the Feds.

We had landed our helicopter on the football field, while two fire engines and the helicopter-chase truck were parked in front of Bruno's Motel. That afternoon we had suppressed two fires about seven miles away. Our helibase and district office in Winnemucca were several hours away over dirt roads skirting the Black Rock Desert, famous for Burning Man, land speed records, and the odd airplane landing. We ate dinner and added twelve people into the swirling Vegas-like mass. We firefighters stuck out with our work boots, tee shirts, and green fire pants. We on the helitack crew especially stuck out with the large-pizza sized emblem of a helicopter covering our backs. Some fire crews forbid drinking and on larger fires, the incident commanders ban drinking or leaving the fire camp to drink. I have always disliked having a job where you are made to clock out and still they tell you what to do while you are not being paid. It was invasive and smacked of fascism and the justification that it was to prevent problems was like the police saying they were going to lockdown a neighborhood because of a chance a problem might occur. It did fit in with the military fetish many fire managers had. On some smaller crews supervisors saw no harm in mingling with the locals as a long as we behaved ourselves. If someone came to work reeking of booze, unable to operate, or missed work because of alcohol, then that was grounds for discipline. The supervisors wanted us to boost the local economy, be courteous, and be seen as polite and ordinary. One of the ironies of being a firefighter in the West was that people in small towns treated us either like old friends coming home or invaders out to steal their land, end their way of life. Time having a beer with some locals fostered goodwill because we lost the anonymity of a faceless government.

People danced in the three bars, the community center, and under awnings set up for the occasion. Out on the floor in front of me, a skinny kid from our crew danced with a blonde in over-tight jeans and a halter top that barely contained her breasts as she followed the kid's lead. His shaved head and big ears made him look like a bobble head with a crooked scar running down the right side of his face from a combine harvester accident on his family farm. He was a mediocre firefighter because he lacked endurance and the ability to carry a lot of weight. He was the one most likely to open his mouth at the wrong time and anger other crews.

Once some of us on the crew went to a softball game. The BLM team was made up of firefighters and resource people. Many who didn't play went to support the team. We had gathered behind the dugout with some of the engine folks, when the Fire Management Officer walked off the field. The skinny kid said off-handedly, "It's cool the way you let them play hacky-sack and watch movies on laptops." The faces of the engine folks went pale and their mouths dropped open. The FMO hated hacky sack and had forbid it for his crews because it looked unprofessional for the public to drive by and see fire crews kicking the small beanbag around. The idea that they had time to watch movies rankled him because he believed there was always something to do to prepare for fires. The next morning they had to stand an inspection and run hose-lay and shelter deployment drills.

Wendy and I marveled at the kid's dazzling dance skills. As the kid twirled the pretty blonde, Sasquatch next to me said, "I'm going to go over and kill that skinny fucker." Wendy and I looked from the dance floor to him and back. There could only be one skinny fucker he was talking about. And with our matching shirts and pants, there was no doubt we were together. As with all people who have experienced unit or crew life, the threat was for me to hear. His, *What are you going to do about it?* look told me the next move was mine, and not the skinny kid drop shooting a woman between his legs.

"Now why would you want to go and ruin a good time for?"

He looked down on me with beer-glazed eyes. "That little fucker has danced one too many times with my wife." Mrs. Sasquatch's feathered hair flapped back like a falcon in a dive as she launched her lithe legs around the kid's hips and then jumped into a twirl before sliding along the floor.

Oh, how High School, I thought, but realized he was serious. I had a third degree black belt in Hwa Rang Do and had been around some fights, and had learned to recognize the signals between blustering and blowup. I didn't want any fight or the possibility of a fight. I thought of the gambler's credo: Don't bet what you can't afford to lose. Even though the kid was a dipshit, I couldn't let Sasquatch pound on him. Soon after any fist throwing the rest of the crew would be swarmed by a drunken mob high on school pride. By that same code I had to defend him. We all rode for the brand as they said in the West. It would be a good old barroom brawl out of some cowboy flick.

When I was a kid watching movies, John Wayne walked into a bar and we geared up for a fight. What kid wasn't captivated by the images and scenes of cowboys, gamblers, outlaws, drunks, and dancehall girls, swinging fists, tables, chairs, beer mugs and the occasional fiddle, while an old man banged away on an upright piano? As far as I knew, all kids were enamored with the Wild West and bar fighting and no kid wanted to be the coward hiding under a table or behind a woman, even if he was the comic relief. My father was a great encourager of this image and not because of what he said--when I was kid I saw him take out two robbers with knives--he told his sons never show weakness, never back down and fight dirty because a fair fighter always lost. As a combat veteran and having grown up in Kentucky where family ties were things people killed over, he also had a keen sense of never abandoning your people in a time of need.

In Gerlach, I knew the cops would be called from Reno for backup. And the cops would be called, because this man wanted to fight, and backing down was the equivalent to running past the nose of a bear--it just makes them want to chase you. Even trying to hustle the kid out would be a fight. No backing out gracefully and besides given the kid's habit of saying stupid things he'd probably mouth off or refuse to leave or even try to fight the guy. He had been raised on the same movies. There would be blood and broken bones and every seasonal firefighter would be looking for a new job come morning without so much as a fair trial. The skinny kid dipped the blonde as a Southern-rock song ended and as another started he twirled her out and back into his arms. He was unaware the eyes of the Corps were upon him. I wondered how come he didn't work such a single-minded focus on fires.

*

We all learned to deal with confrontation. The Westerns all broke it down for us: showdown, sucker punch, yellow belly, quick draw, and once you're called out you can't back down, and all problems are overcome through violence or the threat of violence.

The Hwa Rang Do grandmaster I learned under told me that the master's attack was the counter attack and the best counter attack was to diffuse the situation before the opponent swung. Fighting became the sign of weakness except in defense, the final option. Even for the trappings of fighting, it wasn't about showing strength or the threat of fighting, but confidence and being a little wily. Much like fire, he said one had to be reactive and sensitive to the opponent. In fire, we have the fire triangle: heat, fuel, and oxygen. Take away one and fire cannot sustain combustion, so if you can remove all three the fire is a goner and not a threat. A confrontation has much the same qualities: take away the fuel (reason), the heat (anger) by cooling it off, or take away the hot air, (by not running your mouth in a hostile manner).

In the language of fire, many journalists play up the use military terms to sensationalize what we do and we do use that language not because we were militaristic in ways, but because of language itself and how we describe confrontations. We fight fire and even in the modern lexicon we suppress fire. Suppressive fire is meant to keep the enemy's head down and even though we light a fire to suppress fire, fire never consciously take shots at us. The militaristic language in relation to fire fails there. I could say it was the language of sports too or debate or passionate lovers. It was a small realization that the language of bureaucrats and administrators has dominated the language of the Fire Service and less of the mountains and woods: "Smoke chasing" to "initial attack" to "appropriate management response". The first Forest Service Chief, Gifford Pinchot set up the early Forest Service on the military model and not because he loved the military, because he knew to be successful he needed the same loyalty from his rangers and sense of camaraderie that is common in groups who face adversity. The rangers could resist the socioeconomic pressure of short-sighted, local industry and people living in the shadows of those forests. These groups, whether they are infantry platoons, police squads, fire crews, or sports teams all struggle against something together.

It was the language of struggle no matter if we directly attacked a fire, indirectly attacked a fire, or stood back observing a wildfire use fire for resource benefit. But no matter how abstracted the terminology became, underlying it was passion, guts, and a physical and mental challenge like few others. As an English major, the difference between the Anglo-Saxon of the workers in the fields and the Latin and French descended words of those in power always seemed an unconscious statement of how people saw themselves in the fire service class system. We were trying to join with and overcome something and most of the time the thing we were really confronting was inside us. Even Sasquatch next to me wrestled with something inside him, even if he didn't know it.

*

But there in Nevada I thought about calling someone's bluff. This was another point where military and fire terminology part. You cannot bluff a wildfire. When I was in the fifth grade, I caught the bus with my younger brothers at a cattle guard in southeastern Arizona with the six other kids who went to the three building school in Ash Creek and the high school in Elfrida. The oldest boy was a sophomore. I was the next biggest, and the newest, kid. I was still a foot or two shorter, and he picked on me and taunted me with insults, telling me to swing at him. I seethed in my own fear, cowardice. When I finally had enough, I told my father. His advice, "Stand up to him and say, 'you want to fight let's go, but if I kick your ass, you're going to have live with it. You kick mine, big deal, I'm a little kid.'" Dad told me I'd probably get an ass whooping, but to swing like hell and make the boy pay for it because the next time, he'll think twice about fighting me. Even if he wins, he'll suffer. He said, "You have to make him believe that every time he comes close to you, you're going to make him bleed, even if you have to bite his nose off." My father believed in battleship diplomacy, but also believed that no one attacked another if he thought he was going to get bloodied or lose, unless he had been pushed into a corner and had nothing left to lose. I discovered later, some guys didn't care and liked fighting and being hit, win or lose. Sasquatch looked like that kind of guy.

Such are the ways of civilization. I did call out the bully and he did back off. In Gerlach, I didn't want any fight or the possibility of a fight. Firefighters have a risk management matrix composed of many checks "if this then that," assigned numerical values, which when added was supposed to let you know when a firefighter was over his or her head. The first one should be, "Do you feel completely helpless and about to crap yourself." In this way a firefighter can learn to internalize, bind the body and mind together to make decisions and maintain control. I had to maintain control and risk management matrix told me that if I didn't break up the fire triangle this situation was going to blow up.

Sasquatch took a big drink and emptied his bottle. He set it on the bar behind him. He cracked his knuckles and I asked when he was in the Corps. He looked down on me and said something about the late nineties. Beer foam fringed his push broom sized Fu Manchu and his eyes focused and unfocused on me. It was like looking into the eyes of a bear you encounter along a trail and it's not sure if it needs to run away or attack. I didn't think run was in his vocabulary.

But as Sasquatch looked down and stared, I realized how easy I could take this guy. Not the consequences in the morning and not the other fifty who would jump to his defense, but him. Years of martial arts training and those misguided years fighting over empty ideals allowed me to see his weaknesses. All the training gave me confidence, which was what my grandmaster talked about when he said to keep skills hidden so that the enemy doesn't see you as a challenge, but keep calm and focused so that the enemy unconsciously senses your strength, but remains unthreatened so you can misdirect him. Leading crews in fire warrants the same confidence. The second best advice on leading crews came on mountaintop during a string of seventy some arson fires on the Clearwater and Nez Perce National Forests in north central Idaho.

I had been called out of Elk River to meet up with James, an Idaho Department of Lands, IDL, crew boss, and Neal, a project's officer with a twenty-person convict crew out of Orofino Idaho. On our second day, we had driven from the Incident Command Post in a rock pit where we were all camped.

I rode with James in his state rig while the inmate crew followed in two pick-up trucks equipped with what looked like campers on the back, but had seating for ten. We had an incident action plan (IAP), which had all the frequencies, medical plan, operations plan, weather forecast, and who was where on the fire. On the drive out we talked about our assignment. Working with inmate crews has its own special rules and challenges and some crew bosses acted like petty tyrants who yelled and screamed like drill instructors from Parris Island. Once on a fire, an IDL crew boss snatched a power saw from an inmate sawyer and hurled it down a steep mountain into a brush patch a couple of hundred feet down and told the inmate to go and get it. Some might say that they were convicts and deserved to be treated that way, but these men were either at the end of their sentence, in for petty crimes, and none of them were murderers, rapists, and child molesters. Most importantly, they were people who had been caught in a bad way and in most cases, like a Johnny Cash song, they admitted they had done wrong. Many were trapped by social and economic circumstances that many mainstream Americans don't comprehend. Because of those conditions, the inmates do see the world differently and respond differently than a crew of college students. These men worked to remain outside the prison and for pennies. Someone who needed to act like a despot confirmed for them that authority only wanted to punish and belittle them no matter how hard they worked to prove they were making a difference or how small the crime.

James, a soft-spoken man whose five-five frame was thick with muscle, took his line pack from the back the truck and put it on. We had already briefed the squad bosses on their mission to dig line from the upper forest road and tie into another road two hundred yards down the mountain where an engine crew was assigned to be dowsing the hot spots along the heel of the fire. James and I had talked about how the drill instructor leadership style only came out in some of those guys with inmate crews. "Those guys couldn't getaway with that with a regular crew."

I nodded. "Says more about the insecurities of the boss than the bossed."

We hiked across to the flank of the fire. I wanted to scout my section of the fire, tie in with the engine crew, and then across the heel to talk with crew boss on the other flank.

At the top of the hand-line we saw a squad boss running toward us. The mountain's slope was close to 70 percent. Steep as a dozer blade and this inmate was pumping his legs hard against the earth, dust from the trail exploding under his feet. At first I thought someone was hurt, and briefly thought of a blow up and a burn-over, but the smoke and the rest of the crew still working didn't make that possible.

"Whoa," I yelled. "No need to run."

He reached the top, bent over and sucked in a huge breath. "We're under attack."

"What?" My first thought was that some antigovernment citizen, of which there were plenty, had taken a shot at the crew or threatened one of us with a rifle or had just showed up yelling about the government oppression.

"In New York. The engine guy had his radio on. Someone crashed into the Twin Towers."

Now I thought he was playing a practical joke.

James shook his head. "Let's get back to the truck."

The news voices on every station told us of the terrorist attacks across the country.

"We still have fire to put down."

"Should we gather the crew?" I asked.

"No, keep them working. They know about it. What they need is to see us calm and composed and working. We may be tore up inside, but if we appear as if we're not then the crew won't get distracted and break down." We would control the emotional reaction of the crew by our appearance. "We are in charge and can't act crazy or out of control. They will do what we do."

"Okay." At first I thought the inmates' anger about the attacks wouldn't be that strong, but I was wrong. To a man when I walked by them they vented their anger and frustration at their helplessness. I listened for a moment and then told them we had our own job to do and the best thing we could do to help the country was to button up this fire. They focused that anger into the earth, into the flames, and shook the roots of the mountain.

All our helicopters and air tankers were grounded by order of the Federal government. Nothing flew except the birds and bugs crowding our faces. Across the river, for the want of water drops, a fire blew up and crews had to retreat beneath the pall of smoke and flames rising into the trees as volcanic as the anger in my crew's guts. All over the West, fires blew up in the September heat and raged in the mountains because we couldn't fly. If a Marine Corps recruiter had shown up in fire camp that night, those inmates would have lined up to volunteer for duty.

Appear confident even when you're not.

*

Sasquatch was very much like a villain in a Western who was drunk on his own strength and couldn't fathom any weaknesses of his own. He looked like he wanted to fight and even sitting down could be taken as an insult. I stood to my full height. "I was in the Corps, too."

He straightened, and said, "Oh yeah, with who?"

I knew my lie that I was about to roll out like the Trojan Horse had to be a whopper to keep him from trying to kill the skinny kid, so I told him I was with the Seventh Marines and had been with Task Force Ripper during Desert Storm.

His eyes widened. "No shit." His anger cooled.

"No shit." My brother, Raymond, had been in the Marine Corps for twelve years. He had been a drill instructor on Parris Island and had been in the Persian Gulf. My other brother, Terry, was a Navy Seal during the Desert Shield and Desert Storm. Even a war of overwhelming firepower, deception played a crucial role by cruising a Marine Amphibious Assault Force off the coast to distract Saddam Hussein. A card player's con as old as warfare. Make the enemy believe something to gain a strategic objective and reduce the amount of casualties. I was earnestly attempting both and by doing that put the fire out.

"Semper Fi," he said. He wavered a little and stuck out his hand. I took it.

"Do me a favor?"

"Sure." His slurred speech like he did.

"Don't beat up my little friend. He's on my crew, and I have to watch out for him." He tried to focus on my face as if I had just spoken Latin other than the Marine Corps motto.

I pointed to the dance floor. "He's harmless."

Looking at the dance floor he shrugged.

"I'll buy you and your friend a drink."

Sasquatch nodded with smile. "Semper Fi."

Wendy said she had no idea that I was in the Marine Corps. I imagined Shane who had hung up his pistols and those gunslingers who saw the error of their violent ways and tried to make peace without firing shots. But this was 2003 and the tenor the country was to fight first and ask questions later. Wendy pursed her lips and looked off when I told her I wasn't, as if she expected I should've started swinging consequences be damned.

My elation about diffusing the situation waned. We were still children of showdowns in the streets of shitty western towns. John Wayne didn't lie. He doubled up his fists and punched. Shane took down his guns. Why bother talking? Besides I'd lied about being in a combat unit and felt a little guilty about it. But I considered the pointlessness of Sasquatch's anger and how he reacted with violence because he was in a position of power. He was a belligerent drunk, the kind of man who fought without reason. To him to fight over his wife's honor was as good a reason to fight as any. My options were not fight or flight, my obligation was to stop the fire anyway I knew how. I wanted to go back to the room, sleep, get up in the morning, climb on the helicopter, and fly away.

The music from the Fifties to the Nineties played. Smoke swirled in the light and the chatter was so loud we could barely talk. I was sure groups of people were huddled together all over town, drippy over their ill-remembered school days, creating myths out of the past and re-visioning the meaning of events and laughing at the taunts or the pain of spurned love or all those petty skirmishes that had such great import and life ending qualities then, but now are a joke of adolescent overreaction. Except of course those events that led to a suicide or a crippling injury in an overturned truck along a desert highway or the skinny kid, because he was shy and walked away from a girl coming down the corridor and an imagined insult that enraged her so much that her brother and ten of his closet friends--a high school superpower if you will--caught the kid leaving campus and beat the shit out of him. Things like that stick and do not become whitewashed with nostalgia.

For wildland fire crew leaders, there was no training for this situation. We were left with the admonishment not to look bad in public and some could argue that the Puritanical option of everyone going and locking themselves away in a room was the ready solution. It was my first year with the federal fire service and fresh in my mind rang the Association's criticisms of the "Nanny Service" and treating adults like they were cub scouts or cadets in a citadel.

The skinny kid danced. He didn't get any new scars from a haymaker or a boot to the head. The other members of my crew all went to bed in the motel and not in a jail cell, and got up the next morning with jobs. No one shed blood. The reunion petered out and I'm sure there was some minor drama with so many drunken celebrants, but nothing involving broken tables, chairs, beer bottles, or even a fiddle, and no one died. I never told the kid what happened, and it wasn't important that he know. Although I struggled with how I lied at that moment, I know I did the right thing. Later Wendy told me how it was cool that I thought so quickly. I was responsible for the safety and well being of my crew. They were in my posse, and in the end that was what mattered. Besides the public didn't care about a suppressed fire before anyone spotted it, only the ones that blow up and make the news or police blotter. All part of my job, I put fires out as safely as possible.

Author's photo

Ready to hike to the Nipple Fire.

Author's photo

HT 780 on the dip.

Author's photo

Reading during a break

Author's photo

Burn out.

109

Author's photo

Volcano stump.

Author's photo

Gearing up for the Snowhole fire.

Katzilla and Jess.

Katzilla sawing.

Author's photo

Horse Creek builds.

Author's photo

Horse Creek Helispot.

Author's photo

Taking a break.

Author's photo

Me with the Mexico border in the background.

Author's photo

Border warning..

Author's photo

Bethany looks down on a Montana fire.

Author's photo

Dipping from a pumpkin.

Author's photo

At Three Rivers

Author's photo

Getting out of the way

Chapter 9

ON THE BORDER

A s an engine boss trainee in 2006, I went to Safford, Arizona. The three of us, Chris and Sean were my crew, flew down to rotate with three others from the Clearwater National Forest. Our forest had an engine stationed down there for several weeks already to assist the Coronado National Forest as they'd been fighting fire since January with little relief when we flew into Tucson in May. Just the night before I'd been reading Winnie-the-Pooh to my daughters in the cold Northwest, where they pointed at Piglet and Pooh sitting together saying, "How lucky I am to have something that makes saying goodbye so hard." I'd be gone three weeks.

Summer and the seven-year drought, the worst in over three centuries, dragged on in the American Southwest. The heat exhausted everything in the desert except the vultures that lazed on thermal columns, watching for a rabbit or an orphaned calf to collapse under the weight of dry air. Cacti faded to brown, blue throated lizards panted in the shade, and rattlesnakes moved with ease before dawn. Knots of smugglers and migrants hunkered down in the shadows of rocks, resisting their urge to drink the last of their water, waiting for night.

The National Weather Service (NWS) issues Red Flag Warnings & Fire Weather Watches to alert fire service agencies of the onset, or possible onset, of critical weather and fuel moisture conditions that could lead to rapid or dramatic increases in wildfire activity. This could be due to low relative humidity, strong winds, dry fuels, the possibility of dry lightning strikes, or any combination thereof. If the NWS believes that weather conditions could exist in the next 12-72 hours, which may result in extreme fire behavior, they will notify the fire service of a fire weather watch. A red flag warning is issued for events that will occur within 24 hours.

Firefighters new to the Southwest, after being briefed, will ask when rain is expected and others will ask about the forecast of dry lightning, LAL 6 (Lightning Activity Level). They joked about alto-cumulous-over-time-for-us clouds. None will think to ask what are the chances of getting caught in a gunfight between smugglers and the Border Patrol.

After meeting with the guys we were relieving we took a van and drove out to Safford. For me it was like returning back to an old house where the house was roofed by the sky and the floor stretched miles of sand and rock to walls of mountain ranges. I wondered if the stacks of adobe bricks still stood next to the foundation we dug as we lived in tents out there. The basin and range of the Western North America had been formed over a geologic shoving match between expanding tectonic plates. In the nineteenth century the army geologist, Clarence Dutton likened the region to "an army of caterpillars marching toward Mexico."

We drove between the vast armada of mountains, called sky islands that had risen over the Sonora Desert of Arizona, New Mexico, and Mexico. The archipelago transitioned between the Sierra Madre Occidental in Mexico to the Rocky Mountains of the United States, they contained a bio-diversity from semi-tropical to arid desert to temperate forests.

On our first morning the temperatures on the valley floor at 3,000 feet in elevation cracked one hundred by nine. We received a briefing from the Fire Management Officer about the local hazards and what was expected of us. We were the reserve unit and had to go out and patrol into the Pinaleño Mountains, looking for smokes, unattended campfires, and ready to respond anywhere we were needed. He gave us a list of Border Watch Outs, a map and directions for our first patrol. Another Idaho engine from the Payette National Forest had also been detailed to that district office and would head for a different area of the Forest. We left Safford, three of us shoulder to shoulder in the seat of the Type VI engine, essentially a pickup truck with a water tank and toolboxes instead of a bed. We agreed to swap driving by days and rotate the middle position. Sean had been a lineman on a college football team out of Montana and Chris, while not the size of a lineman still had broad shoulders. No luck to get thin guys on this crew and we rubbed a lot of shoulders in that truck during the three weeks. We wound our way out of the dusty grasslands and into the scorching foothills and dry washes of ocotillo, saguaro cacti, and acacia bushes. We ascended the mountains through chaparral, oak forests, and conifer forests. Sean gaped in wonder not knowing vast stands of Ponderosa, white pine, Douglas fir and spruce with aspen grew in Arizona, a place he always equated with deserts. He shook his head when he discovered that the largest contiguous stand of Ponderosa pines stretched across the Southwest like a knitted blanket.

We drove a couple of hours to over ten thousand feet in the mountains where the temperatures under the evergreens remained in the eighties throughout the day. All of the ranges had different eco-systems. Not only did they overlap geologic formations, but deserts, straddling the Sonora in the West and the Chihuahua in east. Some had very little vegetation, or had pinyon pine and juniper instead of the towering pines, while others still yet had thick stands of gambrel oak with a thin forest. All of the ranges shared rugged and steep terrain that was both hard to negotiate and treacherous to the unwary traveler. The volcanic rocks, pushed up from the earth's guts, stripped the lugs off of boots, shredded clothes, and sheared skin off unprotected flesh.

We reached a lookout on top of a peak and on the next peak over was a giant telescope /observatory. An old man in a snap-up cowboy shirt and faded jeans ambled down the steps and shook our hands and invited us up into the tower. The country opened up in front of us and we saw firsthand how the Apache chiefs Cochise and Geronimo eluded the United States Army or holed up in fortresses of rock escarpments that the army couldn't breech. On the peaks and ridges of the mountains a lookout commanded a view the entire valley floor and observe a troop of cavalry as it approached and watched which trails it was forced to follow and alert the tribe or set an ambush for the hapless troopers approached. Growing up I'd heard a story of a squad that refused to advance up a narrow trail that only allowed the troopers to pass single file because every time they did were forced back by arrows and rocks hurled down upon them from the heights. Cochise eventually surrendered not because of decisive military setback, but because he tired of seeing his people in a constant state of siege. General Crook employed Apache scouts to, as one of his advisors said,

119

"Fight fire with fire." The general harried the Apaches and gave them no respite. Geronimo also eventually surrendered, although later he wished he hadn't.

I have wondered at how the United States Army switched from the persistence of chasing the Native American tribes across the American West to the single-minded pursuit of fire suppression only fifteen days before the surrender of the last war chief, Geronimo. Rocky Barker tells in *Scorched Earth: How the Yellowstone Fires Chamged America* how General Philip Sheridan was a champion for Yellowstone National Park and called for an expansion of its boundaries and opposed the building of railroads into the park. When the federal government cut the budget for the park, Sheridan sent the 1st US Cavalry under, Medal of Honor recipient, Captain Moses Harris to battle fires raging in the park set by hunters to drive game from the park on August 20, 1886. They suppressed the wildfires and the Forest Service later adopted their actions and tactics.

Adding to it in the early part of the 20th Century was William James' "The Moral Equivalent of War" that inspired the US Forest Service to seek out and eradicate every fire after the 1910 fires. Like all things, it was a complexity of attitudes and events, like Sheridan's influence on Pinchot to structure the Forest Service in the military's image, the public hue and cry after the fires of 1910, transcendentalists Romantic notions of what nature should look like and the rise of environmentalists, or the industrial notions of preservation for harvest to build a nation or to secure watersheds for agriculture. Maybe it was the thing that burns in our guts, driving us to engage and challenge ourselves against something outside of ourselves while at the same time challenging us mentally and emotionally. What we strove to control was our bodies and minds to make the right choices under the pressure of a world gone to chaos. The high after that survival was what James wanted to redirect. James' proposed war on nature in 1906 that led the nation to continue its push to extract resources, but reinforced the moral righteousness of it as if fighting forest fires to save resources from destruction for later extraction were a holy cause. The irony being that Sheridan sent the cavalry to preserve Yellowstone only for its own sake.

Chris, Sean, and I wore the uniform and the following morning after our expedition to the mountain tops, rolled down a dark interstate in a truck outfitted to suppress fire where for four-hundred years the Apaches used fire to destroy and burn out their enemies' land and forests both Native and European. Our engine had been ordered to a fire a couple miles north of the Mexican border in the boot hill of New Mexico.

In one of those mountain ranges I saw my first forest fire. Before my family moved down from Gilbert, Arizona to stake out their forty acre dream of homesteading, we had traveled down to spend a weekend on the property. We pulled up to an A&W drive-in and parked. Night had descended over us and we sat in the car eating burgers and fries and drinking root beer. In the blackness I saw an orange glowing as if shimmering caterpillar hovered in the sky. "What's that?"

My father looked to where I pointed. "Forest fire."

I watched it pulse and wondered at how big it must be to cast its thick light so far. In my mind the worm I had thought turned into a flaming dragon writhing on the mountain. The campfires we sat around always mesmerized me, and now this fire, although small because of the distance, writ itself large in my imagination. The noise, the light, the heat and smoke. My only fire exposure had been campfires, and the wind drifted smoke in my face was enough to send me choking with tears streaming. I marveled at who must be up there fighting it at the moment. What were they doing? How tough they must have been to go into the deep mountains to battle the dragon like ancient knights in my mind. Later I'd find out firefighters call suppression, "slaying the dragon." I wondered at how they could even approach such a fire and how could they even hope to stop it from advancing. I didn't know or have the slightest clue except for what I had seen on television and pictured fire trucks squirting gallons of water on flames hundreds of feet tall, palls of smoke hanging in the trees as crews of people marched along forest roads or earth gouged out by heavy equipment, or the helicopters and aircraft streaming water, retardant, and firefighters in the rumble of turbulent air.

"Oh," my mother said. "Fireworks."

Over the town rockets burst like piñatas streaming burning colors. My brothers and sister all perked up watching the tendrils of light flare and fade into ash falling over the earth. The small pops of explosions echoing across the broad basin. My eyes kept being drawn to the fire on the mountain. It pulsed and seethed and even after I became a firefighter I remained captivated by the flames wavering between being and not being, between life and death, and between the light and the darkness of an Arizona night.

Headed for Douglas, we left Stafford before sunrise. Special sodium street lamps that hung lower than other cities' lamps to help reduce the light pollution for the telescope up on the mountain cast an eerie glow.

At the Douglas office we met with the Assistant Fire Management Officer. She gave us a map and directions. As we drove out of town on a gravel road, I had to slow down. Some Border Patrol trucks were pulled off to the side. The emergency lights rolled lazy circles, the dust from our truck drifted that direction so I slowed down so as not to dust them out. Along the edge of the road four women, six kids and a man sat in a line, their hands behind them. "That sucks" Sean said.

"Yeah." The dusty faces of the children made me think of my girls after they had been playing in the garden.

After several hours we passed through a ranch belonging to one of the Budweiser heirs. It was just small house with bird dog kennels, and horses. Later we would meet Budweiser's private fire management officer and go out to his house with a view to the border so we could use his phone. We kept following out the dirt road. Branches squealed along the doors and side boxes of the truck as we negotiated the rutted road until we came to clearing where a couple of other trucks were parked.

An engine crew from Oregon was there. One of their guys suffered heat exhaustion and was taking it easy in the shade. Chris, Sean, and I geared up and met Fernando who was going to line us out and get us working. Short and barrel-chested he walked through the brush like a bull. He led us into the dry wash. Maverick Springs had been developed so that the water pooled in a concrete cistern and had been fenced in with barbed wire and a tube gate. We climbed out of the brush and white oaks and into the sun scouring the desert. Above the wash we reached a trail littered with plastic milk jugs, articles of clothing, a cut up tennis shoe, a backpack and wrappers and paper.

Fernando pointed. "See this shit? We have to clean up after all the illegals. They got no respect."

The fire's sporadic edge matched the density of the vegetation. "You three start digging line up this side. Let me know when you reach the bluff." He measured us with his eyes. "I have another crew on the far side and some others on the way. Any questions?" He left back from where he came disappearing around a bend in the ridge.

I decided to recon our flank as the other two started digging the firebreak. I crossed over into the blackened area where the grass and small brush had been scorched off. It was cool enough to walk on and kept me out of the path of the fire.

The smoke hung in the air, drifted up from tufts of grass like dying campfires and smoldered in cacti and yucca spikes. The heat lingered. It felt hotter under my feet as I walked over the rocks. I hiked past islands of vegetation the fire had burned around. A jackrabbit huddled in one. A knee-high whirlwind of ash spun and collapsed. Small insects flew in circles around hot spots.

If we could tie line in between the bluffs on south and north of the ridge from where the other crew worked we could at least secure the south flank and create an anchor point so the hand crews would have a good solid area to continue north and west. After reaching those bluffs, I'd hike the fire again to determine the next course of action. I wanted air support to give us better chance of keeping the fire as small as possible. Retardant drops would slow the rate of spread so the ground crews could hook the fire across the top, but fires at Sierra Vista, threatening homes meant no aircraft for us. I mapped the natural firebreaks, scree slopes, bluffs, stretches of barren ground and calculated how far they might work before the fire burned around that area.

At the top I paused. Twenty-some miles across the Animas Valley to the East and the Animas Mountains, which was privately owned by the Budweiser heir, and part of the largest deeded property in the United States. South of the Animas Mountains, the Sierra de San Luis extended the Continental Divide into Mexico. To the north and west the higher ridges and peaks of the Peloncillo range dominated the horizon and to the south across the ancient dry lake into Mexico the steep drainage like a chimney in Diablo Creek in the Guadalupe Mountains. I wondered how many people got caught along the trails by the flames and died during fire season. Hell fire on earth.

The local fire folk told us that Mexican government didn't suppress fires in those mountains. The breeze blew over the ridge, and I shivered at the thought of the poor like I'd seen sitting along the dusty

Geronimo Trail, running in broken down and torn shoes with worn soles, a scattering of valuables, water bottles, jackets, sweatshirts, and canned food clattering on the rocks under bushes exploding into flames and scalded to charcoal and fossilized bone. Children in the arms of adults, being jerked by the wrists or hands, panicking, running from the wall of smoke and those who fell injured unable to get up, waiting for the whirl of fire to drown out the roar. I thought of my own near misses and how it was nothing compared to being in front of a fire advancing three miles a minute.

It always gave me pause to watch and consider the burning out of my life and the great black expanse of death where I didn't know what came next. My maternal grandmother sang "Amazing Grace" and that kept coming back to me time and time again in my doubt. When I looked upon her as a child, she had the surety of a math equation, and I felt as a cool hand on a fevered brow. But I waffled between doubt and faith. I even considered atheists acting on faith as they asserted something as true with equally less proof. Even as I got older and haunted by the doubt of nothingness, of no purpose in all the flash and flailing and failing of people, I recalled her as she sung, the beauty of her voice, the confidence of her lyric, the emotional tug in my gut I couldn't explain and feel sure for a moment—a wretch like me I'd believe.

The fire popped as a juniper tree fell scattering embers. Memorial Day and my birthday was approaching being this busy this early in the season, I knew the summer that I wouldn't see my daughters very much. Many times I worried that my daughters' first memories would be devoid of me or, worse, include me only when I was angry or had to discipline them. Some nights it made my guts twist. I'd spent a lot of time away—sometimes weeks or entire months—finding and fighting fire with only a day or two between assignments to visit my girls. Under the summer they grew in quantum leaps, like a selection of snapshots taped to the refrigerator. One day thirty-five pounds, the next time forty. Once I had come home from an assignment to discover that in my absence, Maddie had started pronouncing her Rs. Rotacized, I knew from college. As Kathy drove us from the airport, I could only look into the backseat, while she told a story about the neighbor's cat—the words overflowing like a dam giving way. I stared a long time, smiling and nodding and wondered what moment such a leap had happened. Teaching I thought. If I could just get my graduate degree I'd be able to be home and spend time with my girls. Unfortunately years later I'd still be forced onto the fire line, not able to find a job teaching in the sluggish economy.

The temperature reached 100. I rolled my shoulder and canted my neck to stretch the stiff muscles. Today my body felt great. I hoped soon to be done with fire. Not only because of my children, but because of the physical beating my body took. I was already in my mid thirties when I started in the business. The soreness in my knees, whenever I carried the eighty-five pound packs or the strain in my elbows when I worked all night with a power saw clearing chaparral or scrub oak along a fire front. The persistent everyday pains, better some days and worse others: the knot in my neck like a shard of glass, or the dull ache deep inside my calf. Compounding these were the injuries from dirt bikes, football, and martial arts that welled up in my body like a sulfurous spring.

But for now, I felt I could hike to Mexico and fight the fire there as well. I experienced a mixture of elation and apprehension on every fire. Electrified. "That which we are, we are," I said just to hear my voice. "To strive, to seek, to find, and not to yield." The desert breeze blew my words away. Sometimes I felt like Tennyson's aging Ulysses, older, but still carrying the passion to fly in over the ridge-tops with the fire whirling uncontrolled in a remote area. I loved leading a crew against the fire and bringing it under control. I thought about the contradictory urges: one to be home more with my girls and the other to be away fighting fire. Maybe my whole life had been a problem of reconciling the contradictions that played out in my life. And sometimes those contradictions weren't even a one to one, either or correlation. They didn't square. No matter, I had a job to do for now, so like the dread of death that made me question why anyone should strive for anything facing the possibility of nothingness, I loosened the shoulder straps on my fire pack and continued to fight the fire.

The fire moved across the hill and climbed for the ridge top 1000 feet above. Flames butted into the bluff and crept down the edge of the escarpment. It burned for the ravine. If the fire hooked below, we'd never catch it along the bottom before it burned up another drainage. Ahead of us extended miles of desert grasses and mountain brush, range for cattle, bird migration routes, wildlife habitat that the fire could scorch, and because of the intensity of the drought it would take a long time to recover, if ever. Climate change made the seasons come earlier and last longer and burn harder and higher in the mountains than ever witnessed in history. I blinked. The air wavered as if looking up from the bottom of the Bering Sea.

Along the trail I discovered a small black antenna nestled in a mesquite bush. I thought of the children I'd seen lined up along the gravel road, waiting for processing and deportation. The mothers and fathers so in need that they chanced the crossing for their family. I appreciated the risk, the gamble. Respected, as I knew what it took to undertake the journey, but didn't know what it meant to be that desperate and hoped I wouldn't. I was under no illusion that it couldn't happen to us. The heat bore down on us and the fire had mostly obliterated the shade. I always felt hotter in a burned over area: the heat lingering in the branches, earth and rocks and the look of the blackened waste.

Later when I asked Fernando about the antenna, he told me, "Motion detector. For the border patrol. They know we're out here so we probably won't see them."

"Doesn't look like it could transmit very far," I said.

"Maybe, maybe not, I don't know."

The fire cracked, popped, and roared when it hit the junipers. The leading edge of the fire gathered intensity. The curtain of oily smoke formed into a denser column. The digging got harder. Instead of putting out concentrations of burning material, we scraped away grass and weeds, pulling aside rocks and chopping away brush to create a firebreak. At places we'd stomp out burning grass and use it as a line after running ungloved hands through the ashes. We chipped rocks and the steady rhythm lulled us. The sun reached its apex and leaned its rays down the eastern slope we worked on. The smoke hung heavy in our sinuses and glazed our faces. Our tongues thickened and mucus and grit covered our teeth. The heat made us sluggish.

In the far north Idaho mountains we had fought no fires. Snow still held in the mountains and the rivers still swelled with the freezing runoff of mid-spring. Flowers hid dormant, saving their buds for June and July. We hadn't seen a 90-degree day up north. In the desert we relearned the hardships, hardening the body to the flames forgotten in the dim winter past. We endured scratches and abrasions and the collection of grime and sweat in the body's cracks and crevices. We adjusted to the weight and continuous chafing of straps from fire-packs, and boots that pinched and suffocated the feet. Hands calloused and strengthened as we worked, the pain in our joints like a familiar embrace from a friend long absent. Each became cocooned in our own thoughts as we worked, only forcing ourselves out of the trance of labor to look at the fire's behavior, check the changes in the building clouds, and track the sun as it stamped our skin.

Shade fell on some parts of the fire from rises and dips in the ground. The dingy sheet of smoke rose all along the ridge top, casting a weak shadow on the upper reaches of the fire. In a few spots, black smoke braided into the sky. The fire crossed a ridge. It cracked in thicker stands of trees and brush. Thunderclouds continued to build over the mountains, like black and slate stained sails luffing in the wind.

The twenty-person Coronado IA (Initial Attack) crew arrived and began digging a hand-line from exposed lava rock in a dry wash up the ridge on the northeast side to a bluff. We had pulled off the south side having completed the work and rested in the spackle of shade under some mesquite bushes. We had been going for over 14 hours. One of the supervisors called me on the radio and asked if we could help with the digging.

"Sure," I said. "But we're coming close to maxing out our duty day." The work to rest ratio or the 2 to 1 guidelines had been in effect after it was found that fatigue was one of the contributing factors in the Thirtymile tragedy. I thought again of the findings that everyone on that fire staggered under the weight of fatigue equal to a blood alcohol level of .20. My own experience I had the fire that escaped on me on an Idaho hillside below the horse pasture and driving back and blacking out for stretches of gravel road. In Alaska I had commercial fished in the 48-hour fishing derbies of setting and hauling gear. In those half lit underworlds of perception, where we mumbled as shades wavering in between darkness and light, I marveled at how few of us have washed up on beaches after sundering the rocks or tripping and falling in full flight from a fire turned back on us like a war dog slipped its chain.

Early on it was the typical extreme administrator reaction: no exceptions to the rules. Firefighters dispatched to fires in the evening only had a few hours to work before being forced to stop and watch the fire they could have caught grow away from them or wake in the pre-dawn and watch a fire respond to the rising sun and gain new life after the night cool and higher humidity. Now firefighters can work in excess of sixteen hours in a day, if they have justification, but they have to get prior approval. (Even with this, a Wyoming fire in 2012 went from 5 acres to 80,000 when a crew thought they had to stop working when they could have corralled the flames). On the desert fire where I stood then, the rule was stop or be punished and as a rookie engine boss with the assistant fire management officer from my district as a part of my crew, I didn't want to have it written on my performance evaluation that I didn't look out for the safety and welfare of my people according to guidelines. We three felt fine to go on, but to someone in a desk chair the numbers wouldn't add up to eight off duty and sixteen on duty, and I'd be called to explain myself.

"Come on over. We'll do it like the old days where you just work until you drop."

The condescending tone of his voice aggravated me. "I remember the old days, but I just want to make sure I'm not gong to have to hear about overextending my people later."

"You won't." That was justification enough for me. It rankled me that he acted like I was looking to get out of work. The dichotomy of rigid and inflexible rules used in a fluid environment as set against no rules at all were the products of the unimaginative. On one hand the administration seeking to limit liability and deny responsibility and on the other hand the laissez faire tough, shot through with the Puritan ethic that working yourself to death brought you close to God.

We hiked to the base of the ridge and followed the hand line up. The crew had nearly reached the top and we only helped dig the last portion. The ground was rich with stones: white quartz, rose quartz, rocks that were rusty looking, dull reds, grays, greens, and blacks. The amount of rocks, from the size of sand to the mountains themselves was dazzling. We dug in a kaleidoscope.

On the bluff the sun grazed the top of the mountains. The land softened in the valleys and a thousand feet below us Hispanic men in jeans and t-shirts wandered between our parked trucks.

"Who are they?" I asked.

One of the guys chuckled. "Scouts. They're looking to see where we are and the best way around."

I scanned down the foothills. Those migrants scrambling over the trails would do well to seek high ground during daylight. Many of them hid in the dry washes in the thick stands of brush and stunted trees. The monsoons with torrents of Pacific water were overdue. Rain falling miles away and out of sight had sent flash floods of mud and sand thundering down the arroyos hard enough to wash semi-trucks to Mexico. An irony, I thought, to be drowned in a flood during a drought.

The assistant fire management officer from Douglas brought out fried chicken with all the side orders of mashed potatoes, coleslaw, and corn on the cob. Beams of headlamps penetrated the dark as people moved around filling water bottles and Camelbaks, replacing food for their packs, and sharpening tools for the next day and then grabbing some food. Fernando asked if my crew would stay behind and sleep on the fire and climb back to the bluff at 0600 to get a good look at it. He planned to have the hand crew stage back in Douglas in case they were needed for the fire outside of Sierra Vista where houses had been lost and others threatened.

"You bet," I said. "We'd love to camp out here."

The National Interagency Fire Center called it coyote camping, but I didn't care to use that term in this region where coyote wasn't just the Aztec word meaning small canine animal, but slang for the ringleaders of bands of smugglers who routinely abandoned migrants in the desert to die of heat and thirst.

"Good deal," he said. "We plan to fly the fire in the morning, but if we're not here call dispatch."

I took out my notebook and I'd been warned that contact was lost often enough in the remote location due to bad signals or bleed-over from Mexican taxis and delivery trucks jamming the repeaters. Sometimes, traffickers highjacked the repeater with a more powerful signal, drowning out the Forest Service. I'd heard Spanish over one the channels earlier that day. On any district it wasn't uncommon to have black holes of where a radio couldn't transmit out, but the hijacking of frequencies was new to me.

We three Idahoans watched dust kicked up like red glitter in receding taillights. The dull stamped metal of the crescent moon descended the clear sky like a scythe. Around us the darkness swallowed the details of the land. The night sky brightened over the black void. Stars materialized. Diffused light emerged from the horizon, heightening the separation of land and sky. The rocks and sand reflected the sparse light and made the trees and brush darker. Nocturnal creatures arose from dens and burrows to forage and hunt. To the north the wildfire burned in patches like a sleeping army and the main fire burned beyond the ridge, backlighting it, dimming the northern stars beyond.

The fire on the mountainside, a scattering of red, orange, and yellow lights pulsing and flaring a city of hell. The cooling night quieted the fire.

We worked our bodies into the ground and watched the sky. The wildfire's glow dampened down. It looked like the sodium lights of a town over the ridge. The shifting of our weight, the rustle of nylon sleeping bags or a cough broke the quiet. The air chilled, and I breathed it in deeply, loving the feel in my sinuses.

I took off my bandana and put on a knit cap. I couldn't help but think of Neruda: "The stars are blue and shiver in the distance." Distance and time had their own weight not measured by scales or rulers. I shifted and pulled some stones from under my body. Heat lingered in the sand. It felt nice. As if I were returning home. "Tonight I can write the saddest lines."

Even when exhausted my mind clicked and clicked, especially with the uncontained fire on the mountain and an arroyo full of foot traffic. I laid out some fusees next to my fire-pack for any camp visitors: the roving bear, coati mundis scavenging in the packs, and people. I took a couple of pulaskis, stuck them in the ground and strung orange flagging between them so that if any vehicle traffic showed up they wouldn't run over the sleepers. I felt better with those things, but knew sleep made anyone vulnerable and to react to danger out of dead-sleep was chancy. On nights like this, I would sleep and wake, on average, every forty minutes until dawn when I'd sit up off the cold earth.

The night deepened. High clouds scudded across the sky to the east. The air was still and cooled under the open sky. Somebody dipped water out of the spring and someone had rattled the fence, climbing over it. On my back, I stared into the sky and watched a meteorite skip across the atmosphere. In this stretch of desert I bet there were more people than in Central Park right now. The chill of the cooling desert seeped into me. I rolled over and switched on my headlamp. The other two looked asleep, their small dome tents hunched up in the middle of the clearing. Part of the silver surfaces reflected the light and beyond him the purple eyes of jackrabbits blinked and milled among the bitter brush and mesquite.

Voices carried from up the arroyo. The group at the spring had moved on. Many men trekked north and spent years away from their families to support them. I would do the same. Borders are an artifact of the last war made by people with money and power. The poor have to work and work hard as they have for centuries. All those headed north wanted nothing but to feed their family with some dignity and, like the Okies struggling out of the Dust Bowl, met derision by people no better than them, but born to better circumstances beyond their control wielding the myth of superiority. I found it sick that the same people who mythologized the Dust Bowl migrants and the Irish immigrants disdained the Hispanic migrants. My parents had us living in tents on the other side of these mountains and a little further north chasing the original American Dream. People in run down trailers looked down their noses at us. Least we ain't them, some said. At least we risked, I said back. The gate clanged as somebody walked into it. Another round of furtive whispering broke the quiet. Antoine Saint-Exupèry wrote, "What makes the desert beautiful is that someplace it hides a well." A sublime beauty at that.

Some of the migrants never found that beauty and died along some blasted stretch of desert. Seeing the kids with the women along the dusty road put the hex on my mind. I imagined my daughters graveside, black dresses and lace, the flowers, a summer's day during a dry spell, an explosive season where the tears and sweat of the dead dried minutes before the flames reached them and my girls standing, maybe crying, maybe all their tears spent during long absences and my failure to give them any reason or faith to carry them past their grief. My passing on only my emptiness, a doubt of God and no hope of a life after to smolder in their heads and maybe like the fire, billow and bloom under the light and heat of tomorrow after being suppressed in the dark night. I too traveled to work and wasn't forced to have my daughters dragged through the desert to end up huddled along a dirt road with their mom and aunts because they had sickened of me being in *El Norte* for so many long months or stretched out years like so much burned over earth.

The soft ticking and shifting of burning wood carried down the mountain and settled my mind. I awoke in the gray dawn. A thin veil of smoke drifted over the wildfire. The others still slept or at least remained in their tents. The surreal night of consciousness, waking to shift my weight when a limb numbed and tingled or rolling out of an aggravating position to one that was less uncomfortable or snapping out of unconsciousness and the vivid dream world where animals pressed around me, mumbling strange warnings and journeying to see my daughters down some glory road without end. My body and mind skipped and jerked like an electron so that when I awoke, either from the pounding of my heart, the crick in my neck or a noise out in the desert, I felt I had slept until the next night. After rolling my shoulders, I canted my neck, but no vertebrae popped, only the sharp pain. Stuck.

It was 0458. I stood and stretched. Dirt coated my pants, shirt, and I scratched my scalp under my knit cap. I tore the top off a packet of instant coffee and dumped it in my mouth, then chased it with a swig of water. The cool water caused my teeth to ache a little.

I didn't feel like eating, but hated feeling hungry, so after a minute took out a freeze-dried packet of granola with blueberries, added a couple of ounces of water and stirred it together and ate anyway. Might as well fuel the machine. It was going to be a long day. I never understood people who didn't eat until lunch and then nibbled at an energy bar or some crackers. If I didn't eat, I got cranky and didn't feel I was running at my best. I spooned the mix into my mouth and chewed, working my aching jaw. I must've ground my teeth to feel this sore.

When I finished eating, I changed the batteries in my radio. It annoyed me when someone called dispatch in the morning and the radio cut out. Most people used the radio during the operation and left it on all night in case of a call, and then forced the district to wait while they changed batteries in the middle of a broadcast. Too many mornings, during a fire bust, I sat on the hillside waiting for my turn to give a situation report while someone created dead air. I squeezed the transmit button to see if I could hit the repeater, and got the satisfying radio fuzz back.

I stood and twisted my waist and shoulders, breathed out and touched my toes. My hamstrings were tight. I sat back down and unlaced my boots. Sleeping with my boots on made my feet feel stifled and chaffed. I peeled the outer wool socks off and then the inner anti-blister layer. My legs were soot covered above the upper edge of his boots. With the tops of the wool pair, I wiped my feet. Even with soot smudged cloth my feet cooled and dried. Once I had bad athlete's foot, my toes were raw and cracks formed across the balls of my feet. It took two weeks of powder and cream to get rid of it and each hike during that time was like sand filled my boots. Now I had extra socks and a small bottle of foot powder, and worked the talc into my feet and between my toes. After putting on clean socks, I sprinkled some powder in my boots and put them back on. I wiggled and flexed my toes.

From the breast pocket of my fire shirt, I fished out my travel toothbrush and ran some paste over the bristles. I rinsed and spit, wiped my mouth on my sleeve and put everything in the pack. The other two emerged, rising from their own underworld of sleep.

The eastern edge had burned out during the night along a wash and was pushed back on itself in long ragged fingers by the squirrelly winds between the playa and the foothills. It always impressed me how much burned in the desert and how fast a fire could move cascading embers igniting spot fires, racing toward each other, clashing in a whirlwind of smoke and flame.

We gathered our packs and tools and worked through the brush. The sun still hung below the horizon, but the air began to warm as we hiked. Some mornings it was harder to get moving around than others, but by the time we had hiked a hundred yards we felt awake and clearer. We began to sweat, but picked up the pace, working our legs and bracing our tools in front of us with both hands. Nothing moved in the desert dawn. The rocks and gravel crunched under our feet. We hiked to the top of the bluff we had dug line to the evening before. The fire didn't smoke. It looked out, but only slept until the sun got a chance to heat it.

A jet began to cut a pink and rose-colored contrail across the eastern horizon. The sun crested the Animus Mountains, tipping the peaks and striping playas with light. Long shadows stretched out from the west facing slopes. The foothills and arroyos around us were still in the shadows, but the sun gathered intensity as it cut across our spot.

I picked up a rock and held it in the light. It was milky with rust colored seams. "Pretty," I said and put it in my pocket.

"Rock collecting are you?" Sean asked.

"I bring my daughters cool rocks from fires. They gather them together with their dolls and pretend they've found gold and magic crystals." I danced my hands like I had dolls. "Malibu Barbie, meet Treasure of the Sierra Madre Barbie."

"Funny."

I thought about how many times I had waved at them as the helicopter lifted off and nosed toward a fire. My girls still thought it was cool most of the time and were excited about seeing Daddy fly off and still loved the stones I brought back and the candy out of my MREs I kept in my flight helmet bag. I'd remind them to share the stash equally as Winnie the Pooh said, "Sharing is caring." I smiled at the thought of them the last time I came home rummaging in the pockets and coming up with a spoon and Kathy's disgusted hiss as Madison put the spoon in her mouth. I needed to get some more candy.

Up on the bluff we saw dozens of miles and nothing moved yet. The missionaries came, those great destroyers of other cultures and as the Spaniards arrived with their horses, guns, religious zeal and lust for gold into this area, the Apaches also arrived from the plains, forced down by horse cultures. The Apaches brought fire to drive out other tribes and hindered the Spanish efforts at settlement for centuries. I often laughed when people said they wanted to bring back the "natural" fire regime, when for hundreds of years, the Apaches kept this area virtually depopulated of people, settlers and other tribes, by driving off livestock and the torching the land. That was the natural fire regime for centuries. If the Apache were allowed to reinstitute their use of fire in it's "traditional" role, it'd solve Tucson's water and subsidence problem. Citizens would soon be dead or immigrating wherever they could, maybe even fleeing to Mexico.

At the top we took some photos. Mexico in the background. It seemed not a different place from where we stood with different laws and ways of seeing the world. We could walk there from where we stood, but if we did we'd find ourselves in a different mercy system.

Just after 0700, the steady thump of rotors filled the arroyos. I knew it wasn't the Border Patrol looking for stragglers caught in the dawn flooding the dry lakes and arroyos, but the FMO seeing how we faired down on the frontier.

That evening after a full day on the fire, we'd drive into Douglas along the Geronimo Trail where in 1846 during the Mexican-American War, the Mormon Battalion passed through on their grueling march of 1900 miles from Iowa to San Diego, securing the Southwest for the United States. They never fought the Mexican army, but nearly did in Tucson where the Mexicans retreated upon their approach. The FMO and his wife took us to Agua Prieta for dinner. She joked with her relative the Border Patrol officer at the crossing how she was smuggling a few white boys. We all laughed. Ridiculous to think we'd need to be smuggled into Mexico, and I wondered if what made a country great was not just the measure of its economic success, but its capacity to share in that success with others not so fortunate by birth. We knocked around Old Mexico a couple of nights, drank in the Douglas hotel where Poncho Villa rode his horse up the steps, took our pictures in front of the Bird Cage Saloon in Tombstone, and by some vestige of childhood memory rediscovered the isolated stand of white oaks in Turkey Creek Canyon where they buried Johnny Ringo after finding him dead of a gunshot wound to the head. This place has never been an easy stretch of the world for many and if weren't for drilled wells, air conditioning, and the United States Army it would still be largely vacant of people.

On that bluff after the helicopter had reconned the fire and flown off, I took off my hardhat and retied my bandana over my head to keep sweat out of my eyes. The freshening air and physical activity energized me. The day had dawned with reds and pinks setting the dry lake glowing like an ancient caldera before bleeding out to faded blue. For some reason being in those mountains with those dawn colors reminded me of the Fourth of July. I might not get to see the fireworks with my girls, and as it turned out I was right. I ended up on another fire assignment in Arizona where I saw another bar Poncho Villa frequented to play cards. I deployed with crews in Montana and Idaho to suppress fires. But I wouldn't stay until the bitter end of the season when rain, snow, and budget cuts chased us into unemployment. On my last day that season I would learn of the crash of 5EV. I'd head back to graduate school off kilter from the crash. Maybe in a couple of years I'd be teaching and out of the smoke and heat and broken distances of for good. For the time being it was all good in the Hundred-Acre Wood. I hadn't discovered desperation yet. I didn't know any better.

Chapter 10

FIGHT OR FLIGHT OR SUCK IT UP AND TAKE IT

I radioed dispatch and reported the fire out, the last of its four stages in the official record: uncontrolled, contained, controlled, and out. Out meaning it is "dead-out" without possibility that it will smoke up again. An early crew-boss of mine said we guys should be able to drag our balls through the burned area without getting burned. The second week of August, 2006, and we'd been going since May and it seemed a long time since I had worked the fire on the Mexican border, although it'd only been in June.

Julie and I had landed in a clearing on a high ridge three days before a hundred yards from the fire above the Salmon River and Indian Creek where a remote ranch had been built. Julie was a nursing student from Missoula who loved fly-fishing and knitting. While I always carried a book in my flight helmet bag, she had a skein of yarn and needles. She was also the great niece of the iconic writer, William Kitteridge. We hooked the Bambi-bucket to the belly of the helicopter so he could drop water on the fire before a storm, building to the southwest, tacked over us. The pilot flew on the high edge of the helicopter's performance. He had flown in the army as a warrant officer because he had never gone to college or attended Officer Candidate School. Every time we flew he banked hard, skirted the treetops, and went as fast as he could go. His accuracy in dropping water on fire or placing cargo nets or landing in remote spots was a beautiful display of pilot and machine. Short and stocky, he wore tan flight suits that were a little tight. We started calling him the Velvet Chipmunk in a spoof of army call signs for rescuing downed pilots.

The fire had been about two tenths of an acre right on the ridge top where it broke to an 80% slope. On the first evening, I smelled smoke on the up-canyon wind when I was downhill from the fire. From where we were on the ridge top and in the trees, I couldn't see all the way down the ridge. We hiked down and saw flames jumping to three to four feet high, but lucky for us the rate of spread was low because of the rain that had fallen on the edge of a thunderstorm right after we had landed. I scanned the trees that stretched below us into the ravine over a 1,000 feet and hoped a smoldering pinecone hadn't tumbled down there, waiting to build into an inferno. The conditions were right, and the only thing we could do was rotate down to look for smoke in the distant trees. I called for two more firefighters and flew in two guys, Rick and John, from the Dixie, Idaho engine crew.

On our last night a lookout on a nearby peak radioed to warn us of a storm coming down the drainage and to "get ready for a big cell to pass right over your fire."

"Thanks," I said into the radio.

With the coming storm I wasn't worried about the winds blowing the fire back up or scattering embers in the wind. I had called the fire contained earlier, but not out as I wasn't positive it was dead out. We had knocked our fire down enough, and had been diligently searching for any hidden hotspots, but even a root could still be burning underground until it reached up into grass or the duff of pine needles and leaves and flare up again. I'd seen fire burn along roots under a hand line and reignite on the other side. I told the other three to secure all of their gear and garbage so it wouldn't blow down the hill—objects from toilet paper to flight helmets had blown off mountains.

We ate and readied for the storm. I laid my pack-out bag up hill for my head and my sleeping pad and bag below it. While we waited I read and Julie knitted. John stared with a smile. "You guys carry books and knitting?"

Julie never lost a click of a needle. "You have to be ready to wait it out."

"The flight helmet bag gives us a little extra room," I said. Although I didn't care if I were on a hand crew, an engine crew, or a helitack crew, I always had a book in a gallon Ziploc bag in my pack.

"Anything else we can do to get ready?" Rick asked.

"Only so much we can do. Secure your gear and hope none of the trees close to us takes a lightning bolt or falls in the wind."

They both looked overhead. It reminded me of the first time I fished in a gale storm in the Gulf of Alaska. It was no wonder fishermen and sailors developed superstitions against seas that build skyscrapers of water, busting steel ships in half, or winds that drove a ship into shoals. We firefighters had superstitions too, but ours were to invoke Big Ernie, the god of fire, to give us fires to make money. Even if we were on the ground we could still get electrocuted from lightning hitting close. Trees could lose limbs and tops or come crashing down even in a light wind. We four were nothing to nature and in a world of risk, no skill or quickness of wit could save any of us.

When the storm hit it brought a torrent of rain and a flash so bright my eyes hurt and the thunder, shivered the ground like a ship hitting hard on a sandbar. The crash followed so close that it cut my breath short. Limbs whipped and dust, ash, and pine needles filled the air. I struggled to keep my space blanket tucked in around me. The sound of water rose up and, as the ground saturated, streams ran through our sleeping area. I never expected a small flood on a ridge top. We became soaked. I stuck my head out and turned on my headlamp. My crew of three lay mounds of rain-flies and space-blankets rippled in a high wind. The sky flashed washing away my light and the thunder crushed the air, changing the pressure in my head.

Then hail fell in marble sized ice chunks. They smacked hard and stung through my space blanket and sleeping bag. I pulled my hardhat over my head and tried to keep my shelter pulled close around me as the wind worked edges loose. It gusted and let up as if the mountains were taking a breath and blew again. A tree crashed to the ground, and it slid, plowing earth and brush in its path until it slammed into other trees. The whole forest creaked and rubbed limbs, and wind whistled in the needles and funneled through the Salmon River canyon like the whole world rushed by. Lightning flashed again. Each time the sky lit I tensed, anticipating the heated shock that would electrify my blood and melt my wet sleeping bag around me. I imagined people finding my smoking corpse in the morning next to a splintered tree. Some people prayed to God, but I never could because my father said if God really watched out for people then why did his friends "get blown to shit," in the jungles of Vietnam. "Praying is as useful as screaming. It'll make you feel better, but it won't save your life." Under the wind, water, and lightning I resigned myself to the feeling that I couldn't control where a tree fell or where a thunderbolt might find the ground. I remembered my first big storm in the Gulf of Alaska. Four ships sank, and as we rode the forty-foot swells, beating for the Inside Passage, I trusted in the skipper's nerve and luck. Fear tasted like battery acid in the back of my throat, but where does one run on a boat battered by the sea?

Forty-five minutes the storm beat us. The clouds pushed off leaving the stars brilliant in the blackness between the pine boughs. The water quit running, leaving us all shipwrecked survivors washed up on a northern beach. I fell into a deep sleep and awoke in gray light of false dawn with fog rising out of cold ground.

*

After hiking to the helispot for pick-up we flew to the Red River Helibase. I thought about when I had first flown there and meeting Jenny before we paired up on the Mile Post 59 Fire. Now she was rappelling at Krassel and was flying to her own fires south of the Salmon River. I had promised Nate that I'd work for him, so passed up the chance to be a heli-rappeller that season. Keeping promises in fire insures that when you say you're going to be somewhere, the other person knows you will make it, and, if not, send out a search party. The pilot hot-rodded down the drainages and popped over ridges like he had flown back in the Gulf. Rick and John, neither of them had flown before their ride to the fire, were wide-eyed and smiling, which wasn't always the case. Sometimes we had to ask him to ease up, but he complained, "Sissies," he'd said. "The thing was designed to fly this way." One time we were going so fast when he banked the helicopter the seventy-four pound Bambi-bucket shifted in the cargo compartment knocking the bulkhead hard enough to spook me and wonder if we had lost the engine.

In fire aviation, we were never to pressure the pilot. Even if we had seen a different pilot land in the same heli-spot, we were forbidden to say, "But so-and-so did it." That was considered pressuring the pilot and grounds for reprimand. This also unconsciously set some of us up to never question the pilot: the pilot is infallible. One pilot made it clear, "oh we can be wrong, but we do have final authority. Besides, most people rarely flew and were unsure of what was normal and afraid to look weak or scared by questioning the pilot. Also if the pilot was questioned a lot it created a toxic atmosphere and undermined the confidence needed to work together. Our pilot had flown night missions in the Red Sea, Iran, and the Persian Gulf and had been decorated for his flying in combat. He had flown in more dangerous and worse conditions than we would ever see. I trusted him, and enjoyed the fast fancy flying. Most pilots were pretty sedate fliers, but also didn't have anywhere close to his experience or skill.

Nate, my supervisor at Musselshell called on the radio, telling me to phone dispatch as soon as we landed. I had first worked with Nate when he was the supervisor for Doug and Feltner's crew. We approached the base in a large meadow were I'd first met Feltner. A barbed wire fence bound the helibase on the north, and a stream flowed west, lengthways down the center of the pasture. Logging trucks rolled down the two-lane road and local kids cruised by.

On the south side of the stream, a farmer mowed hay with a Case tractor from the 50s. By the access gate, a crew had pitched a tarpaulin and set-up some tables for the aircraft radio operator, the helibase manager, and anyone in transit with logistics or in need of a flight. The base was laid out like I'd first seen it in '03. To the east of the command post, the heavy helicopters. To the west of the command post, the smaller ships, The rugged, timbered mountains, deep, narrow draws and river canyons, combined with the remote roadless areas, made the helicopter a perfect tool.

After the helicopter landed and unloaded our gear, I went to the callbox mounted on a fence post and contacted Grangeville. The dispatcher asked me how soon I could get my crew ready to fly. Three new smokes had been reported in the vicinity of Nipple Mountain in the Gospel Hump Wilderness. I said we'd need at least an hour to resupply with food, water, batteries, power saw fuel and oil, wash our faces and change our socks and underwear. She laughed and told me to call when we were ready to launch.

The crew and I loaded into a Ford crew-cab and drove to the ranger station a few miles away to find supplies. Before leaving, we spread out our sleeping bags, pads, packs, spare clothes and gear to dry in the sun. The night before these pieces of cloth and material were the only things between the storm and us.

I drank a cup of coffee and felt refreshed. When we arrived back at the helibase Nate told me the plan had been changed. Julie, Rick and John were going to make up their own initial attack squad. I was going to fly with Bethany and a guy from another crew named

Martinez. Martinez's boss wanted me to supervise him as an incident commander trainee because they had no one available to train him. I wrote a few notes in my notepad and then Nate said that we also had to use Grangeville's ship.

"What's wrong with ours?"

"We're going to fly Julie."

"Good for her. Sucks for us."

The pilot for Grangeville had been known to randomly shutdown his helicopter, tell the manager he was on break, while crews in the field still needed support. I also didn't have much confidence in the helicopter manager.

Nate laughed. "Sorry. I know how you feel."

Adam had flushed skin like he had been sunburned. "We need to launch right away."

"All right. Get your guy to load his gear. I turned back to our heli-tender. "Bethany, I need you to load your pack and our saw."

Bethany was a ballet dancer who at a hundred and five pounds had to dead lift her pack to her knee, slip her arm into a strap and spin her back into it. Once she had it on she could hike for miles.

We got in and buckled up. The pilot stood by the fuel truck drinking bottled water, chatting to the driver. He laughed, waved, and headed for a port-a-potty. He walked slightly hunched over. When he emerged he lit a cigarette. His white beard and moustache were yellowed around his mouth. We sat in the hot ship sweating. I had been surprised that some pilots could get away with acting like that, while others did everything they could to take care of the crew and work as efficiently as possible. After thirty minutes, we finally launched and ten minutes later we had the first smoke in sight.

We flew past the first one and caught sight of the second several miles away. The pilot and manager argued over which fire was worse and where the third fire could have gone. It was not uncommon for a fire to smoke up and lay back down again, especially after a heavy rain. It might not smoke again for two weeks. We spotted a potential landing zone on a ridge and the manager called its location into dispatch to make sure it was outside of the wilderness and permission to land.

I asked, "Can we get a closer recon and a tight orbit of each of the fires to see which might be the greater priority." The pilot kept flying too high, wide and fast for me to size up the fires.

I re-keyed the mic. "I'd like to get a better look."

The manager said, "Which do you like?"

"This one coming up," I said. I figured we could get a better look at that one. He flew high and circled high to the south and then east. "Can we fly over so I can get a waypoint for the fire into my GPS?"

The pilot said, "I got it."

"Can you just hover over so I can just push a button?"

"It's too dangerous to hover. I don't like to be in the dead man's curve." The dead man's curve was the High Velocity Curve where a helicopter was at maximum performance at an elevation below 500 feet above ground level where it can't auto-rotate to a safe landing. Of course in the steep forested mountains the chance of auto-rotating to a safe landing was as good as dropping straight down through the trees. Later when I worked at Krassel, Money advised, "Always be looking for a place to crash."

He began reading the numbers and I copied them down. I wanted to say what good was a helicopter that won't hover, but didn't say anything because it'd be considered pressuring the pilot. He could've flown a low speed flyover or fly a tight orbit, but kept flying for a ridge. I wished we had been able to fly with our pilot and our manager.

The manager chuckled. "This is Nipple Mountain, so you're the Nipple IC."

Bethany grinned at me. The helispot was outside the wilderness boundary so we were cleared to land, but hadn't received permission to use a power saw yet. We would unload it and if denied permission to use it we would leave it at the helispot and request someone with a crosscut flown out to us.

He started descending. I made a mental note of where the smoke was and asked, "Can you give us an azimuth to the fire?" As odd as it may seem, smoke from a small fire disappears once you go below the tree line. I had hiked up to fires by following a compass and not found the smoke until I smelled it. Under the canopy, the world shrank and the sky closed off the world to a wooded cell.

"Two Forty-Four."

I wrote it down below the latitude and longitude. When the ship sat down and the pilot gave us the go ahead, we exited, fastened the seatbelts behind us so they wouldn't flop around or accidentally get caught in the door and beat thousands of dollars worth of damage into the helicopter's body. We unloaded our tools and packs and left them by the skids to expedite our time under the rotors. After walking a safe distance into the trees we knelt to watch them fly away and retrieve our gear.

The helicopter didn't lift off. The pilot and manager talked with each other and started waving for me to come back. Shit, I thought, something's wrong. The manager started pointing at the ground in dramatic gestures. I looked for loose equipment or debris, but nothing but a log embedded into the ground. I approached the manager's side and he popped his door open. He yelled over the rotor and jet engine noise. "Move that log. We can't take off with it there."

"That thing isn't moving."

"Just move it."

It wasn't even under the span of the rotors. I went back to the log and motioned Bethany and Martinez over. "He won't lift until we move this," I yelled.

Martinez and I got on either end while Bethany grabbed limbs in the middle. We rocked and jerked the log out of the ground, breaking off several limbs. My gut dropped, hoping the limbs didn't get swept up into the rotors. Heavy, we lifted it in crouch, trying to keep any more limbs or bark from coming off, and hauled it to the tree line. The pilot and manager kept pointing and we went back and cleared the limbs out. The manager waved me back over.

"He wants you to cut those saplings before he takes off." He indicated some pines barely up to my waist, ten yards from the helicopter.

"Jesus, tell him I'll cut them after he leaves. They aren't a problem right now."

He glared at me, but I went back to the trees and knelt down. I'm not having my crew swing Pulaskis or sawing saplings ten yards from spinning rotor blades. They didn't lift right away. I could wait him out. Eventually he'd have to leave or stay the night and he was not the type of person to do that. He'd get back to the chow wagon and a motel bed in Grangeville. Almost two years later, in March of 2009, Nate would send me an email me to report that this pilot had crashed and been killed in an accident over Nebraska. The investigators figured he must have fallen asleep over the stick because he hadn't called an emergency, nothing mechanically wrong was discovered with the helicopter, and he was flying a simple point-to-point flight without any extraneous hazards. Even in winter, I thought, as I read. Even in winter the fire world lost people.

After the helicopter cleared out, we gathered our gear. I set the helispot as a waypoint in my GPS so we could navigate back to it or if we had to call in a different pilot we could pass it on to him. We shouldered on our 80-plus pound pack-out bags getting ready to hike into the wilderness. I shouldered the power saw and said to Martinez, "You're the trainee so it's your show unless I see something that needs addressed, just pretend I'm a squad member." Some trainers just did the job and told the trainee to observe and stay out of the way. I let the trainee "take command." To have the opportunity to plan and make decisions under supervision to insure things didn't get life threatening was the best way for him or her to learn.

Martinez grinned. "Okay."

"Did you write down the lat and long and the azimuth?"

"Not the lat and long. I don't have a GPS, but I do have a compass."

I punched in the lat and long into my GPS and then shot the azimuth the pilot had given us. I had one of those disorienting moments. I knew the general direction of the fire from where we set down, and the azimuth I shot told me the fire on a path at least 45 degrees to the south of that. The GPS didn't help as it showed the track to the waypoint sixty degrees toward the north. I knew the fire was not along either of the paths the pilot had given me. The fire burned somewhere between those two points and the terrain between was steep, full of finger ridges, thickets, timbered with deadfall stacked like houses after a tornado. Even if we were unencumbered by the heavy packs it would still be a struggle.

Dispatch called to inform us the ranger had given his consent to use the power saw in the wilderness. He had over forty fires and wanted them out as quickly as possible. I figured he would because he didn't have the resources to send in a cross-cut saw, the fire burned in an area with potential to explode, and was on the edge of the wilderness so once it hit the top it'd be easy to see from the little communities and ranches in the valley below, which would trigger a rash of phone calls that he really didn't have time to field, but was obligated to answer.

"Martinez, I got the saw. You lead the way." I wanted to see what he'd do. He didn't ask me about the GPS and what it indicated. He took a bearing with his compass and took off through the woods and over the ridge into the Gospel Hump. I let him go for ten minutes to see if he might realize he had taken the wrong route. I didn't want to go too far as it was tough going, just enough to make it a memorable moment for him in the future. "Where did you learn to land navigate?"

"NOLS." The National Outdoor Leadership School.

"Have you had a lot of field experience?"

"Just with them."

"Let's stop a second."

"Bethany, when we landed, which direction was the fire from the helispot?"

"You know, I thought it was that way." She pointed northwest. "But he had the compass."

I set the power saw down and held my GPS in front of me. "What do you think, Martinez?"

"I didn't notice, but Joe gave us the azimuth, so it has to be this way."

"You didn't notice?"

He looked at his compass. "Well, I did think it was down that way." He pointed the way Bethany had.

"What do you suppose to do now?"

He nodded toward my GPS. "What's that say?"

I pointed even further north.

Martinez shifted his hardhat back. His face was absorbed in thought. I didn't want to say anything quite yet. We needed to get on the fire, but it was skunking around and it wouldn't get up and go yet, so I felt good taking a little extra time. This was where the real learning took place. I knew he was wrestling with the adage, always trust your compass, which was true, because people have been turned around and trusted their guts instead of the compass and had taken off deeper into woods to their injury or death. He also wrestled with what his pilot had told him, because he had been taught, "The pilot is always right." He had me stopping him, Bethany pointing fifty degrees out, and my GPS showing another twenty degrees on top of that.

He looked in the direction he had been walking confidently in. "What do you think?"

I was hoping he'd come up with a plan and then ask what I thought. As a leader he'd need to be able to formulate a plan, brief a crew and then ask for comments and questions. He needed to learn to listen to all of those suggestions and then articulate why he was going to either keep to his original plan or how he was going to incorporate a good suggestion. A failure of leadership occurs when he or she cannot articulate what they want done, how it is to be done, and why. To be able to speak to a crew in that way inspires confidence in the boss and the plan.

"We could angle down in the draw to the northwest. The airflow should be coming up canyon and we'll smell the smoke and we can drop down on it. We could also use the GPS and follow where it leads us. But given he balled up the azimuth, I wonder how close it is."

Bethany laughed. "How far off can he be? Not like a plane."

"We'll find out. We should also drop our gear so we can move faster in this mess, locate the fire and then come back. It'll be faster in the long run."

We dropped our gear and they gridded across a finger ridge and down into a draw. I followed the GPS and they found the fire. When Bethany called I still hadn't reached the lat and long.

"Give me a hoot," I said over the radio.

She yelled and she was down the ravine further to the southwest. I yelled, "Day-ooooo," so they'd know where I was.

At the fire I plotted the coordinate he gave us and it was a half-mile further northeast. We dug a fire-line, and I felled two trees, including a volcano stump, which when center of the tree is rotted and when the tree was felled the fire rushed up from the base blowing flame out of the top. Martinez wanted to saw, but I told him his primary job was the incident commander. He had to be able to monitor the radio, which was impossible running a saw. One of the things that had stuck with me from my days with the Association was that their incident commanders were expected to saw. I couldn't remember how many times someone called for the IC and couldn't make contact because he was busy sawing. Once I had handed sawing over to another crewmember, so I could monitor the radio and found out later that someone on the fire complained to the assistant fire warden that I had shirked my sawing duties.

We worked into the night and dug a good fire line and started mopping up before bedding down. Bethany built a lean-to with her rain tarp and used mine for the floor. Clouds moved in dragging a drizzle of rain with it. We fit three across with our heads uphill.

*

When the bear came, I didn't hear it. Martinez did. He elbowed me awake under the rain tarp. "There's a bear in the garbage." His whisper was garbled at first and not just because I was coming out of deep sleep from fighting fires in remote country for a week, or that I'm hard of hearing, but more to confirm his message.

I shifted on the ground. "What?" It was our second night on the fire, and we planned to hike out to the helispot in the morning.

"There-is-a-bear-in-the-gar-bage." He pronounced each syllable in cadence.

"You're fucking kidding," was all I thought to say. I had even joked the night before how I was going to sleep between them so any bears would have to eat them first. I lay there and strained my ears.

Bethany on my left rolled over and whispered, "What?"

"Martinez says there's a bear in the garbage."

"Shit," she whispered.

The tarp on the uphill side, the bear side, had been staked to the ground, so we couldn't see or attempt to see in the thick darkness of the forest. I listened some more and in my extreme fatigue, I thought of all the statistics of bear attacks. I figured we had better than a ninety-five percent chance the bear would walk away and not amble over and lick my face looking for the peanut butter and jalapeno cheese spread that was no doubt still on my breath and in my moustache and goatee. As odds go, it was a safe bet to lie there and see if the bear came down the hill to us. I thought about the bear's nocturnal ramblings, and then I fell asleep. Fight or flight or sleep it off.

Earlier we'd been awoken by a storm coming through that knocked trees down in the already deadfall-laden wilderness and, like three nights before on Indian Ridge, running off through the dark wouldn't solve anything and fighting a lightning bolt makes as much sense as wrestling a bear on its home court.

Bethany drilled me with a bony elbow and asked, "What are you going to do?"

I heard her clearly: "you." I didn't have a gun or pepper spray, a bell to ring, a pot and pan to bang and the tools were up the hill with the power saw and the bear. As these items ran through my mind, I realized I had fusees in my line pack I used as a pillow. I had a chronic neck pain and needed to prop my head when I slept or shivered in fear when not sleeping.

"Well," I drew a breath, "I'm going for it. We'll eat him or he'll eat us." Although I did know the one in front always got ate. I worked a fusee out with the tearing of Velcro. I slipped out of my sleeping bag, thrust my feet into my boots, wrapping the laces around the ankle in what we called the breakfast lace, and readied the striker. I crawled out from under the tarp and before I was all the way out, I struck the fusee. The thick, acrid smoke caused me to choke and as I thrust it into the air yelling, sparks of magnesium flew like dozens of cigarette cherries flaring in night. The metallic magenta light sputtered, casting ragged shadows into the darkness. Sparks landed on my arm, and the smoke gagged me. I angled fusee to the side. Up the hill, by the garbage was nothing but empty space.

I walked above the hooch and scanned the trees looking for any flitting between the shadows and the light. It reminded me of being at Fort Irwin during a field exercise after the parachute flares hung high in the night making the desert a quivering black and white diorama.

Martinez came up behind me with his Leatherman knife. "I swear there was a bear. It walked up the fire line. It chuffed and snorted. I heard it move the bag around," he said.

"I don't doubt you. I made a lot of racket getting the fusee and putting my boots on probably spooked it. Either that or my snoring."

"Is it gone?" Bethany asked from under the tarp.

"Yeah, it is," I said.

"You guys looked all freaking weird with that fusee blowing, like you're in some surreal movie."

"Let's start a fire that'll keep the animals away," Martinez said.

"We had us a forest fire right there," I said pointing to ¼ acre burned spot we had suppressed. "That didn't seem to bother it."

He didn't hear me. He was already gathering wood and digging a pit. I didn't stop him. It'd make him feel better. When he had the wood set up, I dropped the fusee into it and we sat. We talked for about fifteen minutes before I crawled back under the tarp and slept. In the morning at 0700, I had him call dispatch to declare the fire controlled and out. He wanted to stay a few more hours, but I advised him that the fire was out and we needed to get out and back in the rotation. "Besides," I said. "Everyone out there knows about how long it takes to put this fire to bed unless something wicked happens." Also the longer you waited the more likely the helicopter would be unavailable because of other missions. We packed up and hiked to our helispot.

The day before I had hiked back to the helispot using the waypoint I had set in my GPS and then back down to the fire. I wanted to make sure of the most efficient route back and the time it'd take so Martinez could plan our demobilization. I had been hiking with heavy packs and power saws and been sleeping on the ground for five weeks. One more week, and I was headed back to the University of Idaho's MFA program.

At the helispot my pilot called. I was relieved it was our guy. "Nipple Fire IC, I can't see you peeking up. Where are you?"

He flew to the north of us. "At your eleven o'clock."

"There you are poking up. The temperature must have dropped."

*

Three days later I walked in the district office to file fire reports on the fires I had been in charge of during the fire bust. I didn't know the Fire Management Officer or his assistant and when I introduced myself, they both grinned. "You're the bear guy."

I laughed.

The FMO said, "Martinez was in here two days ago and he was all excited. Said he'd never seen anything like it. Said he never thought about using a fusee to scare a bear. Tell you the truth, me neither. Makes me think to keep one handy in bear country though."

I laughed again. "To be honest, I didn't know it until it happened. Just luck like not getting hit by a falling tree."

*

As a short-timer, I didn't initial attack another fire, but ran cargo and personnel transport, even flying out to remote places to bring in crews and supplies or take them out. I didn't mind. I'd started in May fighting fires on the Mexican border and worked my way back north. All week we talked about driving the thirty some miles to Elk City for a pizza party send off on my last day at the helibase. I still had to drive back to Musselshell and drop off all of my equipment and clean out my room, but my crew would still be in the field.

The morning of my last day I had to write a SAFECOM for Heather, the helibase manager. A Safecom defined on the website: The Aviation Safety Communique (SAFECOM) database fulfills the Aviation Mishap Information System (AMIS) requirements for aviation mishap reporting for the Department of Interior (DOI) agencies and the U.S. Forest Service. Categories of reports include airspace, incidents, hazards, maintenance, management and mishap prevention. The system uses the SAFECOM Form AMD-34 or FS-5700-14 to report any condition, observation, act, maintenance problem, or circumstance with personnel or aircraft that has the potential to cause an aviation-related mishap. SAFECOMS may also be used to identify good 'acts, events, and circumstances' as well as unsafe situations."

I had been witness to "an incident with potential," and she wanted it documented because there had been problems with the contractor all summer. I and a guy, Jack, from another crew had been flown up to a helispot to backhaul the trash of several crews who had been camped out, fighting fire in a roadless area. We had asked what his jettisonable payload was for the conditions, (the weight he could safely lift and carry on a long-line below the helicopter at given altitude and temperature). We built all of the loads under that weight and called him back in when we were ready. He came in and I directed while the guy I was working with waited for the helicopter to place the hook on the end of his long-line next to the first load.

Jack hooked the load and walked away. When he cleared the area under the ship, I radioed the pilot to lift. We watched as the line tightened the leads of the cargo net and pulled up. The load popped off the ground and then set back down. The pilot kept trying to lift, but the load was too heavy for him and by the time he had skipped six times, he cut the load and flew off. We had everything weighed, so we weren't overloading the net. He might have given us the weight he could pull for a different altitude, temperature, or balled up the calculation all together and had given a bad number. Those were the only options I knew of then. I have since learned that some contractors had misreported the weights of their aircraft so when its contract weight read 17500, it actually weighed eight hundred pounds more-

-just enough to cause a helicopter to cut a load or crash a helicopter, which had happened in Northern California during 2008 when an Sikorsky S-61 heavy helicopter went down killing nine firefighters near where rappeller Marovich would fall to his death. Although Carson helicopters disputed the report the investigators discovered a discrepancy in the reported and actual weight of the helicopter. I don't know why the weights were misreported, but some speculate that between contracts some equipment is added and no one bothers to re-weigh the helicopter and just uses the old number or that was weighed stripped out for logging operations and not weighed after the USFS required equipment was installed.

After a day of loading and unloading cargo and directing helicopters the operational day came to an end and we went to the end of day briefing.

When Heather was done talking, I was ready to head out for some pizza. Nat stepped forward. "One other thing."

His voice cracked and he looked not at any one, but down and away as if picking a place to step in the darkened forest. He cleared his voice again and told us the crash of Five Echo Victor.

We drove to Elk City. I thought about when I had turned down the position at Krassel last May. I wondered if Doug was still alive, and I thought of Jenny. The next day I'd find out they survived, but it wouldn't't be until next summer that the fragments worked themselves into a story of love and sacrifice. Even then with official reports placing blame on the pilot's flying, and the helicopter contractor blaming the crew for not securing the cargo well enough, some chose not to worry about the who—blame didn't raise the dead. We focused on physical factors and how to prevent it from happening again.

I couldn't help but imagine being in the helicopter with the doomed crew careening and tumbling down the mountain, fingers digging, muscles rigid, bouncing heads off the bulkhead as the pilot struggled to bring the ship under control. The chief investigator for the National Transportation Safety Board said the pilot never stopped flying the aircraft. They could tell by the position of the ship on the gravel road, the only space wide enough and flat enough to land in the steep forested mountains that plunged into the rivers a tumble with rocks and boulders. Fighting to fly. The only safe place to land, and they hit so hard they burst into flames.

I left the next morning with a hangover. My head killed me. I ate breakfast. I drank coffee. Smoke fringed the mountainous horizon. I loved to fly to fires and I loved flying fast, low, and working with a high performance pilot. I tried to reconcile my pilot with the one south of the river, who I didn't know. I had to fill out a SAFECOM against a contractor with a history of problems who they couldn't replace after one issue, but couldn't hover over a fire to get the right lat and long because of the theoretical chance of engine failure. Helicopters crews were told that instead of being flown off fires, we should hike out to a road and be picked up by drivers sent by dispatch because that would limit our exposure to danger by flying, even though a person is more likely to be killed in a car crash than flying.

The Fire Service uses check-rides to insure a pilot was up to standards. At Copeland helibase outside of McCall, Idaho, the Forest Service relieved a pilot from duty because his flying skills were deemed inadequate. To date there was no mechanism for replacing pilots who were shoddy crewmembers and made the lives of those around them miserable.

By the time I got to Musselshell, I found out Jenny and Doug had not been on the helicopter and alive. I drove to Moscow, Idaho, and played with my daughters that evening. The next morning I attended the "Comp Camp," for graduate students with all of those hopeful people who wanted to study English or creative writing and maybe teach some day. I sat in the classroom and when asked what interesting thing happened to us this last summer all I could think to say was that with the exception of last night, I hadn't slept in a bed in the last six-weeks.

Chapter 11

TILTING AT COWS

Sophia ran out of the thicket followed by Madison. My daughters were six and three. Sophia worked her long legs like the deer she hoped to lasso, and her long, light brown hair streaked with summer vacation sun flowed behind her. Redheaded Madison was a foot and half shorter, and had the agility of a tree squirrel. "There are dragons in our castle," Sophia yelled. Our tents were pitched in a tree-lined meadow, a short distance from the Musselshell Work Center. Ringed by mountains, Musselshell Creek formed a bowl and the camas plant grew wild spreading purple over the grass as it bloomed. The Nez Perce tribe had harvested camas bulbs here after they had been chased off the prairies in the late 19th Century. Chief Joseph, carrying the burden of hope of a people to live in one place, made his break for Canada through there before the United States Army hounded the freezing and starving band to a standstill in Montana where he uttered those famous words, "From where the sun now stands, I will fight no more forever." Like most of the West the land was broken with hopes and defeats. Just south of the work center Lewis and Clark staggered out of Bitterroot Mountains starving and lost to be saved by the Nez Perce not but 72 years before that.

The Forest Service built a cabin there in 1902 and had been there ever since. My family camped out most of the 2006 summer and only went back to the apartment in Moscow, Idaho, when I detailed to a fire in another state, although once they did stay for two weeks after I had left for Arizona. The girls swam in the creeks, searched for mussels, and gathered sticks and other treasures. They loved to pile wood on the fire and sit around and tell stories while roasting marshmallows and, as the fire died into pulsing coals, gaze into the deep space of sleep and dream. They also chased free-range cows like I did when I was a kid and my family lived in tents in the southern Arizona desert.

That was a pivotal moment in my life as not only did I begin to become teenager out there, but also I went from a three-bedroom house in the suburbs of Phoenix to a tent and it kicked off a series of years of itinerant jobs my father held and a lot of living in the outdoors. With an exception of about eight months, we lived from 1975 to 1979 in a tent or a camper bolted onto the back of a □62 Dodge truck like my mother's Okie ancestors. People have often wondered at my ability to sleep on any piece of ground, from rockslides to muskeg.

My girls too have lived in a camper or to be precise a fifth-wheel so they could travel to my fire jobs and then to North Carolina where I attended a year of graduate school. The trip was a bust. We left after nine months, and lost the fifth-wheel in the process. I had been awarded a Jack Kent Cooke scholarship and so I applied and was accepted into the University of Idaho MFA program. Before returning to college, I had had a year round, stable fire job, a permanent position they called it, in Elk River, Idaho.

On April 11, 2000, doctors cut Sophia from her mother's womb to save their lives. I was supposed to be away for fire training, but didn't go so I could be with Kathy as she gave birth. I have always rolled my eyes at men who say that having children has made them better men, which having known them was its own special fiction because they were the same men I had known from before. No better, no worse just flawed men. I guarded against overly sentimental and romanticized modern man because this was all usually rooted in talk and not a profound change. But seeing Sophia, I thought of Walt Whitman and a poem I had memorized when I had believed that memorizing poetry made me a better human being, which was its own special fiction. "Oh me Oh life," I thought and recited the poem over her head in the half-light of a hospital afterhours. "That life exists and identity, that powerful play goes on and you may contribute a verse."

I knew I needed to return to college and earn a degree, and it had to be in writing. Telling stories had been the only thing that had been consistent in my life. As a kid, I made up the tale of an immortal bird, named Bird, to entertain my younger siblings. In junior high school, I scribbled derivative science fiction and pathetic love poetry to sway kisses out of girls. In high school I harbored dreams of becoming a

156

writer, but had been knocked off track. Not that I wasn't well read, because my family was well read. My mother began teaching me to read when my father was in Vietnam when I was two. But I didn't know how to channel that desire into reality and the small mining town schools didn't focus on that just as my father hadn't. All the small adding up of things that my family said over the course of a childhood, pushed me in particular directions that in the end made me a gypsy, thinking I was a writer.

I'd been writing horrible poems that I thought were wonderful and being a working class guy and eschewing college as my father had preached because any loser could be a writer without it. He wanted me to study chemistry or engineering, which I was ill equipped to do in both desire and skills. His examples of unschooled and self-educated writers, Hemingway and Twain, were in fact either geniuses or those who had extensive literary connections or both, but I wasn't smart enough to realize that. Also that it was a myth that they were "self-taught." I ended up identifying with characters like Larry Darrell, the questing saint of Somerset Maugham's *The Razor's Edge*. I had neither genius nor literary friends amongst the Elk River crew, although later in the BLM and the Forest Service I'd find many literary friends.

I understood years later my father wanted me to join a profession that made a lot of money. As he saw it, a realistic and stable living as an engineer, but his insistence and pressure unmoored me. I drifted from one working-class job to another looking for a wage and along the way had some adventures. My writing--all of it bad--never grew, but stagnated.

I was an accidental firefighter. Coming to the job because I'd knocked around trying to piece together a living. I needed to find a real job and that seemed it. Seeing Sophia gave me the startling vision of myself as poseur, one who sought identity in professions to fit into like an actor changed clothes and make-up for a role. I could be a writer and a firefighter. What struck me like a furnace wind was that I needed to quit making excuses of why I wasn't going to college by claiming I had to work in the fall or the spring. I needed to quit buying into the working-class myths of unemployed college grads, college grads not working in their majors, book smart college grads without common sense, all of which made college a waste of money. I needed to take the chance. Without risk, I would never grow and in taking that risk,

I had to face my fears of what burned inside me. I owed that much to Sophia.

My daughters have grown up around firefighters and have lived in remote areas during the summer and through the fall until the next summer. For most of the history of the Forest Service, it was not uncommon to have families living at the work centers during the summer break, but with the rise of modern transportation, crewmembers could drive back into town. The two career family made it so that a spouse couldn't live out in the mountains for a summer, and with the closing and relocation of bases into towns, many sons and daughters of firefighters would never spend their summers loose in forests filling the draws and meadows with the laugher of children at play.

The day after Sophia was born, we brought her to a cabin at the fire camp on the outskirts of Elk River, Idaho, a defunct mill town turned recreation destination of the "new West" with a population of 156. We had only moved in the month before at insistence of the Fire Warden, Walter, and anger of the assistant, Jody, who didn't use it except when he didn't feel like driving home some nights, but still he looked on it as his own vacation home. I understood that. I also understood we needed a place to live as the house we were living in had been sold to a University of Idaho professor and he wanted his vacation home vacated immediately so he could begin redecorating, forcing me and my nine-month pregnant wife out.

The helipad at Elk River was a patch of grass about fifty-yards away from where we lived on the other side of a fringe of timber. The pilot, Ray Reel, over-flew the deck of the cabin where Kathy would hold Sophia, their up turned faces startled with delight as they waved, while I flew to a fire or a recon. One of Sophia's earliest words was helicopter, and I have teased Kathy that the order of the words Sophia learned was "Dad," "Helicopter," and then "Momma."

I had planned on staying with the Association. The Association paid several dollars less an hour than any other firefighting organization because they believed a person would work harder if they made less money. It was fools' reasoning because hard workers always worked hard and slackers always slacked no matter what the pay rate. When that came out the mouth of someone, it made me feel my work was underappreciated after spending the summer grinding out fires on short rations and sleeping under a space blanket and a shallow trench for a bed or working forestry through the chilling spring and fall rains and snows, but I stuck it out because I thought I was a part of something unique and better than the federal fire organizations. And still hoped to find a place where I belonged. The winters were spent laid-off doing part time work like logging, construction, and working as a lineman.

When I was compelled to go back to school I scheduled my classes on split days off. I didn't ask for any extra time off and for fire assignments I had arranged with my professors at Lewis-Clark State College that I'd keep up with the work. Every one of them understood, and I never had a problem them. I studied during down-time on fires. One firefighter laughed in shock when I pulled out the 2057 page *Riverside Shakespeare* from my fire pack.

With the Association, I kept up my forestry duties and fire responsibilities and through the fall, winter, and spring this shouldn't have been a problem, but it was. My need for those days off interfered with hunting trips, and Jody, my immediate supervisor, had said that I was only getting special treatment because the Chief Warden, Walter, liked me, but that he and Mike, the guy next in line for my job, thought it unfair. I knew I had reached the end when Walter called me and told me that Jody had reported that I had been shirking my duties.

I demanded a meeting. We met in the office. Long front windows let in the fall sunlight. Three desks with papers and reports were against the walls with maps and firefighting posters of Smokey the Bear and reprints of Charles Remington cowboy paintings with fire slogans. Jody was surprised that I had called Walter to ask for this meeting. But I had records of all of the work I had done for plotting gates on maps for the Potlatch Corporation, and kept records of my herbicide project with the chemical used and where and the purchasing orders. He told Walter, "I just don't see how he can work fulltime and go to school fulltime." I felt as if he were saying, "If I can't do it then it must be impossible."

"This is ridiculous to be told I'm not working. You can also call Laura and Jim about the meetings we've had in the field and in the office." Laura was the USFS resource specialist and Jim was the chief Potlatch forester who I had been working with on the projects.

Walter dismissed the complaint as "just a misunderstanding."

Jody refused to say why he had come up the accusation and why didn't he talk to me about it until Walter left. "I didn't like you because

Walter liked you." The signs of my being forced out had been there the whole long time. All the years of his anger at being passed over for promotion by Walter had left Jody powerless so it was only natural to take it out on me to get back at Walter. In fire, a breach of trust like that made it difficult to trust your life with that person. I worried about the small adding up of small things to a day when I would be forgotten and die or become injured on a fire. I was going to be forced to choose between college and the Association. Although I knew I'd lose my insurance and my steady job, I called Walter and gave him my two-week notice. I had started my second semester and my professors had lit the fire that had been smoldering in me to teach my whole life, but didn't realize until then. Jody wasn't even formerly reprimanded for his actions and before my two weeks was up they offered my job to Mike. I gave myself over to the pursuit of writing and art, leaving Elk River. The struggle began in earnest.

*

Sophia and Madison chattered in their high-girl voices. I smiled. I had only walked to camp for lunch from the work center. A dad's job requires many specialties. Every summer I hoped for a season that kept me busy, but that also meant being away from my family. I had already spent three weeks in southern Arizona, two weeks in central Arizona, almost two weeks in eastern Montana, and had spent some time off on projects like flying building supplies for radio repeaters or the remodeling of backcountry cabins. It was a terrible contradiction of hopes. I needed to make money to help make it through the winter and not have to work as many hours for a wage so I could concentrate on my studies and spend time with my family. I didn't want the ripping fires that devastated tens of thousands of acres and galloped over ill-planned sub-divisions. I loved the small helitack fires, flying through the mountains and the trees and landing in a wooded clearing, unloading and hiking to the fire with a couple of people, and then spend a couple of days working—nothing but the steady beat of hard labor like blood through the heart.

Every winter saw us short of money and working multiple part time jobs. I kept thinking it would be worthwhile in the long run. We just couldn't give up. The mantra of one more month was in my mom and dad's proverbs as was the Merle Haggard song, *If We Make it Through December*. Funny the sins of the father might not be paying for a particular sin but adopting the habits of particular sins. Like me, my daughters were not growing up in any one place, but followed me to different fire jobs and colleges and universities, thinking I'm going to make a better life for them, just as my parents chased their dreams to make their children's lives better. All that happened was more debt and more moving. I kept telling family and friends: "I'm a writer. At least it's something I can exploit later for material." A delusion that I don't think fooled anyone but me.

The children of firefighters even if they lived in the same house their whole lives, live a transient existence. Mother or father sent on assignments from spring until fall, two weeks, three weeks, six weeks, to come home for a couple of days and go again. Many firefighters are college students or men and women figuring out want they want to do after college or instead of college. They were childless and embrace the gypsy life like a working vacation.

My mother stayed in the same house her entire life, the house she was brought home as an infant. She'd leave as a young bride, and my grandmother lived there until she died. My grandmother, though, had moved from St. Joe, Texas, to a farm somewhere around Holling, Oklahoma in a covered wagon while the country mobilized to fight the Kaiser. She grew up riding dirt bikes her older brothers worked on and flew in a bi-plane that came barnstorming over the prairie. She played high school basketball and, after graduating, went to California for nursing school, and ended up settling in Glendale before World War II, leaving her extended family behind until the Dust Bowl and banks turned them off the land and onto the highway and out of homes and into tents. My mother's family told her not to take off with my father to pursue the dream of homesteading down on the border. She fought and explained to them and left, and failed, but she said, she never regretted it. I have to think grandmother never regretted bringing my mother into world with a doomed husband hundreds of miles from the family farm.

*

The cattle had hunkered under the quarter acre thicket of alder brush where they had trails and chambers stomped and wallowed out. My daughters saw the brush as their castle and the cattle as dragons. My job as king was to sally forth and dispatch the dragons. I laughed.

*

As an infant, my mother lost her father. She has no memory of him, but he planted a juniper tree in the front yard of their modest Glendale, Arizona home even as he hacked up chunks of his tubercular lungs. I've dug fire lines with the smoke laying hard over us, coughing so we felt it deep in our guts and our throats burning as the tears stream from our stinging eyes. I imagined he felt like that as the shovel bucked against desert clay. It was a hell of a man who planted a tree to grow with a daughter he knew he would never see grow. How easy, I thought, to do nothing. I knew he had to because Death had lingered around him for a long time. I suppose he came to terms with it over the years of his slow dying and planted the tree to tell Death, "Yeah, you got me, but my daughter will have this tree." His daughter and sons and their children all played in that tree as we grew up.

I have driven by mountain ranges and told my daughters that I helped plant thousands of trees, prepped thousands of acres by fire, burned decadent stands to regenerate the earth, and stopped fires from demolishing the forest to lunar dust. I cannot point to a single tree and say I planted that for you. We never stayed anywhere long enough.

*

I collected a couple of sticks from the woodpile and gave them each one. I said, "Follow me and do what I do." Lead by example not only in how to live, but also in action.

*

Toward the end of our first summer on the Mexican border, my sister, the youngest, prepared to start kindergarten. My two, younger brothers and I did not know what to expect at the small school. Aside from range cows, three wild horses, and the few cowboys riding through, we saw nothing except the wide desert basin and mountain ranges. We cut limbs from mesquite bushes and chased cows across the open range. They'd wander through our camp, shitting all over. We'd yell and scream at them to push them on as they ran, tails lifted, crap flying behind with my sister's black and white Chihuahua darting between hooves as it yipped. In our horseless West, we were cowboys of the poorest order. We didn't even have a real herd dog. Cows scattered every which way, and usually one turned back and stampeded through camp in its ignorant terror of small boys.

My daughters formed a phalanx behind me. I warned them to watch out for the one that might backtrack on them. I walked to the nearest opening and started yelling, "Yah, dragons." I banged the stick against the brush and the lounging beasts labored to their feet in clouds of dust and the rustling of dried leaves and branches. It smelled of cow shit. Sophia and Madison's small voices rose up in unison, "Yah, dragons, Yah." They swatted the brush. At first tentative, but it built as one hit with the stick and the other hit harder and a cacophony of percussion broke out and they got carried away in a small moment. "Yah, dragons. Get out of our castle you rounders, you hooligans. Yah!"

The herd of fifteen cows and calves moved away, looking over hulking shoulder roasts, rib eyes, and ground round. My girls, no doubt sensing a full rout, charged. They dashed past me. Their sudden border-collie movements and shrill whoops put the cattle to full flight in swirls of sun-baked dirt and yellowed grass. The girls dropped their sticks. And as armies who have sensed the field was theirs after a crisis of strength and fear of defeat, they pursued in frenzied confidence, discovering the ecstasy of their power. As the cows bucked and farted and loped, I stopped amid the war whoops, watching the bronze and copper colored hair flying, a king satisfied.

My daughters quit running about 250 yards away. They looked tiny against the 100-foot trees and in their energy seemed heedless of what lay beyond the wood. I had never been overcautious in the world. As my daughters grew, I considered what it meant to be cautious. I had my own stories of people being overcautious in wildfire and invited disaster just as surely as the most reckless. Still, though, as the girls wandered back from the far trees, flush with victory to take up residence in the liberated thicket, I realized I had spent my life being overly cautious until Sophia's birth. I had always avoided having a family for fear of death and for the dread of leaving fatherless children in the world. Maybe listening to my mother's melancholy wondering about her father as I grew up had impacted me in a way I never realized.

When my grandmother died, her children sold the house. My sister went back by some years ago, pulled by that cord of curiosity we have about the shrines of our youth. All she said to me was, "Don't go back. They tore out the tree. Don't tell Mom."

My daughters have set up an empire in the thicket, an empire of dread queens already fading in that summer day. I think of what fire had taught me about people, leading, and risk. Not chance, but bona fide risk where a person has something at stake to lose. Later I would discover another reason I balked at having children in my youth. It took me dragging the girls to other helibases and watching them wave at other helicopters and trucks or giving them a hug and a kiss at the apartment before driving off for six weeks to two months. That compounded with moving to get an education and moving yet again to try and find work and returning to fire to try and not lose the truck that hauled the fated fifth wheel. When I risked, I risked for three other people now and not just me.

I feared rootless children. A family knocked around and on the road was an eyesore to a society that valued the dream homeownership and settling down in one spot and becoming a piece of the landscape like the mountains and trees. To be a rolling stone was coined disparagingly and the gypsies were considered a problem in Europe for centuries. Even we of the frontier beginnings saw not wandering, but a trip from A to B with a cabin at the edge of the wood, homestead. Drifters were not to be trusted, showing some lack of character, not to be able to become rooted. We perhaps have feared that thing because of the unknown they embody like a fire getting up in the trees and scattering sparks where it will.

But wasn't that desire my parents' flaw? They uprooted their kids from the cushy, stable suburbs, and a good job being a municipal judge to recreate a stable life that would be even more so because they planned to farm and ranch for our needs. That romantic ideal of living off the "fat of the land," and striking a little more independent figure in the world. To date, my quest for a greater stability has led to greater wandering. My daughters would have grown up in the same community if I'd stayed with Association, but their lives would not have been as rich nor would their father have discovered who he was supposed to be. My daughters didn't make me a better man, but they did give me my identity and the guts to do what I needed to do.

My daughters had become fire gypsies and never fought a fire. They had become best pals with firefighters, learned the language of fire, and knew the cold distance of an absent father brought on by a hot summer. They also discovered the beauty of the remote wilderness camps and the excitement of watching their father and their friends rappel from helicopters, and cheered them at the finish of a three mile pack-test, our backs hunched under 85 pounds. They were children seasoned by fire. I hoped it was the fire of rejuvenation and hope and not the fire that scorched the soul into calluses. I might not be a better father than anyone else, mine included, but no one can make that judgment in the midst of a life trying to survive like making split decisions on the fire-line. No one goes out hoping to fail. We try our best and sometimes in the process do more harm than good and only see it in hindsight, if at all. I can only hope these little girls grow into women who see me for the flawed father that I am, but one who tried his best.

*

Sophia sent her sister out as a messenger, inviting me to eat lunch in their castle. The forest around them rippled with an afternoon breeze. Dust from their rout of the cattle drifted away. The sun heated the meadow. Moisture in the air rose over the mountains and billowed into voluminous clouds threatening to fling lightning over the forest. Fires were coming. I took a sandwich and water bottle into the shade. They showed me sticks they had collected and which were magic and which were not. I wanted a place where they could watch trees grow I had planted for them, but that was okay. I can point to mountain ranges where they had camped and played the summer away, and tell them, I worked there so I could attend school to learn how to cultivate the right words to contribute a verse and plant stories in the world borne of wandering after hope and fire.

Chapter 12

REBEL CREEK

The helicopter circled the head of Rebel Creek less than fifteen minutes after being dispatched from the tarmac in Winnemucca, Nevada. The fire smoldered an area about the size of a truck hood of brush and grass. Someone in the small crossroads town of Orovada, Nevada had reported small puffs of smoke. The land was part of Wilderness Study Area and although not officially a designated wilderness, the district ranger had to grant us permission to land as it still came under the rules set forth in the 1964 Wilderness Act. Since the creation of the Wilderness, the primary way firefighters have been delivered to these fires is by aircraft, first with the smokejumpers and then with helicopters. Helicopters at first landed and the crews disembarked with equipment to stay for several days and then hiked out. In 1972 a rappel program was established and has gone from being discontinued to reinstated to limited use over the course of years due to accidents and eventually a fatality.

The district ranger for the Rebel Creek fire denied us permission to land and we returned to base. Instead he called for a load of smokejumpers out of Battle Mountain, NV. When the jump ship arrived on station the smoke had died down and because of the altitude and speed they had to maintain in their fixed wing aircraft, they couldn't spot it so they returned to base. A three-person engine crew rolled from their guard station to see how they might help and began hiking up the mountain.

In the early afternoon, the heat of the sun bore down and the up-canyon winds fanned the fire into over a dozen acres. The citizens from Orovada called again, angry that they had reported it that morning, watched a helicopter circle and leave and a jump-ship circle and leave

167

and nothing had been done about it. The jumpers were dispatched again because it was thought that they'd have less of an impact on the land, but when they arrived they called for the helicopter to shuttle in two twenty-person crews and supplies to last a week, and use the Bambi bucket to dump water on the growing fire. Not bad considering that the original crew of two people could have landed, put the bucket on the helicopter and suppressed the fire and been flown off by lunch or hiked down to the road several miles away and not aggravated some of the locals who only see the worst in any government agency and felt the concept of wilderness as an outsider intrusion and considered wilderness "land of no use."

Within sight of the smoke rising over the mountain, two of the citizens of Orovada, Raymond Gabica and Kirk Studebaker had fought the Rock Creek fire before it turned into tragedy in 1939 only a couple of drainages over. They knew the steep ground. Only the month before I walked Rock Creek on a staff ride--a tour of a fire tragedy led by an expert where a group of firefighters go out and hike the ground and learn what went wrong and where and how maybe we could prevent a similar disaster when faced with the same situation.

It was humbling to walk that steep assed country, negotiating the thick sagebrush, the ankle twisting rocks sliding under my boots and imagining the headlong rush down the canyon, running away from fire. In 1939 a Civilian Conservation Corp crew hiked into steep mountains. They had already been delayed in arriving at the fire from miscommunication. They broke into two squads, one went high and the other made an approach from the bottom. This sagebrush was old growth, over ten feet tall. Before they could reach the fire, a thunderstorm built up over the mountains and drove a fifty-mile per hour wind down the slopes. Ranchers who had already been on the fire scrambled for their horses, unhobbled them, and rode as hard as they could. In an interview Raymond Gabica told how they tried to wave the firefighters away using their hats in hand, but they were too far away to hear the men galloping for their lives. The CCC squad panicked and scattered running whichever way and one of guys tripped and broke his ankle. Two others tried to carry him and after realizing they couldn't outpace the flames and still carry him, left him. Those two caught up with another injured man and tried to help him to safety. The fire caught them and in the end they all got burned over. Another man broke his glasses and couldn't see. He ended up turning north and climbed hundreds of impossibly high yards onto a ridge side when the fire overtook him, and three members of the squad reached the two-lane highway and safety. The ranchers made the highway where they had parked some vehicles, but their horses kept running, tails flaming as they kept one stride ahead of fire flowing downhill as if from a fiery flash flood.

One of the things we talked about was leaving behind a crewmember so you'd survive. Some said you couldn't know until you were there and others said, you couldn't judge someone for not killing him or herself for another. Standing on a hillside like that, knowing a bunch of men died there, put the chill in me. When you look down on the land from the head of the creek, you see all the ways they could've gone and how short the distance to safety was from where the fire killed them. You think you could've saved a life and not lost yours in the process.

John Maclean uncovered in his book *Fire on the Mountain*, that smokejumpers, Don Mackey and James Thrash, were safe when the fire on Storm King erupted in 1994. They chose to return down the line and help others make it to safety. They were concerned about the slower crewmembers and instinct took over and sent them *back* down the mountain. It wasn't just jumper hubris, which they had plenty of, but that they were products of a culture that made it a point of honor to protect those under your care. Those jumpers returned because they had to. Everyone connected in some way. In fire, we are all connected by hardships and live in a community of those who struggled and suffered together in a common cause. They went back and they died because, to twist John Donne:

> *No firefighter is an island,*
> *Entire of itself.*
> *Each is a piece of the continent,*
> *A part of the main.*
> *If a clod be washed away by the sea,*
> *The world is the less.*
> *As well as if a promontory were.*
> *As well as if a manor of thine own*
> *Or of thine friend's were.*

Each one's death diminishes me,
For I am involved in humankind.
Therefore, send not to know
For whom the bell tolls,
It tolls for thee.

No firefighter I know can read or hear of a death and not have felt the resonance of that bell pealing and as such might run those extra steps thinking we can save one from falling and fall ourselves. The day we trudged the ridges of Rock Creek it was raining and the wind blew hard out of the North carrying spits of ice, but we definitely had the sense of it. When we hiked back down and past where the men were found, I looked around at the steep hillsides, saw how far they had to go to survive, the real walking distance, the real running while dragging a man with a broken leg over broken country distance.

But what of the squad on the high ridge, the dangerous place to be during a wildfire. We taught all rookies that finding yourself above the fire with unburned fuel between you was a bad spot to be in. I imagined the crew boss looking down open mouthed to see the mad downhill dash, the run for hope, the men stumbling, the men picking each other up. The hillside below that was supposed to be the safe approach because fires moved up not down. The horses galloping with smoking tails like some Western myth of ghost riders in a frenzied charge, mounted with cowboys hats in hands waving to literally beat Hell. In the desert, up those canyons and arroyos sound reverberated and echoed with the screams of men and surely the wild screams of horses, the pounding of hooves, the gunning of engines as ranchers fired up old trucks, the calling of names by survivors from the road and the high calls of birds on the wing, the raptors diving down to scoop up rodents and snakes rooted out from the fire's advance.

And what of the other half of the crew standing on the high ridge watching? Surely some yelled, some struck dumb, as they watched men disappear into the arroyos or reappear as they climbed for ridge tops and to see the awful race against the flames bearing down the mountain. Did they see the men reach the highway? Did they see the men limping and carrying another in panicked flight as the flames washed over them? Surely some stood anchored in shock or fear, some beginning the head long dash for the bottom through the charred skeletons of sagebrush to find men they had lunched with a short time before being reduced to carbon and ash. Did at least one of the men look skyward, not for God or providence, but to watch the thunderstorm to see if it bore crooked fingers of lightning for them to dodge, scattering new fires on the hillside to outrun, or bringing other winds to reverse the flow of the fire that had just killed five of their crew? Maybe they watched clouds that once towered 45,000 feet dissolve into blue skies like sugar cubes in a glass of water.

On that rainy and cold day we hiked up to the ridge and then down into the creek bottom. We couldn't see the way out, only the natural inclination to run down hill and follow the stream course. I tried to imagine holding my breath as the heat scalded my lungs shut before the flames wrapped around my body. A pain I couldn't even imagine, and I had been in the thick of smoke and flames. I considered not making it back to see my daughters, leaving them just kids, their memories of me as faded as an old shirt worn too long under the fiery sun.

*

At Rebel Creek when the jumpers called for helicopter support we landed in the field and set up a helibase that belonged to Kirk Studebaker. We flew in and flared a landing. The kid with a wicked combine scar on his head and I flew to the top of the mountain. He still hadn't been signed off on his helicopter crewmember (HECM) task book and this was his chance to get some tight helispot time. We needed to fly off two full hand crews, plus the eight jumpers and all the gear and trash we'd flown up there over the last two days. I'd had more complicated missions, but for a rookie it'd seem like figuring out the subway system in Manhattan after growing up in a small Oregon town. A mess, a confusion, but doable with some guidance.

The engine crew that had responded had hiked several hours to the fire from the bottom where the road ended and opted to hike off. The engine boss said, "Sure the jumpers get all the glory, but we got here before them and denied the use of the helicopter. We'll hike. It is a wilderness study area after all."

I took my trainee to the side. "Listen," I said. "If one of those jumpers or hotshots starts dorking off during your briefing, remind him or her she can hike down. Now of course they'll get all I'm tough and I can hike down on you, but remind them that they'll have to explain to their supervisor why the whole crew had to wait on their dumb ass while they took their little nature walk."

He nodded.

"I'm serious. You're the boss up here. They listen or they walk."

He nodded again. He gave the briefing and as we flew people off, I had him readjust all of the loads as the helicopter burned fuel so we could load more weight with each flight. It went smooth and he picked up how to revise the manifests and look to where he could slip gear or people on as the helicopter's allowable payload changed. We flew down on the last load. The grass in the field waved under the rotor wash as we maneuvered past humming power lines and the pasture fences. Old man, Studebaker was over in his house. He had allowed us to set up the helibase in one of his pastures and dip water from his pond. I wondered if he thought of the fire he'd outrun.

*

In the middle of August Carmen and I landed on a small fire southwest of Winnemucca. In a repeater shadow, I couldn't talk to dispatch, so after the flames were knocked down, I climbed up the ridge to see if I could make contact. The wind cooled me as I took out my GPS, my personal unit, as I couldn't get one from the warehouse. It cost me a tenth of one office chair that some admin type now occupied, but I figured worth it. They could rest easy at work and I could call down water from Heaven on a spot fire before flames overran the arroyos and rangeland. In the southwestern sky, lines of clouds clustered and started to build vertically, forming great white and gray cliffs like sandstone. They filled out and gathered mass and volume of swirling white vapor, then darkened to the colors of worn gun bluing.

I traversed to a bench and found a rock foundation of some old miner's shack. Desert grass and the stalks of dead flowers freckled what had been the floor. It might have only been canvas over a wood-frame erected over the square that the miner packed up when he lit out or maybe the stones were knocked down and scattered. Maybe the miner realized the rock he built his house with was ore bearing and ground it down stone by stone, leaching out the precious metal with cyanide and mercury. Terrible thing for a home. An old bedspring rested in a corner, and rusted cans were piled at the foot of it. A cross that had probably hung on the wall lay in a pile of rubble in a corner where a mouse nest had been built in the lee of the slight foundation. It was as if the mice had dragged it over and planted it amongst all the grasses and twigs they'd brought. In the hill behind the foundation a shaft gaped, busted stones had been dumped into the ravine and half way down the ravine a rusted truck of some ancient vintage lay mangled in the rocks.

I picked my way past and stopped, recalling Xenophon and the march of the 10,000 after their failed Persian Expedition. I had read it years ago but usually thought about it when I looked at city skylines like Tucson sinking into the earth due to subsidence or stings of homes built in places plainly eroding or with no hope of sustainability. "Who will mourn Nineveh?" Most times, when I looked at up kept houses, those keeping up the appearances against the decaying of the world, it brought to mind all the houses I saw with grayed wood, peeling paint, and yards run-over with weeds and junk. The collapsed cabins with an apple tree in the brushed over dooryard scattered across the Clearwater region we'd run into as we chased smokes. Even new construction brought the images of abandoned and neglected towns because the water ran dry or the ore ran out or the industry left for foreign shores. Ranchers and farmers I'd known complained about all the kids escaping to the city for easier jobs, weekends off, a little vacation time, of movies, stores a short drive away, and all night diners. Those kids didn't want to fight against the slow breaking down of everyday something needed tended, repaired, painted or stained and the everyday struggle to keep livestock alive. The simple life their ass. An old timer, a John Deere green cap cocked up on the back of his head like a yarmulke sat in a cafe that could be in any small Western town, "My dad and granddad sunk their lives into that ranch and then me. I worked this land for fifty years and I'm only fifty-two, but I'm the last." I climbed to the top of the ridge thinking of all the empires great and small eroded to dirt.

A lizard scurried away as I stopped. After I caught my breath, I pulled my radio off my belt. I keyed the mic to see if I could hit the repeater. No squelch tail hissed back through the speaker. Only the wind broke the silence, no sound of cars or planes. Around us stretched hot as hell desert and the stony mountains carpeted with juniper, bitter brush, sage, and the invasive cheat grass that exploded when lit, torching everything whichever way the wind drove it. Carmen's pulaski picked a steady rhythm the sun caught the thousands of flecks on her clothes, hardhat, skin and hair. We pried rocks up then scraped the thick grass and weeds away, exposing mineral earth. We could have been prospectors assaying the frontier, looking to find a strike and make a fortune from our diggings. In a way we were, but our diggings were to smother the gold flames and not uncover the treasure. Our prospecting when we applied to the crew was not to build something out of the wilderness, but only the hope to be out on the line, to be with good people, and fly to fires fast and away.

*

In 2005 Carmen and I would coincidentally end up at Fort Howes in southeastern Montana, on the Miles City District. She landed a position with one of the engines, and I on the helitack crew. It was bluff country with small creek valleys cutting between the high ground that rose to plateaus full of pines. The trees and grass burned deceptively fast. The local population of ranchers was like any others that vacillated between seeing us as government employees and worthy of derision or just people working a hard job. Once on a morning we woke on a fire-line to find the neighboring ranch wives had brought us all homemade doughnuts and pastries, thermoses of coffee, and bright smiles and thanks.

To the north of our fire camp about twenty-five miles was Ashland, a small crossroads town and the gateway to the Crow Agency and the Cheyenne as well as a large Amish population north of town. We were only two drainages over from the Little Big Horn. Miles City on the banks of the muddy Tongue River was named for the General Nelson A. Miles who the army ordered into the territory after General George Armstrong Custer's Seventh Cavalry rode into oblivion.

Off duty at 1700, most of the crew cleared out. A street party in Birney and the Montana Shakespeare in the Park was putting on a performance in Ekalaka, another small Montana town. The night before we had seen them on Poker Jim Lookout performing *Cymbeline*. The troupe drove two Ford Crew Cabs, a Caravan, towing trailers with the modular stage they assembled and disassembled every day on their 2005 Tour Shakespeare in the Park. They traveled over forty-some-odd miles of gravel road to the lookout and set up and perform. Yesterday Colstrip, tomorrow Ekalaka, then Miles City for *Taming of the Shrew*, which I would attend with my daughters, but now, below the lookout tower, treason, murder, mistaken identity. On lawn chairs or on the ground in dry grass we watched: ranch families, cowboys, wranglers, the folks who ran the gas station and IGA in Ashland, the motel, the tack and feed store in Birney, the artist who lived alone down on the Powder River, the People from the Northern Cheyenne and the Crow Agency, a Forest Service fuels crew smelling of timber, bar oil and saw gas, three wildland engine crews, and us--Fort Howes helicopter crew on a fireless, flightless day with no forecast for storms.

From Poker Jim on the Custer National Forest we saw south to Wyoming and the Big Horns draped in thunderstorms like columns of smoke. Fires hadn't flamed the district in days. At curtain call the audience applauded together regardless of rivalries, joined in this one thing. The actors became normal people again. Some of us bought merchandise, cups, hats, and shirts, to help supply gas money. After helping breakdown the stage, we had a potluck and drank with the actors. A dry west wind whipped the cook fires, flaking embers into the jet stream of wood smoke. The mountains and forest shimmered with flames of the falling sun as it lit the smoldering clouds.

We stood in a loose group. Steven motioned to the woman who played Imogen. "I'd really like to talk to her, but I'd be embarrassed."

"Why's that?" I asked.

"I don't know anything about Shakespeare and wouldn't how to talk with her."

"Don't worry about it. Just tell her what you thought of her performance."

"I'm just a range guy. I studied prairie grasses in college. That wouldn't interest her."

"Listen, there are three things you need to know: Comedies are where somebody gets married in the end. Tragedies are where somebody dies in the end. And the Histories loosely based on fact, but jimmied to make her Royal Highness Queen Elizabeth's family look good, her enemies look bad and booster English nationalism. Just come out and admit that's all you know and you'd like to know more."

"Married, Dead, propaganda histories."

"And some sonnets."

"Copy, sonnets."

"Shall I compare thee to a summer's day?"

"I like that."

"It's Shakespeare's, use it. And compliment her acting."

Steven and her hit it off and he had gone to see her in Ekalaka that evening. About an hour after most of the people had left, two guys from Missoula showed up for their detail to the engine crews. Lean with shades of gray in their hair, they both had a lot of experience.

The first one reached his hand out. He looked around at the empty compound. "I suppose everyone is on the fire."

Carmen laughed. "The street party fire maybe."

He looked puzzled. "Who's on the fire up drainage from here?"

"Fire?" We jogged down the drive, away from the buildings and sure enough a thin column rose above the trees. Our pilot had popped a beer, so the five of us who remained loaded into two engines and headed for the fire. As we rolled down the highway a rancher stood next to the blacktop, waving us down. "This road is the best way to where you need to go. Just be sure to close the gates."

"Thanks, we will." Carmen said. We wheeled down the road past his trailer home.

Within ten minutes we pulled up to the base of the fire. It spread up from the road. We slid out and got our fire packs on. Brush and small trees crowded the hillside, so I pulled the saw. Carmen had a pulaski and as I checked the fuel and oil on the saw she pointed to the right heel of the fire. "There's a game trail. I think we should anchor and start up this flank."

The other three rolled up behind us. "Sounds like a plan," I said.

"I'll get a hose lay started with these guys."

"Give me a hose pack and I'll get the first stretch out." I could get three hundred feet of hose laid and then start sawing while the others began knocking down flames and digging line. One of the great things about working with Carmen was her ability to immediately size-up a situation and come up a plan to get us started within a minute of arriving on scene. What made us all laugh later was that she was the least qualified person on the fire according to red card quals. The helicopter supervisor, Conan, was an IC3 as were the two guys who had arrived from Missoula and Matt, a detailer engine boss who had arrived the week before. I was an IC4 and we were all crew bosses or engine bosses or helicopter managers, while Carmen was a fully qualified squad boss. (Incident Commanders were rated 1-5 with 1 being in charge of the most complex and challenging fires, while a 5 commanded smaller fires without a lot of resources or values at threat and generally lasting less than twenty-four hours). But as the others said, "Sometimes it's good to be the one head down and digging and have a good time fighting fire without worrying about anything else."

I sawed up and around through the brush and felled some small trees as the others came up behind me. Carmen turned the fire over to Matt who requested the forest send more people. It had been a slow fire year, so a squad of smokejumpers were in the area doing thinning work with the fuels crew. By the time they arrived, I had completed the saw line around the fire and made ready to sharpen and fuel the saw before helping finish digging the firebreak. The fire had grown to several acres and we had prevented it from reaching the prairie where it might have run in the grass or spread down the drainage. In either direction the fire threatened ranch houses, barns, and swing sets surrounded by fruit trees, fields of alfalfa, wheat, and range grass for livestock and livelihoods. Maybe not as many homes would be lost as in the suburbs of Denver, Boise, Missoula, Spokane, Salt Lake City, or any other major population area, but a loss of home and livelihood in one flaming swath.

At around midnight the first of us to arrive on scene were told to go and bed down and get some sleep. We wouldn't be allowed back on until 0800 in the morning and in the morning we'd get up at 0600 and feel useless. We'd sneak back up onto the fire because that was what we did. We rested enough and then went to work. We wouldn't get paid for it because the administrators wouldn't allow it, even though we worked and spent the night out in the grass surrounded by flagging to keep from being run over, and knew our abilities and limitations. We worked mopping up all through the day and spent another night sleeping out in the grass.

The next morning Carmen, Tyler, another crew-member, who came up that day in a truck for shuttling us back to camp after finishing our shift, and I drove down the road we had come up. We noticed the rancher sitting in his pick up and as we passed his house he started flailing his arm out the window and jumped out.

I rolled down the driver's window. "Hi. How're you?" His face was contorted in anger and I had no idea why, but I had been yelled at and insulted by ranchers, miners, loggers, small town folk, and drug smugglers all across the American West, so I figured he just wanted to vent at the federal government about something we weren't doing right on the fire.

"What do you think you're doing?" His question confused me. Maybe he thought we should still be on the fire. I have heard that accusation too. We firefighters were lazy over-paid babies when we couldn't catch a fire, even if it did grow 20,000 acres overnight.

"Headed back to camp. We've been out here since is started."

"Well, you can't come this way."

"We got to the fire this way. You flagged us in."

"I am sick of you people thinking you can drive across my property any time you feel like it." He was puffed up and self-righteous now and I just wanted to go shower.

"We were coming back from the fire and this was the way we accessed it. You gave us permission."

"You have to go around now." He pointed back up the road a mile where another road meandered through the foothills, eventually crossing the highway. From where the rancher stopped us we sat fifty feet from the highway, but had to open one gate.

"You want us to turn around and drive an extra two hours?"

He glared at me. "I'm going to file a complaint."

"Go ahead. I wanted you to tell me that you want us to drive another two hours instead of fifty feet after we stopped a fire on the edge of your pasture."

He continued to glare as I put the truck into reverse. "You have a good day." I backed down the road until I found a place to turn around and drove my tired crewmates the long way back home.

I reported the incident to my boss. He shrugged. "Yeah, love us when a fire is going, hate us when it's done. I've seen some refuse access when their neighbor's ranch was threatened if the wind was going the other way."

Before General Nelson A. Miles rode into this area after Custer's defeat, the Sioux, Crow, and Cheyenne, other tribes of the Great Plains roamed, hunted and fought each other when they weren't fighting settlers. They didn't stake down particular plots of land in the same sense that we felt compelled to fence everything. With the exception of free range, which was really public land used for grazing, we have felt that if a person owned something then he can destroy it for centuries if he chose to or hold it and block all access even for emergencies. At least when the Native Americans altered the landscape through fire, they did it for the common good of their tribe. We valued the individual over the common good, and in some cases common sense, and as a firefighter I had seen many like that rancher standing along the road ranting about his empire of grass and dirt, when without the might of the Federal army, his ancestors who squatted on the land would never have made it against the tribes. In that moment I lost sympathy also for those who lamented the loss of their traditional ranch life and that they should be protected. They even have the nerve to complain of people coming in from out of state and buying their land or celebrities buying up huge swaths of land and denying public access to thousands of acres. We left Europe where the aristocracy controlled all the land, so maybe it was a natural impulse borne from there. Most have only been in that area three generations or about 120 years, and their ancestors eradicated a set of traditions when they came into the country. Not that going back to some pre-settler ideal could ever happen. It was gone. The tribes fought back and forth and what was sacred ground to one tribe became another's sacred ground and so on. Just ask the Crow.

Like the wilderness, people struggled to preserve an ideal even as it failed. When I write failed, I don't mean that we shouldn't have wilderness or places where greedy industrialists shouldn't be able to destroy for fun and profit. I mean it failed as it props up the prelapsarian notion. A real wilderness should be hands off and no trail building, clearing, or fire crews and no wilderness rangers. Like the frontier, a person went in and took their chances with the wolves and grizzly bears and if they couldn't hack it they died. That was a wilderness. Let roving bands of marauders loose and make it more of the actual wilderness experience. Better than Disneyland.

Wilderness also relied on a bureaucratic system to support it, which meant the possibility of falling under the control of petty tyrants. Not all do, but some. To let the helicopter land at Rebel Creek in view of people who'd witnessed fires there decades before administrators had inserted themselves into the landscape would've been too easy. Easily we could've suppressed the fire before lunch with minimal impact. Wilderness rangers who exercised power through denying were as bad as the rancher who wouldn't let us drive fifty feet, creating a whole different set of hazards. They were both struggling to enforce a broken "tradition" and each was as conservative as the other. We have been caught between two rigid systems of thought and the ones who suffered were those who did the work.

That rancher ranting at us was just staking out his sacred ground that had been somebody else's, and by forcing us to go around he exerted power against the government, which, I was sure, pleased him no end. The rangers who ruled the wilderness in that same fashion were no different from the rancher, both picking and choosing access to the land based on what suited their particular interpretation of how things should be and a concept of what was traditional. Unlike the miners and homesteaders who abandoned apple trees and crucifixes to deer and packrats, the ranger and the rancher both resisted change and maybe harbored fear of the unknown. Two opposites sides, propping up empires built out of false memories and imagination.

Chapter 13

WORKING WITH CONS

In northern Nevada during 2003 we had flown to a fire two-thirds of the way up a mountain. Three of us cleared an anchor point and began digging line. The rest of the crew set up a helibase in a farmer's field in the valley and we began flying people and supplies to the helispot. It'd grown to twenty-five acres in the juniper and grass and it'd take a lot of folks to mop it up and put it to bed.

In the morning I swapped with some others and worked the helibase. Two inmate crews had arrived. I had earned my crew-boss qualification running inmate crews in north central Idaho. I'd get the call from dispatch, drive to a meeting place close to the fire or at an ICP, and met the projects officer and the inmates. I had only worked with men out of the Orofino Correctional Facility, but this group was from a prison in Nevada. The most famous inmate crew in fire was the Flame "N" Goes from Bluffdale State Prison in Utah, the only inmate crew to carry the federal designation of a Hotshot crew. They had a flamingo logo and as far as I knew the only inmates to have logo other than their official department of corrections government logo, much like the BLM.

The inmates I worked with wore red t-shirts and the projects officers wore blue and they were unarmed. The officers were responsible for discipline and worked along with the crews. Inmate crews checked each other's work and no one slacked. If I had a problem with a guy not pulling his weight or acting inappropriately, all I had to do was tell his squad leader--a fellow inmate. If one messed up they all went back to the prison and none of them wanted that. The offending crewmember was straightened out informally, and worked hard the next day.

I gathered the forty inmates and their crew-bosses. I was going to brief them for the helicopter flight to the fire. They could have been any Type II crew I've flown to fires, but they looked harder. Hard set eyes and faces etched with tough living, the low quality tattoos creeping up necks, inked tears on cheeks, on the backs of hands and fingers, and the loose groupings of men talking in whispers with the occasional loud laugh or shout of disbelief, segregated from the other firefighters.

A crew boss learned things not unlike any other type of crew other than what's the best way to smuggle tobacco back into prison or if you take a car instead of cash for a drug deal you might go to prison for a stolen car and feel rightfully framed.

On the evening of September 11, 2001, we gathered by the trucks. The night air was heavy with smoke and the events of the day weighed on all of us from grinding away on a tough Idaho mountainside to the pall of the terrorist attacks on the East Coast. Our bodies suppressed fire in Idaho, but our minds ranged the smoke obscured skies of the future. All the air resources had been grounded. Nothing flew. Fires all across the area had grown without the support and crews had been left without support in the remote roadless areas of the forests.

I asked the first squad boss, "What did you get done?"

"I tied in to the lower road. I helped the engine crew lay out hose, and then I mopped up the perimeter to fifty feet."

Another squad leader laughed, loud and harsh from smoke of fire and cigarettes. His bulk cast a shadow against the darkness of the woods. Tattoos ran down each cheek, and his eyes blotted out in the dark, were usually squinted and blue like edges of ice under volcanic rock. "You're an I guy. You did all that by yourself. Your squad did nothing? How about we did this? How about they did that?"

Some giggled.

I don't know if anyone saw my smile in the dark. "So then, what did your squad get done?" I asked him.

"We cleared all the brush and hazard trees from around the fire." He emphasized the "we" like a gunshot.

We loaded into the trucks and drove an hour or so to the ICP for dinner and to bed down. Our tents were pitched in a gravel pit away from the grass fields the other crews camped in. After eating, I told the squad bosses when I wanted the crew assembled in the morning. As the others dispersed the big man said to me, "You know. I'd go and join the Marines after what those fucks did back east, but they won't have me." He shrugged his shoulders and lumbered into the darkness.

*

The Nevada inmates paid attention and focused on what I told them about the helicopter. "Any questions?" I asked after I finished my spiel.

"Yeah, what are you reading?"

A book stuck up from the cargo pocket of my pants. A Norton Critical edition with a purple-bordered cover smudged with the dirt and grime of fire. I always carried a book to read by headlamp when we bedded down on any fire or when I found myself stuck on stand by.

"It's *Paradise Lost.*"

"What's it about?"

Before I could answer another inmate said, "Fall of man, bro. It's all about the fall of man."

"Cool," said the inquisitor as he motioned around. "We understand that."

Chapter 14

TRUCK ATTACK

L ate in the day at Krassel we received the radio call to fly to the Nez Perce National Forest, just north of the Salmon River. My first chance at an operational rappel had me excited to go and I'd be the first rookie to do so. After rappel training I had been assigned to go out with the Payette Regs hand-crew and in the words of Money, "It was glorious," but I had yet to fly to fire and no opportunity to rappel. The ship had just come back from an assignment in Wyoming, and I was on the up-team that morning and had all my gear loaded and ready to launch. Destination: Dixie Ranger Station. A remote area with a large meadow. Keg would be with me. We worked on the Regs together on the last roll and as a saw team we worked the steep rocky Wasatch Front from the July 3 until the Fourth with Flegal leading the way up into the shadows of flame and moonlight. Keg'd be the IC as my red card was still fouled by red tape and inflexible thinking.

The Nez already had several fires burning and no ships available to fly to it. Region One still had very few rappel ships due to the tradition of smoke jumping, even though helicopters had proven to be better suited at inserting firefighters and equipment with pinpoint accuracy, without scattering gear and people all over the forest and breaking legs, hips, wrists, and other assorted bones several out of every hundred jumps. No one knows for sure how many bones because it wasn't made public. But traditions held sway and many jumpers in high places insure that the "Bros" were looked out for in the fire world. Several years before it was recommended in a report to shut down many of the jump bases and consolidate the jump program because of the effectiveness of helicopters being one reason, much like the military's overwhelming use of helicopters over the use of combat parachuting.

185

We in helicopters could land at a specific spot unload people, put the bucket on to start suppression, or send it for more people while the jump ship would still be circling and dropping streamers, much less the time it took to recover their gear spread in the forest. Political concerns may have had a hand in why the recommendation was never pursued and some of us in helitack believed it was also behind removing helibases away from the forest and consolidating them further away into "Super Bases," thereby making them less effective as a tool in suppressing fire, and in the demise of the light helicopter rappel program. But those really were just nasty rumors, I hoped.

Talking about the jump program was always a sensitive thing. It has been said that anybody who criticized the jump program was just jealous and secretly wanted to be a jumper. I had wanted to be a jumper because I always wanted to parachute and it looked like a lot of fun. Plus after you became a jumper there were huge political advantages for getting into fire classes, fire assignments, and job potential. This was not hearsay, but something many jumpers bragged about. The jumper image is so strong that even when I tell non-fire people I was a heli-rappeller, they respond, "oh, a smokejumper". I had known many great jumpers who worked hard and dedicated their lives to fighting fire, and some I'd even trust around my family, but they do have their share of fools like all groups do. But even as I wanted to parachute and join the relentless public relations and career boosting juggernaut segment of the fire community, I did so knowing I was like men who signed up for the cavalry long after the tank and machine gun made the dashing cavalry officer obsolete. Jealous? Sure, who doesn't love a saber?

From Krassel we lifted and flew north. The late afternoon sunshine filtered through the haze of fires burning all around us. We flew over the Zena-Loon Fire, burning toward Krassel from the North, stretched to almost 200,000 acres and eventually grew to 217,263. It hadn't crossed Lick Creek yet or jumped the South Fork of the Salmon, but it was coming like a bad prophecy for Krassel Helibase, which we would defend and save. The Cascade Complex on the Boise National Forest to the South burned toward Krassel and in the end of August converged with the Zena-Loon, gobbling up 242,709 acres, including the Incident Command Post that was evacuated when the fire overran it. Our helicopter landed on a section of the Rattlesnake Fire on the Nez

Perce National Forest and it eventually burned onto the Payette totaling 102,212 acres. Further east smoke from the Showerbath Complex in the Frank Church Wilderness northwest of Challis was burning toward 130,784 acres. Smoke rose in columns in every direction and at night smoke sunk, dampened by the cold air, filling the valleys and draws creating a gauzy curtain, obscuring the mountains. All across Idaho firefighters set up pumps, cleared brush and trees, and dug fire lines around rural towns where normally the local population regarded them with suspicion for being a part of the government, but now embraced them. It was something to see a guy with a "Don't Tread On Me" flag begging for federal firefighter help.

We crossed over the Salmon River and the dry high ridges covered in yellow grass and higher up scattered ponderosa pines thickened into the forest. We followed a creek into the mountains to the coordinates and found no fire. We talked with the air attack plane for the complex and he guided us with landmarks until we were in the right area. The lat and long were off. We found the smoke and circled it to size the fire up, find a rappel spot, water sources, escape routes and safety zones, hazards, and trails to hike out. We went to configure in the meadow south of the ICP. The Grangeville helicopter sat idle in the grass and beyond that the yurts and trucks of ICP. Martinez from the Nipple Fire and the bear incident was there and came to say hi. We took the doors off, unrolled the small cargo net, the tuna net, filled it with our pack-out bags, saw, and tools, and put on our harnesses. Before we finished, a guy came over from the ICP wondering if Keg was with us because he had a call at the ICP. Money told him to go ahead.

Smoke grayed the dome of the sky. The mid-day sun dulled and washed out colors until it dipped a few degrees off the horizon when it electrified the sky in a gaudy swath of Saturday night neon. Reds, golds, radioactive orange creme-cicles, deep indigos, deepening to night and the haze of stars. I kept going over in my head the procedures and making a plan for the coming night, what to expect in the next two days, and looking forward to working on my favorite type of fire. I liked being on hand crews and engine crews and I felt a lot of satisfaction being a part of a crew that defended homes and livelihoods, or as a team that accomplished a hard job and stretched out on the ground to sleep, but the little fires on some isolated ridge or draw in the backcountry or the wilderness were my favorite. We were cut off from seagull managers, those who came in and squawked, shit on everything and left, and not fed into the industrial machine of large fire camps of twenty-four hour generators, trucks and dust, and people who felt the need to chat four times normal conversation decibels on their cell phones. No, out in the deep woods armed only with a radio, fusees, and hand tools struck some chord as if I were back down living in the Arizona with the snakes and the poor migrants tripping the sharp stones to *El Norte*.

Many nights I lay in primal dreams, wind in the tops of the trees to be awoken by wolves howling or heard nocturnal animals foraging in the brush. It'd been many years since the sound of packs hunting or even the thought of bears drifting in and out of the forests had terrified me. It was ironic that the most if the anti-wolf and anti-bear hysteria came from outdoorsmen and women who reveled in their rugged toughness and frontier hardness and shivered and shook at the mere thought of a wolf roaming the woods. They must be from weak stock. They wanted the "wild" experience, but didn't want it wild, much like the poor tourists who wanted signs posted at trailheads that cougars might be prowling around. Moose attacked more people a year than wolves and bears combined. Bees and wasps killed more people than any wild thing cruising the forests and prairies.

Even forest administrators, supposedly steeped in science, have irrational reactions. A group of resource people was working in the Sawtooth Wilderness when they became concerned about wolves in the area of their camp and radioed for advice on what to do. The reaction down at the main office was to immediately scramble the helicopter and "rescue" them. They landed the helicopter in the wilderness, loaded and flew away. There have been firefighters denied food resupply on a fire by a long line operation, as it was an intrusion, even as fixed wing aircraft flew over headed to land at airstrips in the wilderness. Turned out that an elk carcass was not too far away and the wolves were only checking out the humans to make sure they weren't going to steal the buffet. Solution would have been to either move camp or just stay the hell away from the carcass. The big wolf kill-off during the Twentieth Century was not because wolves threatened people, but because they threatened livestock. I felt a deep sorrow for those poor timid souls who felt they must wander the woods armed in fear, and trembled at night in their sleeping bags. They had neither faith in science nor God.

The mountains rose ragged and hard above the meadow. Maybe my own nostalgia for living in a tent on the desert or some deeper human instinct to journey into the woods on Campbell's journey, to discover and test and not have a sanitized forest fit for the weakest. A journey without challenge or struggle was nothing to me.

I appreciated fear, though. The Fire Service does have a qualification called "Gunner," for working in Alaskan bear country and the job was to carry a shotgun or a .44 magnum and watch out for the big omnivores. I've asked and researched and so far haven't found any one who has had to lay low a large predator or a cow moose or shot up a beehive in self-defense. I have been afraid, but I refused to let me fear get the better of me. When I was greenhorn to the forest and before being forced to confront the wild unarmed, I felt to be armed was the only way to engage the wilderness. I was wrong. Instead I learned something different. A person with a rifle in the woods always seized up my stomach a little. Human hunters averaged wounding over a thousand people a year and killed just fewer than one hundred people a year. Typically these were ones wetting themselves at the thought that wolves killed on average 0.1 people or bears wiping out 0.5 of us forest trekkers. Even the domestic dog can take down an average of 31 people a year and they don't even have to be loose in the forest. More than once some person had started blasting away at gophers, beer cans, or songbirds, and sent rounds over my camp. Once a poacher shot in my direction. I had known fear in the forest.

Keg came walking back from the ICP. His stride measured and solid, but he stared ahead with serious intent. "I need to go back."

Both Money and I stood still trying to register what he said.

"They're taking my nephew off of life support."

Shit, I thought. "All right."

Money started unclipping his spotter harness. "Let's put the ship back together."

I followed his lead and took off my rappel gear, stowed it, and helped put the doors back on the helicopter. I was caught in between emotions of wanting to get my first operational rappel and fight fire to having to leave for a dying nephew. It was totally unexpected, so I felt like shit as fought between the disappointment and the grief that Keg must be feeling. After all, his nephew was being taken off life support. What accident had he suffered, I wondered. I imagined my own nieces and nephews, my own daughters kicking around playing softball, bike riding, swimming in summertime waters, kids struck down by a car or some disease rising up out of the gene pool, laying abed attached to tubes and wires not knowing an adult poised ready to slip the switch off. What brain-crushing malady had struck the poor boy down?

We buckled our seat belts and plugged in our flight helmets. The pilot lifted off and we made our way south. Money said, "We can fly back and get someone else. We can still rappel this thing before pumpkin time." Pumpkin time was thirty minutes after sunset and the time all Fire Service helicopters and single engine aircraft must be on the ground.

Excellent for me, I thought. I still had a chance to rappel. I still felt bad about the nephew and struggled between the joy of being able to go back and feeling bad for Keg and his family. The pilot cut in. "We won't have enough time. I flew in from Wyoming this morning and will time out." In the fire world a pilot could only fly eight hours a day and must shut down before going over the time limit. In most cases a manager shut a pilot down earlier so as not to even chance violating the rule.

Of course, I thought, I'm not meant to do this right now. My guts and brain swung between the unique feelings that people who were denied goals know, but torn between having to be denied by something no one could control. The death of child and a relative took precedence over anything I could want in fire.

Keg switched on his mic. "I should have known it was going to happen. They've been talking about pulling him off life support." He explained the boy was eleven days old and had been on life support the entire time. My inclination was to say, if you even suspected why did you jeopardize the whole mission? Why didn't you pull yourself off the up team? Why am I flying back to base when the pilot will be timed out and can't fly another team back? I didn't say it for all the reasons one shouldn't as a baby lay dying. I realized he had stuck it out with us as long as he could so as not leave us short handed in the remote camp. Maybe too by working he put the coming tragedy out of mind and being on fire perhaps the inevitable remained without the power to manifest itself. Out in the deep woods, head down grubbing the dirt, slaying the dragon, the world stopped and nephews didn't die.

As we flew past William's Peak Lookout and into the South Fork drainage we saw smoke from two other fires on Tea Pot, a mountain right above Buckhorn Creek only a few miles up stream from Krassel. They must've just smoked up as none of the lookouts had called them in yet. We sat down at Krassel to let Keg off and then launched to recon the fires. The fire on the north side we could hike a ridge from the road. No trail cut up the side, so I searched and identified landmarks to locate the right ridge for when we drove back. It burned about two-tenths of an acre in the timber maybe a third of the way up the slope on a finger ridge. The flame lengths only reached a foot or two and the rate of spread was slow. The jumpers would fall on the fire on the south side of the mountain in the morning. In the late morning they'd call for the helicopter to fly off the fire in the afternoon. In the afternoon, they called dispatch to check on the availability of the helicopter and McCall Dispatch answered, "Only if you sing the "Little Teapot' song." As we laughed the jumper-in-charge's voice came over the radio: "Maybe later. Our fire's escaped and we need bucket drops right away."

At Krassel Money and I landed. The sky darkened and I briefed Dano and Kat about the fire and our route. They had already begun loading a pick-up truck and only needed me to toss my gear in the back. Jess would follow us later. This was my first fire on the Krassel district. At the trailhead we parked and I gathered the saw and saw kit to pack up the hill.

"You want me to get that?" Dano asked.

"Nope. My red card's still all balled up. You're the IC and she's the trainee, so I'm the sawyer." They nodded.

We located the ridge I had seen from the air and began the hike up. The soil gave way under our weight as we scrambled up. Climb two feet slide one. The dust swirled and dried our mouths, but at least in the twilight the temperature had begun to drop.

We reached the bottom edge and I scouted down and back up as Dano and Kat scouted the other way. We met on the far side in a draw.

"What do you think?" Dano's face gleamed with sweat.

Kat scanned the trees. "We should definitely anchor low with the saw line, but we can knock down the flames along the front to stop it from growing."

"Sounds good to me. But let's keep eyes up." I pointed to a couple of snags.

In an hour or so Jess joined us, and Kat briefed her on what we were doing. We worked late into the dark, our headlamps mixed with firelight casting orange and white between the shadows. The thing about working on a fire was that it grew and the planned route might be gone by the time a crew could complete the line. In the best situations the sawyer gauged the rate of spread so that folks digging the line had a chance to complete the firebreak before the fire burned over the line. Much like an expert shot, a sawyer needed lots of fire experience, and the gut's inclination to where to pull the trigger.

I completed the saw line and grabbed a tool Dano had carried up for me. I joined the other three in digging the firebreak. "Bummer you didn't get to rappel," Kat said.

"At least I'm on a fire with my friends and not sitting at camp."

Kat dug at earth. "Hey, can I name this?"

"Call dispatch and see," Dano said.

I shrugged. "Don't see why not." Many dispatch centers preferred to name the fires themselves based on a geographic feature.

Kat made contact with dispatch. "Instead of us calling it by a number, I'd like to name this fire."

"Sure, what you thinking?" I didn't know who drew the overnight shift at dispatch. Being isolated at Krassel, I didn't get to hang out a lot with other people on the Payette, but all of the dispatchers over the radio were good at what they did and always friendly.

"Yeah, dispatch." Kat let off the mic for a moment and then re-keyed. "I'd like to call this the Big Lebowski Fire."

We all smiled. I had no idea what she was up to. We all leaned in to hear dispatch's response. Even the fire burning in our containment lines seemed to pause as it drew air, waiting on the radio to open up. Kat looked at each of us, doubt started to cross her face. "Maybe, I should call back that I'm joking."

The radio crackled. "Sorry it took me so long to get back to you, but I couldn't stop laughing. I'll put it on the board and see what they say in the morning."

In the morning the fire named after the cult film was a big hit. Later the district ranger would say it relieved the tedium of all the Deer Creeks, Beaver Creeks, Elk Creeks, or some bluff, and other like named fires. However, he was relieved it didn't go over a hundred acres and make the National Situation Report. It was nice to know that sometimes even in the higher reaches of Forest administration, that they abided a little bit.

*

My last fire at Krassel in 2010 burned in the Frank Church Wilderness. A seven-mile hike from the trailhead to a place called Copper Camp along Big Creek. John Patton and I gathered together at the Krassel Office. The summer had drawn out long and slow. I had only one other fire assignment and it had lasted exactly twenty-four hours as a crew-boss for the Payette Regs. We had assembled at 1800 in McCall, drove the ICP for the fire north of Eagle, Idaho and were immediately released when we arrived. The fire had been stopped with heavy tankers and helicopter bucket drops in the grass after it had demolished hundreds of homes built in the foothills. The next day we returned to the Payette and were assigned to limb trees for forest health on a unit close to McCall, the one I had already been working on for a week. We were released at 1800.

Patton had been a Krasselian before he had become a jumper and he had even gone through rappel training again when I was a rookie, so he could keep up to date. That day I had to get a lot of work done aside from the fire. My good friend Mark Sanders had called me from a university where he was the Department Chair. Turned out they needed a nonfiction professor in a hurry as they had been left high and dry. I had planned on working at Krassel through the fall and then returning to Amundsen-Scott South Pole Station. I immediately said yes and notified both Doug at Krassel and my South Pole supervisor Paddy that I planned to be teaching starting in August. My elation between the fire assignment in the Frank Church Wilderness and the opportunity to teach at the university kept me floating high. Not only would I be teaching, but I would also have the opportunity to maybe keep it going and quit having to bash my body in fire and finally quit traveling to work and be with my daughters. I had to submit a raft of paperwork, including the contract that needed to be signed and sent back ASAP. I emailed the Director of Composition, Liz, about what she wanted concerning the syllabus and the texts and made sure to alert all of them that I was going to be out of touch for at least fourteen days in the backcountry. The staff and faculty that I dealt with during that crunch time were all responsive and helpful and it all came together because Liz, Gina, and Becky were so on their game. Mark arranged air travel for me and when I emerged from two weeks in the wilderness, I had two days to be in the piney woods of East Texas. When I met Patton at Krassel before driving out to the Big Creek Ranger Station, a couple hours further out to the end of the road before the wilderness boundary, I felt like I was departing to the last fire I would ever be on. Everything was finally falling into place.

At Big Creek we unloaded all our gear at the barns. The packers would load our gear onto livestock for our fourteen days, except for our line-gear and tools, which we would pack in ourselves. We spent the night with our friends the packers and then got up early the next morning. The mountains cracked the sky, bleeding light into the crisp air like the frosted breath of a sleeping child. August with October morning temps. The whole nation paused in firefighting except for a few fires, but nothing like the fires that burned up the country in '07 during my rookie season at Krassel. But it was only a lull in the cycle of the big picture spanning centuries and not the short attention span of someone looking out a window, remembering the summers of their youth.

We drove to the trailhead, got our gear, locked the truck and hiked. At the campsite six other firefighters waited for us. Four planned to leave when we arrived and two planned to stay for another few days. I won't lie, I was excited and carried my fly rod with me as I knew I'd be forced to take mandatory time off not being able to work over sixteen hours a day. My job was to be the Incident Commander Type Four trainee and the Fire Effects Monitor trainee, or what we shorthanded to Femo. Essentially I slung the weather (so called because we used a double-thermometer, which fixed to a small aluminum plate with chain attached to a small wand to hold while a firefighter swung the thermometers in a circle. The point was that after wetting the cotton covered bulb the swinging cooled it by spinning it until it read the lowest temperature. By using the dry bulb reading in relation to the wet bulb reading on a chart the relative humidity could be determined. An important bit of information for firefighters predicting fire behavior) and recorded the weather every hour, wrote down the observed fire behavior, and measured the growth of the fire. It was a pointless task book as any firefighters who'd worked fire a couple years should be able to do it or turn in their fire boots.

The Fire Line Handbook issued by National Wildfire Coordinating Group warned firefighters to avoid saddles on ridges and slopes greater than 50%. Fire ran fast uphill, increasing the flame lengths exponentially with the slope's steepness, and the saddle funneled the fire and smoke as wind rushed through, combined with the up drafting of heat. In other words, if you found yourself under a saddle on a steep slope and fire below you, you were fucked.

I reconned the Copper Creek Fire and made my report to dispatch. At 6,350 feet up the ridge the fire had come to a halt just below a saddle on a slope of 80%. Heavy material, such as big logs, concentrations of brush and snags smoldered and flamed up in the interior of the fire, but nothing threatened the entire fire north of the creek. Hiking around the fire on the south side of the creek, which being the northern exposure remained shaded by the ridge most of the day, lay even quieter. I hiked up and down the 404 acres (in this year of slow fire activity it was the second largest fire on the Payette that season), and by the time Patton and I hiked off it fourteen days later, it grew another staggering five acres and that within the first two days of our arrival.

I hiked around it every morning as small planes buzzed into the remote landing strips, and in the afternoon Patton and I took our crosscut saw, an axe, and wedges and cleared trees that had fallen across the trail. Some had toppled from bluffs and hung in the air like bridges; while others made a steep ramp a motorcycle daredevil could jump the mountain with. It took a lot of care to remove them safely. We moved a giant ponderosa three foot in diameter by driving wedges under it until it rolled off the trail and into the ravine. I loved thinking about how equipment as old as the wedge moved tons of tree with the force of one guy stacking and driving them with the back of his falling axe. The beauty and elegance of hand tools sung in my blood.

We cleared the trail over a day. Relatively close to a trailhead parking lot, the District wanted to keep us monitoring and act as a presence for the public who only saw smoke and thought danger. And the public came and asked.

Three businessmen on their yearly get together camped down from us and we shared a couple of nights around a campfire with them. They had some misconceptions about fire use and fire history, but they were inquisitive and listened as Patton and I talked of fire as both life giver and taker in the wilderness and how it's role wasn't only by lightning, but human presence over millennia. We talked of wolves and wilderness and all agreed that the proposal to sell off sections of public land was an idiotic idea. Maybe congress should convene around a campfire.

One afternoon a teenager with an AR-15 hiked by with two other guys and set up camp in the trees upstream from us. He had hiked past us a couple of days earlier. Usually I saw men and women carrying side arms like revolvers in cowboy rigs as they rode by on horses or backpackers with bear spray or small pistols. During hunting season, I knew it'd be high-powered rifles with scopes as the pack trains of mules stretched into the wilderness. I wondered about the use of modern firearms in the wilderness where it was supposed to be primitive and the "dogma of comfort," to quote Aldo Leopold. At least the hunters wouldn't be astride the loud and smoking four-wheelers breaking the mechanical dawn.

An old neighbor from the University of Idaho hiked by, and we chatted for a few minutes as if we had been old friends, although we rarely talked when we lived in the same apartment complex and when we did it was about our kids who played together. I was surprised to find out he was with the guy toting the AR-15 as he'd always been a hippie, but it was a family trip with cousins.

As we patrolled the fire along the trail, horse packers, kids, guys in spendy fly gear, and an old woman with legs of iron went by looking to discover something. Why else would they put that much effort into it? We greeted anybody we saw with a smile and a wave and many kept hiking or riding by while some stopped to ask about the fire or how the fishing was in different places. A cross section of America from hippies traveling with armed teenagers to high-speed sales men unwinding and getting a little dirt on their shoeshine. Industrialists and environmentalists and Neo-Cons to Liberal Leftists traversed the Frank Church. It was a gross misconception and a disservice to say that only environmental elitists used or loved the wilderness. A bigger travesty was to say it was a "land of no use." It was a land that strummed the

196

earliest impulses of new beginnings from those crossing the Bering Land Bridge to Huck Finn's plan to "light out for the territory." Even as I worked there I felt I the crossing from an old way and into a new phase, but true to the mercurial nature of journeying into the wild, my life reaped a boon I never foresaw, but only after sacrifice. The nature of wilderness lay in its ability to transform us in unexpected ways. I went in seeking one thing and found another. What made the wilderness beautiful was not the scenery, but that it could end your life.

During those two weeks, I looked forward to the coming semester. I planned out my classes in my head, wrote lesson plans and writing exercises in my fire notebook, and considered the books, stories, and essays I loved and wanted to use. I thought of all the things I had learned from my teachers and the things I kept learning as I read more whether author interviews or texts about writing. This fire out in the Frank Church The River of No Return Wilderness, I resolved to be my last. I didn't want to come back except as a hiker, a backpacker, or a fly fisherman with my daughters in tow.

Toward the end we took up our crosscut saw, an axe and wedges again. The trails crews hadn't cleared Raimey Creek trail yet, and the district thought that since we were out there and the fire growth was minimal, that we should clear the trail. I wondered about the public relations reason for keeping us out there, but wondered if the trails people were trying to get a trail cleared on the fire budget, which they did. No matter to us, we were happy to clear it. I have had friends who have worked trails and as I cut and axed my way up the trail, I felt the rhythm of the saw. I enjoyed the teamwork and the quiet zing of the steel teeth cutting into the wood with each stroke in a Zen-like repetition. Earlier that month I had been limbing and thinning with a power saw on a unit outside McCall. Running a power saw all day wraps the sawyer in a shell of numbness with the constant noise, even with ear plugs in, and the smell of motor exhaust. It reminded me of being with the Association and sawing all-day and ready to respond to a fire in the afternoon or evening. On a wildfire the scouting of the line, the fire, working ahead of a crew created a different feeling of awareness than the repetitive motion of limbing trees or felling snags. It wasn't that the stakes were higher, but it demanded an increased and constant state of vigilance. The old sawyers called the crosscut saw the misery whip. The difference was that they were production sawyers trying to fell as many trees as possible and pulled hard against the bark and wood trying to keep time with another man and then swing the axe as fast and accurately as possible. A monumental work ethic kept a man swinging and pulling for all he had for 12 to 16 hours a day.

As we worked our way up the mountain I thought of my trail clearing friends and how nice they had it to work ten days out in the wilderness and then four guaranteed days off without worrying that any plans they made would fall away because of a fire assignment. They took their days off and didn't have to worry about having their gear with them in case they were called by dispatch. Then the work. They could work a nice steady pace in the quiet of the wilderness, and not the intensity and chaos of the fire anytime day or night, whether in the wilderness or a suburb. A friend of mine who had worked in the Frank said, "It's a sweet deal if you can get it." She later left trails and went into fire. I thought of trails, but I knew it would never work out. I knew that I'd see a smoke and feel the tug of it and feel like that boy sitting in a car in some Arizona town as fire walked across the far mountains.

After two weeks Patton and I packed up and hiked out. We readied the gear for the packers and left it under the trees. I looked forward to teaching in Texas. I'd worked at Krassel four seasons and never rappelled a fire or even helitacked a fire. I did fly to divisions of fires in progress as part of the Payette Regs, but any fire I actually fought as an initial attack firefighter I attacked from a pick-up truck. Every season since my first in 1997 I had flown to a fire. The morning of what I hoped to be my last fire, the air carried fall on it. Elk bugled in the rut, and the brush, and grass were wet from over two inches of rain that had fallen the past couple of days. Overnight frost held on the grass and ground that hadn't felt the sun's warmth and leaves began to blush the colors of change.

This last fire I didn't even work to suppress. I observed it and took the weather, spent time being a liaison to the public, and worked on clearing a trail. It was all good. "Firefighters first," we always said. In actuality we were Forestry Technicians first, but that was the way it'd been since the early days of the Forest Service, but times were changing. No one in the early days would have monitored a fire. The Fire Service found itself in changing roles from all out suppression to monitoring for resource benefit. As I hiked that trail with the creek rushing below, I thought it appropriate that this kind of fire be my last. Something about the transition and a new way of thinking about the world appealed to me. Something about regeneration and growth from the flames and how I had re made myself not through the fire in the forests and deserts, but of the fire of the mind in college and the light of Prometheus breathed into me a greater understanding of the world. I had sacrificed my fire career to education and the hope to write books and teach others. As I legged it up the last slope to the trailhead and the waiting truck, I felt the burn in my muscles and it felt good.

Chapter 15
ETO

An emergency tie off was a procedure a rappeller executed when the rope fouled or knotted, preventing a person from descending. The rappeller needed to arrest the descent by braking with her hand, dally the rope to the Genie, pull the rope between the body and the harness and tie it above Genie. After insuring the knot was locked, the rappeller cut away the rope dangling below so that it wouldn't get tangled in trees or brush when the pilot lifted and flew or get tangled in the rappeller's feet when lowered to the ground. The pilot had an easier time judging depth with the body at the end of the line.

I stood on the skid and looked down the length of rope. We were taught that we needed to be able to spot the hazard and arrest descent so as to make sure enough rope was between us and the obstruction. If we slid too close to the knot there wouldn't be enough slack to tie off or if the rope was fouled in a tree and we kept rappelling below where the lower part of the rope had been caught on a limb, we'd be caught in the danger V, with us at the bottom. It took phenomenal strength to be able to pull up enough slack to even get a small amount of rope. During tower training everyone got a chance to rappel into a danger V, so we could see just how hopeless it was to be caught in one. I descended the first time into the danger V with the rope tied off to the first level of the tower. I pulled up on the rope above and managed a little slack, but as soon as I tried to force some between my harness and stomach, it slid out. I couldn't maintain my weight suspended in the air and manipulate the rope in any meaningful way. It didn't help that ropes were designed to slide and the palms of rappel gloves had been slicked by rope passing through. A rappeller had to keep many things in mind even before reaching a fire.

After cutting the rope below, we brought our arms overhead as if doing jumping jacks and the helicopter lifted to clear the trees. Above the tree canopy we slapped our hands together above our heads, and the helicopter flew to an area large enough to lower us to the cold comforting earth, where we cut our tether to the ship and ran. If the helicopter encountered trouble anytime during this operation, we were jettisonable cargo, and the spotter had a special knife to cut us loose, whatever the altitude. The best helicopter ride I ever took was the training ETO and the 200-yard flight down the Krassel airstrip dangling below the helicopter like some spider looking for new territory.

When I performed my first training ETO, I forgot to simulate cutting away the line. I realized it as the ship started forward and I gripped the can. After I landed I had to do 50 push-ups to reflect on the consequences of how small mistakes can kill a person and even bring down a million plus dollar aircraft with its crew. One small lapse in awareness was what we all sought to avoid.

During the tower training a trainer held up a length of retired rope for the rookie to cut so that rappeller felt what it was like to make a clean cut and insure that the knife was properly used. The rookie then took that length of rope and kept it until the end of training. At anytime if the rookie was found to be without it, the result was fifty push-ups. I hung in my harness from the tower a few feet above the earth. Doug handed me the rope. I measured out a full fathom and cut it. Doug laughed. "Most cut a couple of inches to carry in their pocket."

"I wanted to make a belt."

Some made anklets or bracelets, and Dano made a choker. Some only cut a couple of inches, enough to put in their pocket, which when they showed up to PT in only running shorts and a t-shirt made it a little harder.

After graduating in the spring from the MFA program at the University of Idaho I looked forward to ending my life on fire. I strengthened over my rookie season. In the winter, I considered my options. I wondered if the time had arrived to get out of fighting fire or did I still have the strength to use my experience and add a vital presence to the crew? With fighting fire I made enough money to help supplement my meager lecturer's salary and there was still that urge to run a power saw on a running wildfire or fly into a remote area as a smoke column scarred the sky. The better paying teaching jobs weren't coming due to the sharp downturn in the economy. The nation cut education and even as administrators gave themselves bonuses they scaled back on teachers. We in the lecturer pool worried if there would be enough classes for all of us to teach and indeed they laid-off a few of us. I applied to many universities and colleges, but planned to return to fire. I trained hard through the New Year and into the spring. My friend Blix kept me running snow or shine. A little snow wouldn't stop me. I concentrated on my legs and lifted weights and hauled seventy pound packs up and down trails and sometimes I let my daughters climb onto me and piggybacked them miles through the parks.

I did more pull-ups and sit-ups than anyone on the crew, much to the dismay of the twenty-some things, my second season. I helped ChaHow, Flegal, and my rookies Rich and Aaron. During that season I became a teacher of rappellers. The crew taught each other. Money uttered the sage words, "When you're flying, always be looking for a place to crash" and, as we flew, he quizzed us on potential emergency landing zones.

My second season at Krassel, when I found myself hanging below the helicopter performing the emergency tie off, I didn't forget to simulate cutting away the rope. I held on in the rush of air as the ship flew down the runway, not ready to be jettisoned.

Chapter 16

AFTER ACTION REVIEW: 2012

The rookies gathered around me. The first young woman walked up to me and stuck out her hand. Leslie flashed a quick smile. Straight dark hair fell about her round, Asiatic face to her shoulders. I knew she might have trouble on the three-mile run coming up the next morning. She had graduated high school the week before in an agricultural town outside of Twin Falls, Idaho along with another young man, Rob, a tall thin runner with a short hair and a desire to do better each day and was headed to Boise State University. Rachel had her blond hair up in a ponytail was attending Lewis-Clark State College (my undergrad alma mater) and looked forward to traveling. Sophia's blonde hair fell below her shoulders and carried her runner's build with purpose. She had earned a biology degree from UCLA, and when she couldn't find work in a biological field applied to wildfire. Mike had worked trails for the Forest Service for many years, one of the original trail bike and power saw guys, and decided he wanted to get a red card so he could fight fire. A big man, he would struggle with his physical fitness, but understood what he needed to do to do the job. Derek, a fisheries biologist stood the tallest, with a shock of brown hair and tanned skin from fieldwork who also wanted a chance to cross over from resource work to fire for a change. We were Squad Seven, anticipating the next five days as we all anticipated the up coming season as fires raged in the Rockies and the Great Basin.

I had not expected to be teaching at Guard School with a squad of rookies. A week before starting on the Sawtooth National Forest, my new boss, Ray, asked me if I'd help at fire school and be a mentor and a teacher during the weeklong training. The faces of my new squad around me were all new and fresh with zero fire experience. Already the barrage of information, guidelines, checklists, and administrative rules started to overwhelm them. As I saw it, my job would be to distill down the information to essentials that I knew they'd need to use as touchstones. I would make them identify objects in the environment, memorize cloud formations and what they meant, see the terrain as a firefighter, smell the wind without it being abstracted into a numbered set of guidelines. Influenced by Paolo Freire's *praxis*, I strove to make them understand reflection and action. I took Freire's lead and took it a step further. It's not enough to say the water is dirty but to ask why the water is dirty, and who is responsible. It is not enough to say we need situational awareness, but give them the historical and personal examples so they could begin building experience to recognize danger by using all the senses and critical thinking before the fire forces align into an explosive situation.

I had four days to give these rookies the tools to call bullshit on any fire assignment, how to mitigate danger, and articulate it to whomever might be giving the orders. They needed to be empowered to take their safety into their own hands. They needed the tools to become a solid member of a team in a state of chaos and flux and my job was to make sure they had a solid foundation to build upon. Luckily the training cadre teaching at the guard school took their positions seriously and carried a lot of experience in the fire world. It was 180 degrees away from my experience with the Association. The man in charge, Ryan, blended both field and classroom, and whenever possible opted away from, "death by PowerPoint."

They all looked at me and I told them that at 1900 they would meet me in front of my cabin, the one with the sign Wapiti above the door, with all of their line gear and we would talk more. I gave them a quick briefing on the facilities and where they were to find a bed and sent them away. My guts stung. Their safety started right there for them and not in some cloistered office in DC where officials sought to mitigate their liability when a tragedy struck. I wanted them to apply what they learned from their instructors throughout the week on the practice fire scheduled for Thursday. It wouldn't be just head down digging or learning how arduous the job could be in pleasant conditions, but heads up and how to process what they experienced.

Guard School was held at the Methodist Camp along the South Fork of the Boise River in the Soldier Mountains, where they had been hosting the weeklong class for thirty-four years. The mountains were rugged and a mix between sagebrush and conifer forests as if the land couldn't decide between being a high desert or a full on temperate forest. It rained and snowed on us, and the nights left frost covering anything exposed. My rookies met in front of my cabin, now known as Club Wapiti. They gathered early, milling about and chatting. I waited inside until my watch read 1900 and walked out with my line gear in hand. I set it down. Earlier I had wrapped the waist strap around its back and folded shoulder straps over the top, and clipped all the buckles. It formed a neat bundle with nothing loose to drag or get caught in doors of trucks or helicopters. I placed my hard hat on top that was clipped into the carrying strap with a carabineer.

"Make your gear look like mine and line it up behind it."

After several times of me saying, "no that's not right, it doesn't look like mine," they stopped and looked closer.

"The details," I said. "Look at yours and then mine and the pattern."

When they got it right, I nodded. "If your gear is squared away and I as a helitack guy walk up looking to fly people, I'm choosing you and not the crew that looks like a yard sale. If you fly first, the other crew might not fly at all due to a change in plans. Who wants to fly?"

They all raised their hands.

I went over my expectations for the next few days. Do not be late. Do not sleep in class. Have all your equipment with you. I will teach you before and after class extra lessons. "Now what's in your line gear?"

They weren't all outfitted correctly. "You'll need a lighter in case you need to burn out a safety zone to save yourself. You'll need fusees to burn out a safety zone to save yourself. You'll need a compass to find your way and save yourself. You'll need a pen and paper to write down the weather when you get it, write down the fire behavior, write down current weather and fire behavior, write down your orders and the frequencies for communication and latitudes and longitudes for destinations safe and unsafe as some of these will be to fires and not safety zones, write write write everything, it might save your life. Writing helps you focus and pay attention. Writing helps you remember what's important and isn't just a reference for you to look back on, which it is of course. You can't memorize everything you need to know. You'll need to have your Incident Response Pocket

Guide to be able to reference those many things, especially the page on how to refuse assignments so you can save yourself.

"You'll need enough food to last until morning if you get stuck out overnight, and for overnight a sweater and watch cap to keep warm if they don't resupply you because people get forgotten, trucks and helicopters break down or a wilderness ranger decides now you are an intrusion and you are on your own, and you may need to save your own life. Never forget your yellow, your hardhat, or your gloves—it has happened. You need a magnesium fire starter, a length of parachute cord, a headlamp with spare batteries, a knife, a bastard file, a first aid kit, more than a gallon of water, you need anything you can think that may save your life. Remember this is not the French Foreign Legion of March or Die. We march and survive.

"Take a book to read, as we aren't barbarians. I have a book of poems in my line gear and while it has never saved me from a fire, it has saved my life. Never forget your fire shelter. There are many like it, but this one is yours. The shake and bake bag has saved hundreds of people from dying all the way back to the buffalo hide Lewis and Clark wrote about in 1804. A mother covered her son with a fresh skin and told him to stay until she returned. He waited under the dank, dark hide, and his life was saved. Your mother will not be able to cover you with a fire shelter. Have it handy and know how to use it. Remember your fire shelter is designed for one, but a young woman at Thirty-Mile took in two tourists and saved their lives. The old couple later sued the Forest Service and won because the road wasn't officially closed, although they drove by several fire crews and engines, and past the fire burning on both sides of the river. Let that be a lesson to you: people ignore the obvious. Fire people cannot legally stop anyone from entering a fire area or order evacuations, but we can take them into our shelter, even if it causes us severe burns. You must look out for each other. The most important thing you possess to save your life is your mind. You are responsible to see the building clouds and feel the wind switch on your skin like the caress of a lover who has fallen out of love. At the end of the day we are responsible for each other. All the gear and checklists cannot save you without the trained and seasoned mind to wield them. You must learn to spot the breaks in the pattern of chaos. This starts now and will never end as long as you are on fire. The goal is that we all come back. You slay the dragon. The dragon does not slay you."

*

When I look back on all that happened to me in wildfire and the petty bureaucrats and tyrants who made other people's lives difficult or held somebody down for no reason other than they could, I bristle because I have felt that sting just as surely as a poor supplicant before a minor official in a Russian novel. Still, the generosity and close familial bonds I have formed with people stun me. The by-word of the Fire Service has become micro-management, as it was the only way an administrator can consolidate and wield power, even if it is pointless.

In 2011 Region Four arbitrarily decided that firefighters lost rehire rights if they hadn't fought fire with the Forest Service for twenty-four months. I had seventeen months with the USFS and nearly eighty months in fire and forestry with other agencies. I lost my rehire rights and wasn't able to go back to Krassel. I was shocked and hurt to be severed from a crew I had invested so much in and yet, I knew someplace in the regional office a bureaucrat sat safe in his or her chair never to bind so closely to a crew and know such people who'd risk everything for you and come to your aid even in winter when no fires burned. I have the tattoo in memoriam, as did Flegal and ChaHow, and Bage and Feltner and Jess and others and something of crew cohesion that can't be taught or administered. It made me wonder about all the talk of crew cohesion that fire management reinforced when they undermined it in the same breath. The great Antarctic explorer Ernest Shackleton offered his entire *Endurance* expedition, ship, stores, and men, to the Crown before the outbreak of World War One with the request that they be used as module, "So as to preserve its homogeneity." He understood crew dynamics the way an administrator never could. The bureaucrats had taken all the hiring out of the field supervisor's hands and fouled it up.

Administrative foul-ups weren't new and neither was the schism between administrators and people working in the field. Ed Pulaski was denied medical treatment for his eyes after saving forty men during The Big Blow up due to a "bumbling bureaucrat." "College" educated foresters in 1905 were dismissive of "Paiute forestry," that rural people and Native Americans had been using for thousands of years, and instead of looking to restore burning in the forests after the conflagration of 1910 spun the story to suit their personal ideology and in the face of what people on the ground actually doing the work had suggested. From DC, administrators set policies for western forests that had not the least interest in doing what needed done, except to advance their careers. Gifford Pichot wrote about many cases of incompetent employees hired due to cronyism and nepotism. These forest supervisors proved to be too weak, corrupt, and without any forestry skills to perform their basic job much less manage a complex district. In his book, *Breaking New Ground*, Pinchot wrote, "An elderly man who had been cashier in a bank, was a close friend of the Commissioner. He frankly admitted he had no knowledge of forest conditions and didn't know one tree from another. But Binger made him Forest Inspector, the most important and responsible post of all." We have learned how wrong they were, but no one stopped to analyze how they might be doing more harm than good. Maybe they didn't care because their mind was made up. Even today people without helicopter experience tell crews what helicopters they can use based upon the price and not by what capability was needed and saddled crews with ineffective aircraft. Those who have to live with the consequences excluded from the decision process.

It was not lost on me that I had shifted between two radically different fire organizations when I left the Association, who still modeled themselves on the 1905 fire regime of logging, thinning, slash abatement burns, burning pastures, and clearing, and aggressive fire suppression not save in ideological construct of what nature was supposed to look like, but just like the Native Americans who used fire to suit their needs, they only gave the society what it wanted: to make money, build houses, homesteads and feed timber to cities bursting with the great exodus of people looking to start anew in the American West. To them the forests were to build nations and not to stand around and gawk at or as Pinchot said, to "make it pay."

They also carried the vestiges of 1905 and the interloper Federal Fire Service bringing their French educated Pinchot and his disciples into the woods who didn't know "jack shit" about the "real work" and American forests. Pinchot favored the military's attitude, no doubt a residual effect of the Civil War, toward local populations and sent his young rangers to places where they had no ties to local interests and therefore were less likely to be swayed by local desires of what to do with the forest and ranges under their supervision. A good move as he was right because locals treated public land as their own and bad as it created a great schism between the public and the Federal agency which was looked upon as an occupying army in many areas of the West.

In the end the shopkeepers will have the last say. Those dour folk with their ledgers of budget and loss (no profit for the government) made the final call. All the debate and research into land management, forest health, the impact on watersheds and those tricky paradigms of "natural" fire and wildfire use fires for resource benefit and the folly of full suppression because it didn't allow fire to clear understory of saplings and brush, regenerate fire dependent species like red stem ceanothus and lodge pole pine, or regenerate the grasses that disappeared due to both overgrazing and lack of fire had been squashed. So much for all the work and debate about the forests health by environmentalists, conservationists, industrialists, fire ecologists, and all the scientists and profiteers. The accountants said we couldn't afford for a fire to get large enough to become a project fire. All fires were to be aggressively suppressed, no exceptions. A matter of money you see.

At the same time that we were asked to suppress all fires they cut the crews down in numbers and told us no helicopters were allowed in the wilderness. Many have wondered aloud if a smokejumper made that decision because they were still dropping streamers, scattering gear, and breaking legs all over the wilderness. Bureaucrats decided to use fewer fighters to suppress more fires, forcing them to commit longer to suppression efforts while browsing the catalogue for the latest eleven hundred dollar office chair. I wished I joked, but in 2003 the Winnemucca Field Office destroyed its fire budget buying office furniture including chairs at the cost of eleven hundred dollars a pop.

A joke amongst firefighters has been that the GS-13s save money in the budget by taking away the pay of a GS-3 and even higher up they will cut the crews themselves making harder work for those on the ground while preserving the administrative heavy Fire Service. When I heard of the crew cuts coming to helitack crews to save money, I knew the 2012 season was going to be epic. Recently on the Boise National Forest the supervisor proposed to cut all of the GS-5 seasonal

211

jobs from fire and make them all GS-4s not realizing that many GS-5s come with years of experience, in some cases thirteen. She would effectively gut all the experienced firefighters from her forest because many of them would leave for other areas. This was the equivalent of cutting all of the sergeants out of the military. Maybe she doesn't care because she didn't have to live with the consequences or work on the ground with all the inexperienced people, making a greater hazard to other crewmembers. It also meant a loss of efficiency, making the job harder to get done and a product of this was not to complete all the tasks that needed done, taking longer to do and costing more money, or where a crew at full strength with experienced personnel might be able to stop a fire while the inexperienced crew could not, much like what happened at the Mile-Post 59 Fire when my crew took a mission the others couldn't execute due to experience. Inexperience was tied to many tragedies as the Willow Springs investigation pointed out. But administrators cut a dollar on paper in the spring and lose hundreds over the summer and somehow felt successful. In 2012, in order to save money, firefighters will only be allowed to take one class, effectively stifling their career and also stunting the educational growth of firefighters coming up.

Squad Seven met me in the classroom, each in their own crew shirt. "I want each of you to take out your IRPG and turn to the first page that is the color of a daffodil lit by early morning sun."

Some smiles and laughter as they found the page detailing how to refuse a mission. "Whenever you feel sketched out about something and you do not have a clear picture on what your mission is and how you can accomplish it safely, go over these four points."

1. There is a violation of safe work practices.
2. Environmental conditions make the work unsafe.
3. They lack the necessary qualifications or experience.
4. Defective equipment is being used.

"Go to your supervisor, your squad or crew boss and they should tell you how these things are mitigated. I've refused a mission. A division supervisor wanted us to dig line down a ridge to stop a grass fire. We knew the fire would over run the saddle before we could even reach it and trap us. In fact, it over ran the saddle as we were turning down the assignment. In another case we took an assignment after a crew turned it down because even if they didn't have the experience, we did. Keep in mind that you can suggest other alternatives. It is incumbent upon you to be thinking tactically about what you and your crew can do. Your supervisors and you need to be able to say what the mission is, how you are to accomplish this task, and what's it supposed to look like when it's all done. This is called Doctrine. These three things must be clearly understood by everyone no matter how complex the operation. "

I wrote on the white board:

Doctrine:
Task: What is to be done.
Purpose: Why is it to be done.
End State: How should it look when done.

They sat in the row of chairs in front of me and nodded.

"You also need to be aware of accepting assignments others turn down. You need to know and understand why people before you said no way. For instance the crew boss on the Thirtymile fire accepted being the IC of a rapidly changing incident after Hotshot supervisors turned down being the IC of the fire. Now it's true that not all Shot supervisors are the end all to be all, but if somebody with that kind of experience on a crew known for getting shit done said no, you have to ask yourself, what makes me the one to carry out this assignment. If you can't answer that, then that is a red flag waving before people die."

I pointed to Sophia. "So will you go down the ridge and stop the grass fire before it reaches the saddle?"

"No."

I pointed to each of them and they all responded, "No."

I went back to Sophia. "Why?"

"Because rate of spread is too fast for us to make it to the saddle before we can get there."

"What else can we do?"

"I don't know. I don't have enough information."

I clapped my hands. "Excellent. Never just say something to look like you are offering a solution without adequate knowledge." I turned to big Mike B. "What would you do?"

With my marker I made other ridges on the far side.

"I suppose I'd ask for what it looked like up canyon."

"Sure. Can we fall back a safe distance, put in a control line and maybe burn out?" I pulled out my lighter. "Who used matches to save his life and hoped to save his whole crew?"

"Wag Dodge at Mann Gulch."

"Good. What else?" I drew some people, a truck, and a helicopter.

"Who else is available?"

"Yes. What other resources are around and can you talk to them."

I erased the board and drew another series of canyons and drainages with people. Leslie commented that she liked my artwork. I laughed. "Okay cartoons," she said.

"This is Rock Creek in northern Nevada. The year 1939."

I detailed the historical events and my history on that district and the staff ride I participated in.

"Why did the fire run downhill?"

"Winds."

"Winds from what?"

"A Thunderstorm..."

"Right." I drew billowing clouds above the ridges. The crew boss gave his squadie the easy and safe assignment." I used finger quotes when I said, safe. "What kind of winds come with thunderstorms?"

"Erratic."

"Gusty."

"High."

"Yes, and what else do we know about direction?" Some contemplative looks. I hum the game show countdown theme. "You should be able to look at a thunder cell and tell me which way the wind is blowing." I pointed to a ceiling beam above and behind Sophia. "That's the top of the mountain. Thunderstorms build above the tops of mountains because of the elevation. As the land heats, it takes less time for the day heated and night cool air to swap positions and condense into clouds. The point where the air swaps is the mixing height. Cold air drops, warm air rises and clouds form. Heat and moisture create thunderstorms and when they are building, they are sucking in air from all directions. If you face a thunderstorm and the wind is at your back it's building." I pointed at the beam again. "As

214

they climbed that mountain in 1939 the wind was at their backs. Now given your weather knowledge from class what will happen next?"

"Eventually the wind will come down."

"Exactly. The storm will build so high and so thick that it can't keep building and will burst sending rain sometimes, but always wind and lots of it and the bigger the cell, the more wind that'll rush down the slopes. Look back at the mountain and you see the storm building above you. You're not even to the fire. The eight-foot tall sagebrush and grass is thick and all around you. The wind is at your back pushing. Do you feel safe?"

They shake their heads.

"Can you think of an alternative to climbing the slope as a thunderstorm builds?"

"Pull back to the highway and wait."

"Excellent. You just refused an assignment, but in the same breath offered an alternative. But there are other alternatives too, and many they didn't have in 1939."

"You see a storm building and you don't have enough time to hike to it and create an anchor or safety zone, you need to rethink what you are doing. Not only can the wind blast the crap out you by rolling the fire back on you, but it can blast the crap out of you with lightning. That is a trigger point you can use without ever taking another class."

*

Thursday morning we gathered for the training fire. What a sight. Over fifty firefighters dressed and decked out in their fire clothes around the lodge. A bunch of new faces from the district office arrived ready to help with the training and act as monitors on the fire. Even with the conditions, it was still a fire and rookies in a rush could still be hurt. The photojournalist from the Twin Falls paper milled about taking photos. The church staff clattered about the kitchen before breakfast as we lined out our crews. The South Fork rushed down its banks and I thought of my missed opportunity to fish it while I was at the camp. The river ran high, but I'd worked dark to dark the whole week teaching.

My squad marched over and set their gear in a line. I pointed to the sky. "Rachel, what kind of clouds are those?"

"Alto-cumulus."

"What kind of cumulus?"

"Floccus?"

"Baaa," someone said.

I smiled. "A floccus of clouds."

"Letting us know we have moisture and an unstable atmosphere."

"You are correct. For that, I'll buy breakfast."

They chuckled and after eating we formed up outside for a briefing.

The first squad led out and the knots of firefighters fell in and uncoiled across the camp. We threaded between the buildings, across a field of sagebrush to the road. By virtue of being Squad Seven, we brought up the rear. Over fifty firefighters stretched out ahead of us with a clatter of tools and packs shifting with the crunch of boots on the gravel road. Only a mile and half we managed to keep the line tight the whole way without any gaps.

As we approached, I saw smoke drifting up from behind a ridge. "I see the smoke, anybody else?"

My squad looked around. "Got it."

"What does that tell you?"

"It's not burning very hard.

"Why?"

"Light, wispy, gray, not black, drifting and not building."

"What else does it tell you?

"The wind is blowing up the drainage."

"What else do you notice?"

They looked around as we continued to march.

"What do the trees look like?"

"Some are dead."

"Right, we can see dead trees on this side of the drainage so we can expect snags in the fire area. Why is that important?"

"Snags fall."

"Correct. Where's your nearest water?"

"The river."

"You will also be entering a drainage, note the condition of the creek and where might be the best place to set up a pump. Look for places a helicopter can dip water or land. Look for your escape route and keep an eye on the sky for clouds and smoke. Notice the wind on your skin. It will change and you want to notice it when it does."

We marched into a clearing next to the road and the overhead took the squad leaders up to look at the fire. Then we broke into assignments. My squad had been assigned to hike up to the upper end to the fire to corral a spot outside the main fire. We were to combine with squads five and six. The squad six leader was an engine assistant on my district and I knew he had an open task book for crew-boss.

"Hey, B. Just thinking minimum people to need a crew boss is what?

"Sixteen."

"We have at least that with our two squads and if we include five with permission, we can make this a training assignment for you."

"Sounds good."

"Okay, call the IC and tell him you are the point of contact for us."

At the bottom I briefed my crew on our assignment and listened to the overall briefing from the incident commander. "Comments, questions, concerns?"

They had fixed me with their eyes, but said nothing.

"Follow me," I said and led them up the skid trail. The trail had been built next to a creek and on our section of the fire the creek was bordered by a hillside with only grass and sagebrush. I stopped the squad. "Look over there and what do you see?"

"Aspens and an open hillside."

"You see a safety zone. The aspens act as barrier to the fire and you can cross through this thin fringe of trees and the creek and burn off the hillside from the bottom. The IC may have told you that the safety zone was down by where we assembled, but that doesn't mean you quit looking for other sites."

The fire burned above the trail in some spots. The first two squads climbed into the woods to the spot fire. Behind me flames sprung up in a tree surrounded by brush and smaller trees. A facilitator had used a drip torch to light fire behind us.

"Hey, Tony," I yelled up. "We have a spot below you."

"All right, get on it."

"Copy. Here we go squad, start digging line and I'll knock the flames down."

I waded into the brush and knocked all the limbs off the tree and stomped the fire down. Some of the squad still stood. "I just robbed the fire of ladder fuels so it can't climb the tree and send out embers and then stomped the flames. Now you need to dig the hand line just like you were taught." They started digging and clearing away dead limbs and downed trees. More flames sprung up on the opposite side of the copse. The person with the drip torch saying, "I think you put that out a little fast. Here's some more fire."

As I stomped out that fire two more spots sprung up. I directed my squad and showed them how to break into smaller units and maintain communications and keep their heads up. Through the day I showed them how to take the weather and use it as a predictor of fire behavior and then showed them when the conditions lined up to meet the predictions. "See how it burns hotter. Look at how the wind drives it. See how the rate of spread has increased."

During mop up I got down on my hands and knees and showed them how to cover every square inch to make sure the fire was dead out. "There is no more embarrassing thing then to have a fire smoke back up on you." I thought of my own escaped fire and the woman with the scared horse. "It's even worse when houses line the ridge above you."

Leslie dropped to her knees and started kneading the ash and dirt. "This is like being in a sandbox." She smiled. "Don't tell my boss how much I like this though. It might be all he lets me do."

I laughed. "You'll go far. You can move out of the smoke if it's bothering your eyes."

"My eyes are normally this way. I'm Asian," she said.

We pulled off the fire. On the hike back I saw the faces changing in my squad. Not used to hiking to a fire loaded with gear and then trying to suppress that fire on a steep hillside and then hike back, they looked worn, but they all looked happy. "Great day for a hike," I said. "At least I'm not carrying a power saw."

Sophia smiled. "That makes me feel better."

At the camp in the evening my squad and I held an After Action Review. They were all confident in what they had learned and experienced. Rachel said, "I was a little dumbstruck when you told us to start digging and stepped into the flames."

I smiled. "A little overwhelming at first."

She nodded. "But then you started giving orders and I just followed."

"At anytime did any of you feel sketched out?" They all shook their heads. Keep that in mind. It can be overwhelming, but if you feel sketched out, stop, take a breath, and look around and figure out why. Give it a name so you can tell someone else. This fire was low intensity and as Ryan said, normally a fire that big will have ten of you not fifty of you."

The next morning we loaded all of our equipment into our trucks and cleaned all the cabins and the campgrounds. We drove out to the fire scene and worked until lunch.

We worked across the fire. The spot we ended on was less than a tenth of an acre and it had been mopped up and the fire line rehabbed to help prevent erosion by cutting water bars that channel water away from the fire into the green and by dragging branches and the dug up earth back over the scar.

My rookies started finding their way downhill off the fire line. They filtered through the brush and trees down to the old skid road. The lowest paid employees of the fire service, but eager of heart and mind to perform to the best of their ability. I stood above them on the hillside. My crew boss trainee had already contacted me: The other squads waited at the assembly area for the final debrief. Squad Seven was the last on the fire working the farthest spot.

The French aviator Antoine de Saint Exupèry felt sorry for all the minor and gray faced bureaucrats making their mindless rounds every day, never to know the company of those who dared and dared nothing themselves in their poor dull round. As he set out across the stormy Pyrenees he felt sorry that they never knew what it was to feel alive. I do too, although, I didn't always feel that way.

My squad single-filed into the trail and walked. I jogged up next to the line and told them to hold on. They stopped and faced me and as luck had it, a mound was centered in front of them as if made for a movie ending.

"Because I am, at heart, a sentimental and romantic fool, I want to take this moment before I let you loose to say that I am proud of you all. You did great out here and aced the classroom (none of my squad scored below a 94%). In the words of Tennyson, you need 'to strive, to seek, to find, and not to yield.' Never yield on your safety."

Mike called on the squad to give me hand for taking the extra time with them, and I just held my hands up. "No, I'm just a guy doing my job, but thank you." In the short days we had become an effective squad. They learned to form a team and learned that their scared obligation is to lookout for each other and pass along what they know, to teach. It must become their life for their life depends on it as does the lives of others. I pointed to Sophia. "All right take us down the mountain." She nodded, turned, and hiked with the others behind her to the clearing where they'd all receive their certificates in a field ceremony.

*

Fire draws us even when the high became a hangover or the money didn't come so fat. Things like the dawn on a remote mountain peak with clouds flowing below, like Lau Tzu beyond the frontier sentry or a night on the high desert with the starlight breaking bright over our heads or the smoke low in the draws with the headlamps of others tracing the ground as we find our way through the nighted forest captured us. The helicopter cutting through mountains as elk look up from meadows, smoke rising from the trees to land on a ridge and after working the fire, descend to the river and a waiting jet boat to ferry us to a beach for the night. Fire draws us even as it humbles us and forces us to hike fast down the mountain and across a drainage as flames snap three hundred feet into the air above the crowns of the trees, blowing fire brands a mile away as we watch, sweating, legs throbbing, and gasping for breath. Fire gives us scale to measure our lives.

On that crisp fall morning in Boise with the helicopter flying overhead I thought fire was over for me. I was wrong. My daughters still endure my absence all week until I drive the three hours on days off, if I get days off at all. Their voices on the phone ring like the soft strings of violins playing Adagio. They have come to understand distance does not mean any lack of love, and still thrill at the rocks and candy I haul home. I never managed to find my way back to the level I'd been before coming to Krassel. Texas didn't work out either, and although I know why, it's not important to this story. My friend Savona Beaudoin-Holmes pointed out, "Rumi says, 'Out beyond ideas of wrongdoing and rightdoing, there is a field. I will meet you there.'" I stand in that field. Not all stories ended the way I'd hoped, but any hard experience, like fire, scorches away the dead and decadent, allowing new growth. My friends stand like a forest after the fire, enriching me in life and in their death. I don't believe in ghosts, but I feel the dead pushing me harder as I climb mountain trails or carry gear and water across a desert trying to stop the flames from rushing around a house. They are the crew always at my back.

220

My rookies each hugged me in turn. I was teaching, just not as I planned. All of us had come to fire for different reasons, but something in our guts kept us marching. None of them hiked with ghosts yet as they had only just begun to learn their names, where they died and how to shake hands with them. I wished them well. Ash smudged their faces and some still coughed up smoke, reminding me of my reflected soot covered face in the window of backcountry cookhouse eating spuds and squash. Who was that rookie who would be shaped and tempered by a life on fire? I hardly know him from this distance.

Fire breathes in air and pulses, shifts colors and light since ancient times. The fire of stars mesmerizes us with cold beauty, while campfires bring us together to share stories not found around a television. It has razed cities to the ground, reduced millions of timbered acres to cinders, and choked summer air with smoke so thick airports shutdown. It spreads death and purification in the same moment. Preachers tell us a great flaming lake floods Hell and God appeared to the prophets like Ezekiel and Moses as flames. Many of the world's spiritual traditions have wedded fire to both damnation and salvation. Fire erupting at the end of a lightning bolt like God's finger invoked myths and prodded early humans, loose on the plains, toward civilizations. No fire, no art. Infernos merging with mountains captivate us firefighters, whether we stand in awe of flames swirling heavenward or gaze from miles away like a kid sitting in a car as fireworks color the night sky. We sacrifice our lives, our relationships, and our bodies. A few months at a time we watch infants rise up to children, who develop into teens that turn away from us, and then become adults. We measure years by seasons and, along with those in our lives, wonder if any of us will disappear into the smoke and flames before it ends. No one is left untouched. Fire consumes us all.

Author's Note:

On August 12, 2012, USFS firefighter Anne Veseth was killed when a tree hit her on the Steep Canyon fire. This fire burned on the Headquarters' District of the Clearwater-Potlatch Timber Protective Association. Veseth was twenty and the sister of one of my former students at the University of Idaho, and fellow firefighter Brian. What makes her death even more tragic is that the day before the Flathead Hotshots pulled off the fire due to unmitigated hazards, such as no lookouts, falling trees, rocks, and explosive fire behavior. They also noted that the Association firefighters weren't wearing Nomex or using the proper safety equipment while operating a power saw. The incident commander, a thorough Association man, told the Flathead's supervisor, "We have different values than you." Indeed. My guts dropped as I had already written about the Association's disregard for the federal fire service's safe practices and their cavalier attitude when engaging fire, the disdain for checklists and not going by the book as it suited them. It had only been in June that I taught my rookies how to turn down missions, look out for bad incident commanders, and hopefully empowered them to walk away from such assignments. My heart goes out to Veseth's family. A daughter, a sister, a friend is dead and it didn't have to happen. God's speed.

RESOURCES

Web Resources to Accidents and Tragedies Mentioned

Mann Gulch Fire Leadership. http://www.fireleadership.gov/
toolbox/staffride/downloads/lsr14/Race_That_Couldnt_Be_Won.pdf

Rock Creek Staff Ride: http://www.fireleadership.gov/toolbox/
staffride/library_staff_ride3.html

N335EV Accident Report. http://www.ntsb.gov/aviationquery/
brief2.aspx?ev_id=20060824X01237&ntsbno=SEA06GA158&ak
ey=1

South Canyon Fire Investigation. http://www.iaff.org/hs/LODD_
Manual/LODD%20Reports/South%20Canyon,%20CO%20-%20
14%20LODDs.pdf

Steep Corner Fire Safenet filed by the Flathead Hotshots: http://
safenet.nifc.gov/safenet.nsf/ea2b334e0484179b87256c00000dbf83/1
b8dc7ac9c2c109187257a5a0060a4e6!OpenDocument

Thirtymile Accident Report. http://www.fs.fed.us/t-d/lessons/
documents/Thirtymile_Reports/Thirtymile-Final-Report-2.pdf

Willow Helibase Rappel Accident Factual Report. http://www.
wildfirelessons.net/documents/temp/Willow_CA_Final_2009.pdf

Wildland Firefighter Foundation. http://www.wffoundation.org/

The Author

Jerry D. Mathes II is a Jack Kent Cooke Scholar alumnus, author of *The Journal West: Poems* and an essay collection, "Fever and Guts: A Symphony". He fought wildfire for fourteen seasons, taught writing at the University of Idaho, and taught the Southernmost Writers Workshop in the World at Amundsen-Scott South Pole Station, Antarctica during the 2009-2010 and 2011-2012 Austral summer seasons. He loves his two daughters very much.

For a free catalog of Caxton titles write to:

CAXTON PRESS
312 Main Street
Caldwell, Idaho 83605-3299

or

Visit our Internet web site:

www.caxtonpress.com

*Caxton Pres*s is a division of THE CAXTON PRINTERS, Ltd.